School Trouble

What is the trouble with schools and why should we want to make 'school trouble'?

In this book, Deborah Youdell brings together theories of counter-politics and radical traditions in education to make sense of the politics of daily life inside schools and explores a range of resources for thinking about and enacting political practices that make 'school trouble'.

The book offers a solid introduction to the much-debated issues of 'intersectionality' and the limits of identity politics and the relationship between schooling and the wider policy and political context. It pieces together tools and tactics that might destabilize educational inequalities by unsettling the knowledges, meanings, practices, subjectivities and feelings that are normalized and privileged in the 'business as usual' of school life. Engaging with curriculum materials, teachers' lesson plans and accounts of pedagogy, and ethnographic observations of school practices, the book investigates empirical examples of critical action in school, from overt political action pursued by educators to day-to-day pedagogic encounters between teachers and students. The book draws on the work of Michel Foucault, Judith Butler, Ernesto Laclau and Chantel Mouffe, and Gilles Deleuze and Felix Guattari to make sense of these practices and identify the political possibilities for educators who refuse to accept everyday injustices and wide-reaching social inequalities.

School Trouble appears at a moment of political and economic flux and uncertainty, and when the policy moves that have promoted markets and private sector involvement in education around the globe have been subject to intense scrutiny and critique. Against this backdrop, renewed attention is being paid to the questions of how politics might be rejuvenated, how societies might be made fair, and what role education might have in pursuing this. This book makes an important intervention into this terrain. By exploring a politics of discourse, an anti-identity politics, a politics of feeling, and a politics of becoming, it shows how the education assemblage can be unsettled and education can be re-imagined. The book will be of interest to advanced undergraduate and postgraduate students and scholars in the fields of education, sociology, cultural studies, and social and political science as well as to critical educators looking for new tools for thinking about their practice.

Deborah Youdell is Professor of Education in the Department of Educational Foundations and Policy Studies at the Institute of Education, University of London, UK.

Foundations and Futures of Education

Series Editors:

Peter Aggleton *School of Education and Social Work, University of Sussex, UK*
Sally Power *Cardiff University, UK*
Michael Reiss *Institute of Education, University of London, UK*

Foundations and Futures of Education focuses on key emerging issues in education as well as continuing debates within the field. The series is interdisciplinary, and includes historical, philosophical, sociological, psychological and comparative perspectives on three major themes: the purposes and nature of education; increasing interdisciplinarity within the subject; and the theory-practice divide.

Previous titles include:

Language, Learning, Context
Wolff-Michael Roth

Learning, Context and the Role of Technology
Rosemary Luckin

Education and the Family
Passing success across the generations
Leon Feinstein, Kathryn Duckworth and Ricardo Sabates

Education, Philosophy and the Ethical Environment
Graham Haydon

Educational Activity and the Psychology of Learning
Judith Ireson

Schooling, Society and Curriculum
Alex Moore

Gender, Schooling and Global Social Justice
Elaine Unterhalter

Education – An 'Impossible Profession'?
Tamara Bibby

Being a University
Ronald Barnett

Schools and Schooling in the Digital Age
Neil Selwyn

Forthcoming titles include:

Irregular Schooling
Roger Slee

The Struggle for the History of Education
Gary McCulloch

School Trouble

Identity, power and politics in education

Deborah Youdell

Routledge
Taylor & Francis Group

LONDON AND NEW YORK

First published 2011
by Routledge
2 Park Square, Milton Park, Abingdon, Oxon, OX14 4RN

Simultaneously published in the USA and Canada
by Routledge
270 Madison Avenue, New York, NY 10016

Routledge is an imprint of the Taylor & Francis Group, an informa business

Typeset in Garamond by Swales & Willis Ltd, Exeter, Devon
Printed and bound in Great Britain by TJ International Ltd, Padstow, Cornwall

British Library Cataloguing in Publication Data
A catalogue record for this book is available from the British Library

Library of Congress Cataloging-in-Publication Data
Youdell, Deborah, 1970–
    School trouble : identity, power and politics in education /
    Deborah Youdell.
    p. cm.
    Includes bibliographical references and index.
    1. Education—Political aspects—Great Britain. 2. Education and
    state—Great Britain. 3. Critical pedagogy—Great Britain. I. Title.
    LC93.G7Y68 2011
    379.41—dc22
    2010019494

ISBN13: 978–0–415–47987–5 (hbk)
ISBN13: 978–0–415–47988–2 (pbk)
ISBN13: 978–0–203–83937–9 (ebk)

Contents

Acknowledgements

I need to thank a lot of people for being part of the research and thinking from which this book has emerged. Thank you to all of the No Outsiders research team and schools, and especially Laura and Fin (ESRC reference: RES-062-23-0095). Thanks also to the staff and students at Bay Tree School, in particular Miss Groves, Miss Appleton, Mr Parsons, Mr Newton and the boys in year 9. Sally Power, Michael Reiss and Peter Aggleton, the editors of this series, have given endless support as well as feedback on drafts and have undoubtedly made this a much better book. Mike Apple, Felicity Armstrong, Tamara Bibby, David Gillborn, Zeus Leonardo, Emma Renold, Jessica Ringrose and Michaelinos Zembylas all read first drafts of chapters and I am enormously grateful for their insights, time and friendship. Colleagues at the Institute of Education and the universities of Melbourne and Wisconsin-Madison who have been part of the 'Three Deans Partnership' have made an important contribution to the trajectory of my thinking over a number of years and I want to thank them all, as well as Geoff Whitty, Field Rickards and Julie Underwood for their ongoing support of the conference that has been such an invaluable place to think. I was invited to participate in the '(Anti)Racism and Pedagogy' workshop and conference, supported by the Hawke Research Institute, University of South Australia and Yunggorendi First Nations Centre for Higher Education and Research at Flinders University, Adelaide SA, while I was writing this book. It was an important learning experience and I want to thank all of the workshop participants for their generous collegiality and also Robert Hattam and Daryle Rigney who organized the workshop and conference. Thanks also to Mindy Blaise, Mary-Lou Rasmussen, Jane Kenway, Anna Hickey-Moody, Dena Leahy, Kalervo Gulson and Patrick Carmichael for sharing ideas and pushing mine, as well as to everyone who attended the seminar at the Education and Social Research Institute at Manchester Metropolitan University where I gave these ideas their first public outing. Finally, much love and thanks for everything to my sister Linny and her family, my mum Pat, and my excellent friends Clare, Kate, Sue, Sarah, Paul, Catherine, Mark, Ron and Kitty Hough.

Prologue

Falling[1]

Tommy shifts in his seat in the exam hall as he and the rest of his year group begin the first of this year's national tests, the test that every student in the country his age is taking right now. As he scans the pages of the test booklet he wonders where he's been for all the years of Maths that he suddenly seems to have missed. He shifts some more, adjusting his grip on his pencil and almost imperceptibly dropping his head a little closer to the test paper as he feels Mrs Church's glare.

Tommy isn't sure exactly how he went from being a smiling kid who loved the world and thought the world loved him back to this. How he went from loving the fact that before he even started school he could write in his baby brother's birthday card and play alphabet games with him, to being this 14-year-old not-boy-not-man struggling to find the heart to start a Maths test.

But he knows it has a lot to do with years of being the last to get to choose what to play at during free class time; years of being separated from the one boy in class he really got on with because the teachers thought they were a 'bad influence' on each other; years of being last to be called on for an answer, no matter how quickly, how high or how long his hand was in the air, or told to stop messing about when he was called on to answer even though he was sure his answer had been right, or at least plausible; years of being pounced on at the slightest infraction – a snort at another student's dropped item, a distracted amble into a classroom a minute after the bell – and of rapid and heavy sanctions if he ever did anything serious. Like the time he had a stand-up row with Mr James when he tried to explain that he wasn't disrespecting him by 'coming along to class at anytime he liked' but had been held up in the corridor by Mr Smyth who wanted to talk to him about a fight between some younger boys that he'd seen that morning. That event ended with him outside the headteacher's office, mum up at school, and an unwanted day at home. Until he found he just wasn't able to ask, the hand just wouldn't go up into the air anymore, the words just wouldn't come out.

Tommy knows school might have been different if his mum and dad had stayed together, if his mum had done better at school herself and got a good job instead of the string of part-time stuff, if she'd been a 'respectable' White woman, a possibility Tommy knows is precluded in Whiteworld by the warm cedar tone of his skin, the curl in his hair, his cheekbone, his mouth . . . He knows that as far as school is concerned he's the messed-up, mixed-race kid of a White Trash mum and a Black dad they assume is absent. According to them she has no sense, no self-respect, no ambition and he's caught all of that and tops it off by hanging with the wrong crowd – which means his mates are other Black and mixed-race kids with lives not much different from his.

Not that he blamed it all on the teachers. He knew he'd stopped really paying attention to the teachers and the school, and with that to a decent-sized chunk of the lessons and even to the textbooks and revision aids that his mum insisted on getting for him. But his attention had been drawn elsewhere. To the friends he hung with at break-time, after school and at weekends; to the impressive form his body was surprising him with since he started growing and working out at the same time; to the girls that suddenly all seemed to want to get with him; to the buzz that came with all of that.

So here was the test paper, demanding to be answered. He knew that the level that he achieved in it was going to decide whether he was going to do the basic or the mid-level course for the next two years, and which one of those he did was going to decide how much chance he had of getting the grade that would get him into college. He hadn't quite followed how it worked, he wondered if the teacher had, but if he did badly in this test and was put into basic level then, according to the teacher, the stuff they'd been doing in Maths this summer was probably the hardest stuff they were ever going to do. She'd said it to be reassuring, but it left a sick kind of feeling in his stomach, something between guilt at having given up trying already and shame that the school, even the government or whoever it was that marked the tests, knew and didn't care that he wasn't ever going to try anything harder ever again.

Perhaps he'd misunderstood the teacher, because it didn't seem right at all. He'd told his mum, who agreed that it didn't seem to make sense, and she told him to go back to the teacher and ask again about it, to ask to make sure he got into the right course, the one that gave him the best chance of getting the grade that he, and everyone else, needed. She'd even offered to phone the school herself and see if she could talk to the teacher about it. But they both put it off, and at Parents' Evening the Maths teacher had told them that while Tommy had a chance of getting into the mid-level class, it would depend on his result in this test, and that it wouldn't really hurt if he went into a basic class because a few students who go into the basic class and work hard and stay focused still get the grade, and she was sure that they both agreed that was what was important.

Tommy turned back to the first page of the booklet and tried not to recall the feeling that his teacher's reassurances were in some way a veiled accusation. He pulled back from falling into the pool of residual confusion that rippled at the corner of his eye, shook off the gnawing mistrust that twisted in his stomach and recorded his answer to the first question in the test booklet.

(DY composite Summer 2009)

Note

1 This account draws on evidence from across a number of actual studies but puts this together in a fictionalized form. This 'storytelling' approach using a single 'composite' character and narrative to bring together experiences and issues from a range of research sources has been developed and popularized within Critical Race Theory. There is debate over whether there should be a place for such storytelling in social science, but I am compelled by the strength and usefulness of this approach (Delgado 1989, 1995; Gillborn 2008).

Introduction

The starting point for this book is the idea that schooling is implicated in the making of particular sorts of people as well as the making of educational and social exclusions and inequalities. And, following from this, that schools are important sites of counter- or radical-politics. From this starting point the book investigates a range of resources for theorizing and enacting political practices that make 'school trouble'. The spirit and the form of my title, *School Trouble*, is borrowed from Judith Butler's (1990) *Gender Trouble* in which she sets out the problematics of gender, demonstrates some of the trouble that gender categories cause, and offers theoretical and political tools for 'troubling' gender. This book hopes to make similar moves in relation to schooling. Its key goal is to piece together a series of tools and tactics for intervening into contemporary education in ways that have the potential to destabilize the endurance of its inequalities and loosen the constraints of its normative knowledges, meanings, practices and subjects. The book does this by bringing theorizations of counter-politics together with a range of counter-political traditions in education. This underpins another key concern of the book – to illustrate resistance politics inside education. The book investigates a range of ideas for and empirical examples of critical action in school as this is enacted in the practice of teachers and students across a series of educational settings and levels of intervention. I engage self-conscious politics pursued by educators, practices that might be understood as sub-political activities that are a part of educators' day-to-day practice and practices that can be seen as implicitly political but might not ordinarily be thought of in this way either by those engaged in them or by those looking on from outside. This highlights the book's concern with the political aspects and effects of ordinary, day-to-day practices, pedagogic encounters and everyday life inside schools, the ways that these connect to 'who' is recognized as a 'good' student and learner and how the constraints on such recognition might be unsettled. In this sense a key target of the politics of the book is, borrowing from Critical Race Theory, the 'business as usual' of schooling.

A fundamental question of the book pivots on what radical- or counter-politics in education might look like now and how we might go about pursuing such politics. In order to think through how we might pursue a counter-politics in education and identify what its goals and tactics might be, we need both a sophisticated understanding of the terrain that we hope to intervene into and a set of political tools that might enable us to do this. In developing a richer understanding of the education landscape

I borrow Deleuze and Guattari's idea of the assemblage to try to make sense of the way that economy and politics, policy, organizational arrangements, knowledge, subjectivity, pedagogy, everyday practices and feelings come together to make up the current education assemblage. I take up Michel Foucault's understandings of resistances, practices of self and fearless speech that invite us to resist prevailing discourses in our everyday practice. I draw on Judith Butler's understandings of performative politics, discursive agency and new collectivities that set out ways of resignifying discourse and suggest political action that moves beyond identities and politics based on these identities. I engage with Ernesto Laclau and Chantal Mouffe's understanding of agonistic pluralism and the struggle for hegemony as a framework for thinking about politics that foreground discourse, take account of the passion of politics, and are collective at the same time as they are multiply focused and do not demand consensus. And I take up Gilles Deleuze and Felix Guattari's understanding of becomings as a way of thinking about a politics that is affective, anti-identity and concerned to unsettle assemblages.

As I make use of these ideas I bring them together to identify a series of modes and arenas for political practice: *a politics of discourse, an anti-identity politics, a politics of feeling and a politics of becoming*. Thinking across these orders and conceptualizations of the political offers a series of interconnected insights through which the possibility for a counter-politics in contemporary education emerges. It allows me to explore the ways that state and judicial power come together with disciplinary power in the micro-circuits of the everyday. It offer avenues for understanding the way that institutions and their practices are made and constrained, providing ways into thinking about the people or subjects of education. It offers a way of interrogating the inter-relations between the apparently disparate orders of institution, knowledge, practice, subjectivity and feeling. And it provides ideas for thinking about how schooling might be different, that is, how the education assemblage might be converted.

The book is organized in two parts. Part One, *Troubling ideas*, explores conceptualizations of identity, power and politics and the place of these in education. Chapter 1 demonstrates the fundamentally political nature of education and charts some of the multiple counter-political traditions in education, locating education in a wider political context and mapping the policy tendencies that this context provokes. Chapter 2 introduces the political tools that I will be making use of in the book, connecting these to their intellectual and political histories and suggesting how they might be useful for thinking about and making sense of political practices in schools. Chapter 3 details the theoretical tools that underpin the political ideas that are being put to work in the book, offering an extensive treatment of these for those readers who wish to engage with theory more deeply.

Part Two, *Troubling schools*, mobilizes these conceptual tools to make sense of empirical accounts of the processes of schooling and to interrogate the capacity of these theorizations to underpin political practices in education. As aspects of the education assemblage are explored, Part Two moves from school knowledge, to subjectivity, to everyday practices, to feelings, to becomings and maps these orders and their significance for politics and identifies radical political interventions that might scatter the assemblage. Chapter 4 engages with the critical tradition of sociology of knowledge in education, offering a detailed analysis of the use of 'gay' storybooks as a political resource in primary schools and one educator's attempts to make use of these to intervene in and unsettle school knowledge. In Chapter 5 issues of identity take centre stage. It demonstrates the processes through which we are made subjects and the ways in which particular subjectivations are resisted in the everyday practices of both students and teachers in school. Chapter 6 explores the possibilities for educators to engage in radical political practices in their everyday practices inside schools. It considers a series of examples of pedagogic interventions, both improvised on the spot and planned in advance, inside particular school spaces and in particular moments. Through an analysis of these everyday political pedagogies I examine their potential to remake students and schooling, as well as the inevitable limits of their reach and endurance. Chapter 7 focuses on the affective dimensions of education and explores the significance of affectivities in pedagogic encounters, once again drawing on instances of pedagogic practices inside schools to analyse the place of feelings and their relevance for and entanglement in enacting radical education politics. Chapter 8 takes up the notion of 'becoming' to consider a series of practices and pedagogic encounters inside one school and explores how schools, classrooms, teachers and pedagogies might be seen to offer students 'becomings' that disrupt the business-as-usual exclusions of schooling. Chapter 9, the final chapter, returns to the question of politics in education asking whether educators might practise as assemblage convertors and whether the education assemblage might itself be converted. Drawing on the analyses offered in the preceding chapters, it maps some of the possible terrains, tactics and 'lines of flight' that counter-political pedagogies and counter-political education might pursue.

Over the course of the book I draw on a range of materials. These include existing education research, policy documents, government reports and official statistics, mainstream film, children's and young people's fiction, teaching resources and lesson plans, teachers' accounts of and reflections on their own teaching interventions, ethnographic observations of practices inside classrooms and other school spaces, and storytelling using composite characters and events such as that offered in the prologue to this book. My key concern is to investigate the various insights offered and possibilities opened up by the lines of counter-political thinking and practising that I explore here. For this reason I do not attempt to offer a 'complete' picture of contemporary life in schools. Instead I make use of a relatively small selection of accounts of pedagogic practice and everyday life in school. I return to some of these accounts and incidents over the course of the book, using them as critical cases against which to try out the conceptualizations of political tactics that I am concerned to explore. This approach allows the reader to consider both the relative promise and problematics of these ideas and to appreciate the ways in which the various orders of the education assemblage are manifest in a single event or encounter. Much of the evidence offered, in particular the school-level research data, is drawn from English schools and classrooms. This means, inevitably, that England is the empirical focus of the book. I try, however, to keep the book looking and listening beyond England and the UK. The book draws on international thinking about the shape of contemporary education and the possibilities for educators to intervene in this, as well as on research-based accounts of the work of critical educators from a range of nations. Furthermore, the trends and tendencies in education policy and practices that are mapped are in many ways global and reach into education across settings and age phases. It is hoped, then, that the book will speak to educators in a diverse range of institutional and geographic locations and, even more, that the book will contribute to dialogic spaces in which educators and others share and explore their thinking about education and politics.

Part I

Troubling ideas

Identity, power and politics

1 The politics of schooling
Converting the education assemblage

School trouble: politics in education

Schooling and politics are inseparable. Schools are shaped by the wider economic, political and social context which is reflected in education policy and legislation that delineates what education is and constrains what schooling can be. In turn schools become sites where these wider economic, political and social issues are played out through organizational structures and systems, the curriculum and pedagogy and the subjectivities available to teachers and students; where educators and students are managed, monitored, compared and held accountable; and where normative under-standings of schooling and its subjects are sedimented. And schools are also sites where abiding inequalities are made and remade, even as these become the focus of policy interventions. Schooling, then, is shaped and constrained by the prevailing politics of the moment; it is fundamentally political even if the politics of educa-tion are often opaque or taken as the normal state of affairs. After 30 years of neo-liberal government in the world's wealthiest nations, a neo-liberal consensus has been established globally and neo-liberal values and approaches to government have pro-liferated and become entrenched. Education has been a key site for this neo-liberal reform and education systems, values, content and goals are now firmly shaped and constrained in these terms. Yet there is discontent with the current education land-scape – from employers bemoaning inadequately prepared employees and parent-'consumers' finding that the 'choice' they have been promised does not result in their choices being realized, to students disillusioned with schooling and fully aware that it may well not lead to the future opportunities that it claims to offer. This suggests a continuing, if altered, place for radical and critical traditions in education. While education might be captured by neo-liberalism, possibilities for change remain – we should not give up on education.

In the prologue to this book I offer a story about Tommy, 'Falling'; it is a compos-ite that brings experiences and problematics identified through education research together in a fictionalized account. Like the autobiographical and *ecriture feminine* in feminist writing (Cixous and Clement 1986a; Kehily 1995), storytelling has been developed in Critical Race Theory (CRT) as a rebuke to the privileging of certain forms of knowledge and evidence in social science and as a way of making recogniz-able experiences that are often outside formal research accounts. With the politics of knowledge a key concern of this book, I purposefully open with a piece that in form and content is contested. The story I offer draws on evidence from across a number of actual studies but puts this together in a fictionalized form in order to bring to life and open up experience in a way that is difficult to do through more established forms of evidence. 'Falling' allows us to see the contemporary education landscape dominated by national testing regimes; the ways that attainment in these tests demarcates educational possibilities and impossibilities; the complexities and opacities of schooling's systematized practices; how responsibility for educational successes and failures is individualized; the ways that particular identities are made and given bounded meanings within and beyond schools; the dynamic between how schools recognize or cannot recognize students and students' own identifications and the practices that flow from this dynamic; the way that the minutiae of everyday life in school is implicated in framing and constraining 'who' a student can be, even when this is nothing more that a simple look; and the way that feeling is an integral part of the experience of these processes. The story of Tommy in 'Falling', then, brings together and allows us to see a range of the processes that I will be exploring in detail through this book and which the politics of this book are concerned to 'trouble'.

What does it mean to 'trouble' schooling and to suggest that schools and schooling are troubling? And why should we want to cause 'school trouble'? Ordinarily, schooling, and education more broadly, is seen as a 'good thing': everyone needs and has a right to education; education is good for the people educated; and educated people are good for the society they are part of. In this sense, schooling and education are seen in close relation. Education is a state and societal endeavour with programmes of study and recognizable modes of teaching, learning and assessment that takes place in institutions from schools and universities to community centres, prisons and places of work. In relation to schools, then, education is the object and the goal, schooling is the process through which children and young people are educated and schools are the principal places in which this education takes place. Yet, as I have begun to show, what counts as education is neither straightforward nor neutral and the processes of schooling are often far from benign.

Research in the sociology of education over the last 40 or so years has drawn attention to educational inequalities and to the ways in which both education policy and the practices of schooling actually exclude certain children and young people from education. Inequalities of access to education and outcomes from education are the most immediately visible. But it is those school processes that create these inequalities that are at the heart of much sociological research in education. The sorts of knowledge that circulate in schools, within the formal curriculum and the wider cultures and practices of school life, are tied up with these inequalities. Which knowledges are authorized and conferred particular status, which are silenced, and who has access to or is excluded from these knowledges, are all bound up with relations of power and are key mediators of students' participation in and experiences of schooling. These sorts of concerns lead us, as my opening story illustrates, to more nuanced problematics within formal education; the subtle or implicit hierarchies and everyday practices that are implicated in inequalities of access, participation, experience and outcomes. These subtle or implicit hierarchies and everyday injustices often have their origins in institutional and educator judgements about 'who' students are. These judgements inform practice both explicitly and implicitly as they are taken up by educational institutions and educators to predict and explain what students can or cannot do, how they will or will not behave, the futures that are or are not open to them. This 'who' is not simply descriptive but also productive of particular sorts of students and learners as it is drawn on by educators as they forge different relationships with differentially positioned students and as they explain and constrain the relationships that these differentially positioned students can and cannot make and sustain. These everyday judgements have massive implications for students' experiences of education, shaping and constraining how students understand themselves and the opportunities, relationships and futures they see as being open to them. In this set of circumstances and relationships the feelings of educators and students – both those feelings that are explicitly acknowledged, named and engaged as well as those that are disavowed – are a powerful but often overlooked productive force in the creation and foreclosure of particular educational subjectivities, experiences, and trajectories.

This way of thinking about schooling poses fundamental questions about whether educational institutions and encounters actually do what they are intended to do; whether these intentions are necessarily coherent or compatible or in the interests of all students; whether it is intentions – 'good', 'bad' or otherwise – that govern what actually happens in the complex realities of everyday life in schools; and what sorts of interventions educators committed to education that is inclusive and fair might make. Ian Hunter noted some time ago now that, given the ways in which mass schooling emerged as an endeavour of the state and continues to be improvised in the face of pressing social, economic and political demands, it can neither be as good or as bad as its promoters and critics suggest. That is, schooling is neither simply a system of reproduction nor is it simply a site of emancipation or equalization (Hunter 1996). What this suggests is that schools are sites in which the forces of the state are manifest and the aspirations of the state are pursued but they are simultaneously sites where these forces and aspirations run up against blocks, whether these are intentionally deployed or artifacts of the sites into which they intervene. As the nature, purpose and effects of education are contested, it and its institutions become sites of struggle (Apple 2006).

A range of alternative visions for education have emerged that respond to readings of the problematics of formal education. These are underpinned by different philosophical and theoretical traditions and are more or less overtly politically orientated in their approach to schooling and their ambitions for a reconfigured education. The 'deschooling' of education and of social institutions more widely has been advocated principally by Ivan Illich and his followers on the grounds that institutional education is socially divisive and psychologically stultifying and should be replaced by education that proceeds from the question of what learners might need to learn (Illich 2000; Kahn and Kellner 2007; Lund 1977; Morrow and Torres 1990). Child-centred, democratic schooling, often referred to as 'progressive education', has sought to establish education contexts in which children decide what, when, where, and how to learn. One of the most well-known and well-developed examples of this in action is the UK independent school, Summerhill, which was established by A.S. Neill in the 1920s and which continues today (Summerhill 2004). Having fought against government moves to close the school in the early 2000s (Shepherd 2007), the school received its first approval by the UK Government's school inspection agency Ofsted in 2007 (Ofsted 2007). 'Radical education' movements have championed the 'common school' as a site for critical education that has equalizing potential (see Michael Fielding 2005, 2007). 'Critical pedagogy' has taken a dialogic approach to education with the central goal of enabling people to come to a critical and political understanding of their social and economic location. Critical pedagogy's key proponent, the Brazilian educator Paulo Freire, anticipated that this process of conscientization would lead to mass political uprising and so social change (Freire 1970). Principles of critical pedagogy have been taken up and developed in a range of international settings with a view to enabling learners to understand critically their social location and so change it. For instance, bell hooks has developed this thinking from a Black feminist perspective to encourage and enable transgressions of normative positions and social ordering (hooks 1994); Sonia Nieto has used these ideas to explore the education of 'out of school' students of colour in the urban USA (Nieto 2004). Sandy Grande has built on these ideas to develop a 'Red Pedagogy' focused on de-colonization working with First Nations people in the USA (Grande 2004). And critical theory and pedagogy is an underpinning principle of Te Whare Wānanga o Awanuiārangi, the Tribal University of New Zealand (Awanuiārangi n.d.). Elsewhere, the 'inclusive education' movement has followed these critical traditions to call for fundamental changes to schooling and schools, in order to render institutions truly inclusive of all students (Allen 1999; Barton 2001; Corbett 1996, 2001; Christensen and Rizvi 1996). And 'feminist pedagogies' have taken-up and critiqued the critical pedagogy tradition in order to develop pedagogies aimed at conscienticizing girls and so provoking girls' and women's critical, feminist action (Luke and Gore 1992). More recently critical race pedagogy has built on the insights of CRT to explore the pedagogic possibilities of exposing the embedded nature of racism and the endurance of Whiteness and so unsettling White supremacy (Leonardo 2005). And deconstructive and queer pedagogies informed by post-structural theory have sought to unsettle and shift the normative subjectivities produced in schools by working both explicitly and implicitly with students to deconstruct these subjectivities and by engaging in queer practice (Atkinson and DePalma 2009; Davies 2003). All of these education movements respond to and look to intervene into the aspects of schooling that are seen as problematic. These ideas about education and the practices they espouse have received varying degrees of recognition and take up in the mainstream of education theory and practice, and while for the most part they have remained marginal, they have been legitimate, recognizable and speakable. That is, they have had a place in educational theory and practice.

The contemporary political moment

I began this chapter by suggesting that the wider economic and political context impacts on and forms a component of the education landscape and that education is political from government legislation to the day-to-day practices of classrooms. It is important, therefore, to consider this wider political context and its relationship to education. The question of politics in education is located in a broad context of global neo-liberal consensus that has seen widespread, although not universal, movement towards the political centre and centre-Right and the demise of communitarian or socialist Left oppositions. While for much of the past 30 years this political shift has been credited with creating the conditions of massive global economic growth, the effects of this are neither evenly distributed nor assured. In the present, this is a political context of economic crisis, heightened concern over environmental vulnerability, and proliferating and prolonged military conflict, a context in which the 'War on Terror' has positioned Islam, in a range of locations and manifestations, as the ultimate global problem.

In the UK, against the backdrop of the War on Terror and global economic downturn it has been possible to see rising discontent with established political parties and processes. Both of the main political parties in the UK have for some time been citing the fragmentation of community and community values, social exclusion, and the disaffection of particular sections of the youth population as major problems for party political and civic participation. These concerns have been variously echoed and refracted by civil society organizations, trade unions and popular media at the same time as the demise of party political engagement has been highlighted. Academic analysis of this disengagement from party politics has charted processes of political evaporation and the emergence of political apathy (Eliasoph 1998) and has examined the connections between apparent dissatisfaction with electoral politics and the day-to-day choices and practice of individuals (Ginsborg 2005).

World-wide interest in the 2009 US election campaign and subsequent 'feel good' responses to the election of Barack Obama as US president suggested a new popular engagement with formal political processes. Almost simultaneously, however, anxiety over the economic situation and a related resurgence in dissatisfaction with the drawn-out military involvement in Iraq and Afghanistan have seen a growing critique of existing policy trends in the UK and a collapse in support for the then Labour Party government in the popular media and, according to recurrent opinion polls, the population at large. It was against this backdrop that in May 2009 the *Daily Telegraph* newspaper exposed what was reported daily across news media as the scandal of the size and nature of expenses habitually claimed by Members of Parliament (*Telegraph* 2009). These exposures have led to ongoing media and parliamentary debate and ultimately a formal parliamentary inquiry (Kelly 2009). In the wake of these events, bigger questions have been raised over the parliamentary political process and the extent to which this is democratic, with mainstream media discussing the bluntness of representational democracy and the nature of democracy itself in ways that are unprecedented in the UK during the post-war period (McSmith and Savage 2009; *Guardian* Editorial 2009). Furthermore, emergent Left alternative organizations such as Unlock Democracy and Compass, as well as coalitions of trade unions and public figures, have attempted to mobilize this moment through moves such as the 'People's Charter for Change' (Brittain *et al.* 2009; Compass 2007; Unlock Democracy 2009). While the establishment of the Conservative-Liberal Democrat coalition government in Britain now appears to have foreclosed the possibility of significant democratic reforms to electoral and parliamentary processes, the demands for such change did suggest a moment of political possibility that had not been seen during 30 years of neo-liberal government. These currents of discontent underscore the abiding possibility of finding spaces to 'talk back' to power and the potential to influence and shift policy direction and even the shape of democracy itself. At global, national and local levels we can still find spaces in which to think and talk about what we might *do differently* in the day-to-day inside communities, in institutions such as schools, and within interactions, including those of the classroom.

Education policy tendencies

This is the contemporary political context in which education is situated. Education is intrinsically linked to this wider context as it informs and shapes education policy, and is the set of relations and concerns to which formal education is charged to respond (Brown and Lauder 2006). It is also the wider politics that frames political practices as these are pursued in and through schooling.

As I have already indicated, the last 30 years has seen the rise, extrapolation and embedding of neo-liberal approaches to public policy and public sector services across nations. These are not just the closely aligned English speaking nations – the UK, the US, Australia, New Zealand and Canada – they also include many nations in Europe, Latin America, Africa and Asia. Indeed, these approaches to public policy, and to the reinvention of the state itself, can be understood as an integral part of globalization and, increasingly, they are themselves global phenomena (Ball and Youdell 2008). These approaches to public policy and the management and transformation of the public sector have had massive and far-reaching impacts that have substantially altered education. Predicated on a core commitment to the importance of a small state, deregulated markets and the efficiency and effectiveness of the market form itself, neo-liberal reform agendas have pursued marketization and privatization in the public sector. There is a great deal of writing that details these policy moves and interrogates their underpinnings and their impacts in education (see Apple 2006; Ball 2007; Ball and Youdell 2008; Gewirtz *et al.* 1995; Gillborn and Youdell 2000; Lingard 2007; Whitty *et al.* 1998). What is evident in this literature are the ways in which neo-liberal policy reform has drawn on the ideas, techniques and technologies that are dominant in the private sector and imported these into the public sector through a massive programme of reform.

Marketization, the creation of markets within the public sector, has been a key feature of these reforms, along with the diversification of provision and consumer 'choice' that are seen as the drivers of and check on these new markets. Another, and often related, feature of these reforms has been accountability and associated mechanisms of performance measurement and management designed to render the sector accountable and allocate budgets according to various measures of performance. These sorts of reforms have been pursued heavily in education, often framed by policy makers in terms of the need to transform and thereby improve education in order to respond to fast-paced global changes and to secure a dominant position in a competitive global marketplace (Brown and Lauder 2006). A more recent turn in neo-liberal policy has been a move towards privatization in and of education, with both private sector practice and private sector for-profit players now established parts of what was state education (Ball 2007). These privatization tendencies have already changed education, from policy frameworks and the organizations involved in the design and delivery of education to everyday life inside institutions. These privatization tendencies have undercut the idea of education as a collective and public good and established it as a saleable commodity and an asset to be competed over by self-interested individuals.

These policy tendencies, and the way of thinking about education, schooling and students that underpin and flow from them, have significant impacts on schools. As much research has now shown, policies are not simply implemented by schools and ways of thinking are not exported in any straightforward way. As they are enacted inside schools, policies and the understandings that circulate with them are variously refracted, resisted and rearticulated in ways that can make their impacts unpredictable and their effects sometimes unexpected (Ball 1994, 2005). Nevertheless, the state does reach into the school and the classroom as polices are implemented and educational knowledges are disseminated and deployed. As such, schools, classrooms, teachers, teaching practices, students and students' experiences are shaped and reshaped by policy and prevailing governmentally sanctioned educational knowledges. In the English context key features of this include the mandated National Curriculum; organizational approaches including 'ability' groupings; accountability mechanisms, targets and performance indicators; an audit culture and its inspection regimes; particular teaching and learning approaches, some mandated and some heavily promoted; the requirement for all lessons to be heavily documented; a demand for approaches to school activities, from school leadership to 'behaviour management' and promoting health and 'wellbeing', to be based on approved forms of 'evidence'; and required ways of working with other agencies from across sectors.

While these policies are claimed to promote efficiency and effectiveness and raise educational standards, in wealthy nations such as the UK, students from lower social class backgrounds and from particular minoritized race and ethnic backgrounds have continued to perform less well in national tests than their White and more privileged counterparts (DCSF 2009a). The precise nature, pattern and persistence of these differential outcomes has become the subject of significant debate at the level of policy makers and education researchers, with argument over which groups are reaping the least benefits from education, why, and how this might be measured and explained (Connolly 2006, 2008; Gorard 2000; Gorard and Smith 2008). The New Labour government incorporated a concern for these inequalities within their education policy platform, with a policy emphasis on 'social inclusion' and 'social exclusion' (Levitas 1998; Youdell 2006a) later superseded with a focus on 'deprivation' (DCSF 2009b). Yet while this focus on deprivation included a concern for what schools can do to improve the relatively low levels of educational attainment of students identified as experiencing deprivation, this discursive framing almost wholly disarticulated the causes of deprivation from wider economic, political and social structures and the causes of these levels of attainment from the policies, structures, institutions and practices of education (Francis and Hey 2009). The new UK government's policy in relation to schools and its wider 'Big Society' platform suggests a further pulling back of the state, as either a provider or commissioner of services, and represents a new iteration of the privatizing and individualizing tendencies that have been associated with increasing educational inequalities.

A critical account of the systemic and in-school processes that produce persistent educational inequalities offered by David Gillborn and myself (Gillborn and Youdell 2000) suggests that education policies that set national tests and demand their ongoing public comparison provoke educational institutions to improvise new practices of sorting selection and uneven resource allocation – what we call 'educational triage'. A key mechanism of this sorting and selection is the deployment of notions of ability and intelligence, notions that are suffused with old ideas of race and class hierarchy and which cement these classifications and their hierarchical arrangement and normalize the uneven distribution of opportunities and outcomes across differentiated groups of students.

As these constellations of policy requirements and governmental guidance reach into schools and classrooms they not only impact what schools and classrooms can 'do' and can 'be'; they also impact the teachers and students inside them. Research has argued that the privatization tendencies that these particular policies are a part of are transforming the people who populate schools. The headteacher as a leading professional is transformed into a corporate manager; the professional teacher is transformed into a teaching technician as pedagogy is remade as the 'delivery' of correct knowledge through the correct application of techniques; the student learning within a school community is transformed into an individualized consumer, the personal beneficiary of education in competition with her/his peers and responsible for her/his own success or failure (Ball 2003a; Youdell 2004a). These policy tendencies and their impacts on schools and their populations, therefore, transform relationships from collegial and community focused to competitive, individualized, instrumental and performance focused (Ball 2003b). It is these transformations that Stephen Ball has called the 'terrors of performativity' (Ball 2003b). Education policy tendencies that embed neo-liberal forms of governance and transform the public sector into a commodity and the public into individualized consumers are shifting what education is and what it means. They are also implicated wholly in the ongoing creation, not the mere reproduction, of educational inequalities and the hierarchical categorization and ordering of students. These policy effects have consequences that reach far beyond the school and are a key reason why education is political and why it is a site of political struggle.

Converting the education assemblage

Using the idea of assemblages, drawn from the work of Gilles Deleuze and Felix Guattari (1983, 2008), helps us to conceptualize the complex terrain of education and the ways that economy and politics, policy, organizational arrangements, knowledge, subjectivity, pedagogy, everyday practices and feelings come together to form the education assemblage. Deleuze and Guattari (1983, 2008) suggest that apparently 'whole' entities, be these societies, institutions or something else, might be understood as assemblages of heterogeneous components that cross-cut state, social, representational, discursive, subjective and affective orders. Deleuze and Guattari suggest that it is the particularities of the ways that these component parts come together that we need to map in order to understand a particular assemblage. Manuel DeLanda (2006) has taken up and developed this idea to try to better understand the complexities of the contemporary world, bringing together and bridging the micro- and macro-levels by moving from readings of the personal and organizational through to readings of cities, nations and the transnational. It is the inevitably uncomfortable synthesis of these readings that enables us to understand the complexity of the assemblage.

The work of Deleuze and Guattari is receiving growing attention amongst education scholars, and their notion of the assemblage has been put to work to understand education and the workings of particular education disciplines and pedagogic practices (see Hickey-Moody 2009; Leahy 2009; Rose 2000; Tamboukou 2008). While my focus is on the potential for counter-politics in education, situating this in an understanding of the complexity of the education assemblage provokes me to engage questions of counter-political practices across its various components: the wider economic and political context, education policy and its effects, school knowledge and its inclusions and exclusions, pedagogic practices and relations, subjectivities and their possibilities and constraints, and the place of feelings or affectivities.

As this initial account of the education assemblage suggests, politics is manifest and pursued in education at the level of party political manifesto pledges, government activity such as legislation, policy, guidance and special initiatives; at the level of formal or systematic activities relating to these at the level of the institution; and at the level of the activities of educators and students inside institutions that might take the form of tactical moves in their day-to-day practice. Thinking about politics as being enacted and played out at these various levels suggests that education and its institutions are shot through with politics: the policies that frame and constrain institutions and educators; the curriculum that is taught; the systems, techniques and technologies that are utilized; the pedagogies that are deployed; the forms of relationships that are manifest; and the everyday cultures that inform the smallest interactions and ideas are all part of a political landscape and implicated in relations of power. Counter-politics that intervene into this inherently political terrain might be enacted at all of the levels of the education assemblage that I have identified, they might take a number of forms and might be pursued and have effects that flow in multiple directions and to multiple ends. Counter-politics in education are often manifest as formal expressions of new social movements whether these take the form of identity politics concerned with categories such as gender, sexuality, race and disability or the form of single-issue politics concerned with matters such as school deregulation, sex education or environmentalism. These politics might take the form of organized lobbying or coordinated resistance over particular policy initiatives, be it lobbying for the creation of policy such as the protection of particular minorities in schools, or the repeal or reform of policy such as the deregulation of state schooling. Counter-politics might also take the form of more everyday struggles and resistances enacted by students, teachers or others in the practices of their daily lives. These forms of practice may be less recognizable as politics, or be identified as sub-political or simply the tactics of everyday life (de Certeau 1988). Yet these everyday struggles and resistances might seek to unsettle the ways in which influence, prestige, status and their exclusions are rendered in schools; they might seek to shift what and whose knowledge counts and what and whose knowledge is silenced, discarded or erased; they might seek to transform pedagogic forms and relationships and who is privileged or disregarded by these; or they might seek to trouble 'who' educators and students are and can be. I explore these political forms in the following chapter. All of these counter-politics might have the potential to unsettle the 'business as usual' (Delgado and Stefancic 2000: xvi) of schooling and so unsettle or even 'convert' (Hickey-Moody 2009) the education assemblage.

2   Tactics for political practice

Radical politics

The notion of radical politics offers a useful starting point for thinking about education as a site of counter-political action. Radical politics in the broadest sense can be understood as pursuing change at the 'root'. That is, radical politics pursues change at the very foundation of society. It is important to remember that radical change agendas can be found on both the Left and Right. For instance, the reforms initiated by the Thatcher and Reagan governments in the UK and the US pursued and realized the radical neo-liberal reform of education that is now commonplace and common sense around the globe.

On the political Left, revolutionary, socialist or communist movements have argued that the economic structure of society and hence exploitative social class relations between owners and workers in capitalist societies should be fundamentally changed. These forms of radical politics foreground the promise of radical change in the dialectic of history. This dialectical thinking suggests that an exploitative capitalist economic and political system bears the inherent tension of its exploitative relations, in particular in its separation of workers from the products of their labour and the extraction of the surplus value of this labour. The resolution of this tension is understood as being immanent in the tension itself which is seen as inevitably precipitating the downfall of capitalism through workers' revolution, whether this is arrived at through the active interventions and mobilizations of a revolutionary leadership or as a result of the tension itself (Boggs 1976; Callinicos 1976; Laclau and Mouffe 2001).

A range of radical movements has built on this revolutionary tradition and there has been extensive diversification of the goals and strategies of the radical Left. The question of whether political struggles should seek communist revolution or socialist democracy has been key here and workers' movements, radical branches of the Protestant church, settlement movements, and trade unionism are examples of practical political endeavours that have emerged from this (Martin 2004; Munro 1999; Thompson 1980). The Marxist Feminist movement has offered readings of the gendered nature of exploitative relations under capitalism and combined revolutionary ambitions to erase capitalist relations with ambitions for fundamental change in relations between men and women (Walby 1986). The Radical Feminist movement has sought to fundamentally change patriarchal relations of exploitation between men and women and envisioned feminist utopias underpinned by this (Dworkin 1988). The Black Power movement has looked to overturn relations of domination and exploitation between the dominant White population and people of colour (Joseph 2006). And Anarchist movements have argued that oppression can only be erased by dismantling the state itself (Bakunin 1990). All of these Left political movements, which have emerged and re-emerged over the last hundred and more years, identify relations of domination, oppression and exploitation, understood in a range of ways, as the necessary locus of radical change; change that would no doubt shift fundamentally the shape and nature of society and the political system that is a part of it. Their impact has a legacy for the contemporary period in which globalization has given rise to new economic, geopolitical and cultural arrangements and a whole series of mobile alliances based on geographically dispersed political, religious or cultural positions as well as situated national and regional interests.

Unsurprisingly given their thoroughgoing critique of society and ambition for fundamental change, the various expressions of radical politics have seldom been met with state, media or mass approval outside those nations where 'revolutionary' change has occurred. Yet despite states' commitments to prevent radical social action, and media and mass rejection of change of this sort, for much of the twentieth century many forms of radical politics have remained legitimate and have been accepted, if not signed up to, by sections of the population. This is perhaps most evident in the case of the strength of Left workers' movements and the engagement of the Left intelligentsia in this. Even during the 'Cold War' period, radical Left politics remained thinkable despite it exercising particular governments and populations who sought to expose and expunge it. For instance, it has taken a relatively short period of time for the anti-communist campaigns of the McCarthy era to be judged more harshly by academic and popular critics alike than the socialist/communist radical political movements that were its targets (Oshinsky 2005; Reeves 1983).

Radical politics, particularly in the form of communism, has a long association with communities and societies constituted by the capitalist West as backward and dangerous Others, an othering that also deploys forms of racialization. The processes of racialization that are implicit in these constitutions are not restricted to contexts where simple phenotypes can be deployed to confirm racial otherness – within the terms of Whiteness, the old USSR and Eastern European nations were constituted as racially Other, as 'not-quite-White'; a not-quite-White racialization that, post-the dissolution of the USSR, is both set aside *and* remade in constitutions of Eastern European economic migrants to Western Europe (McDowell 2009). In this sense Whiteness and capitalist economies undergirded by liberal democratic political systems are inseparable (Leonardo 2004a, 2004b).

While radical politics are widely constituted in Western hegemonic discourse as ideological and so not rational or scientific, this constitution is simultaneously undercut by the development of revolutionary and socialist political philosophy within the West. Radical political thought has an established place in the story of the Enlightenment, whether this takes the form of the work of Marx himself, the radical intellectuals of the late nineteenth and early twentieth centuries, the Labour movement or trade unionism. This is not to ignore the struggles of the White working classes in the West and their class oppression. As the radical Left has moved out of political philosophy and into political struggles it has always been effaced by the political establishment – in constitutions of 'Reds Under the Bed' in the US, the 'Loony Left' in the UK and the wider constitution of the 'Communist Threat' by the Western coalition of NATO countries. Critique has frequently taken the form of ridicule, derision, censure and overt oppression. Yet the discursive space has remained for radical politics to be recognized as being based historically on critical reasoning and a search for an accurate analysis, even where this is judged to have failed. In turn this analysis is conceded as being a legitimate underpinning for education movements (Anyon 2005; Martin 2004; Nelson 2001).

However, in the contemporary neo-liberal political assemblage the legitimacy and speakability, or even thinkability, of radicalism and radical politics has been called fundamentally into question. The impossibility of these politics and forms appears to be inextricably linked with the 'War on Terror' and the discourse of Islamic 'threat' that has become so widespread and apparently self-evident since the attacks on the US Pentagon and the World Trade Center in 2001. This is not a new discourse however. As Edward Said's work has shown, the discourses which constitute a reviled 'Oriental' Other (Said 2003) and a fanatical and 'under'-developed or 'un'-Enlightened Muslim (Said 1997) reverberate with the prevailing histories and meanings of the Crusades as well as Western colonial and post-colonial relations with the East. Yet in the context of the War on Terror, these constitutions of the Oriental-Muslim Other have come to be inflected by a discourse of terrorist threat that is constituted not only as a threat to the lives of individuals but as a threat to the *whole way of life* of the West (Martin and Phelan 2002; Richardson 2004).

A previously legitimate, if marginal and sometimes derided, notion of radicalism has been subsumed within this discourse of 'terror'. This has been effected through the collapsing of the notion of the 'violent extremist/ism' and the notions of 'radical-ism' and 'radicalization'. This expropriation of 'radical' and redefinition of 'radicaliza-tion' as synonymous with 'violent extremism' and as a phenomenon located within Muslim communities, both in the Islamic world and in the West, is evident in the dis-courses of governments internationally (AVID 2004; NCTB n.d.). In the UK it is evi-dent in government policy (Smith 2008), government commissioned research (Brand *et al.* 2008; Choudhury 2007), government sponsored intervention projects (C&LG n.d.), opposition political parties (Mughal 2008), civil society organizations (Gadher 2007) and academic research centres (ICSR n.d.). A key example of the expropria-tion of radicalism can be found in the US Violent Radicalization and Homegrown Terrorism Prevention Act that passed with massive support in late 2007. Violence and radicalization are tied together in the title of the Act and its definition of violent radicalization as 'the process of adopting or promoting an extremist belief system for the purpose of facilitating ideologically-based violence to advance political, religious or social change' (Abel 2008).

This configuration insists that radicalism and violence are tied together; that this includes ideas as well as actions; and that these radical ideas and acts are intrinsically ideological, that is, erroneous and not subject to purportedly 'rational' interrogation. It is important to acknowledge that violent revolution has been a key aspect of debate within communism, a fact of revolutionary uprisings, and a feature of the Western constitution of the 'Communist Threat'. Yet radical movements have also offered notions of peaceful revolution and socialist democratic ambitions and radical political thought has been acknowledged as encompassing a broad set of political ideas and goals. The contemporary tying together of radicalism and violent extremism, then, is an expropriation which takes the idea of radicalism out of its prior meanings and relocates it in a new set of meanings that render radicalism as intrinsically irrational, necessarily violent and automatically terrorist. This can be thought of as a chain of signification that *makes* the meanings it appears to convey. That is, this re-signification of 'radical' within 'terror(ism)' acts to make radicalism synonymous with 'violence' and 'extremism'. At the same time, this re-signification threatens to constitute anybody who might be identified as Muslim as a potential violent extremist (Gillborn 2008). While there is some acknowledgment within the discourse of the War on Terror that 'the idea of radicalization could be used to criminalize protest, discredit any form of "radical thinking" and label political dissent as potentially dangerous' (Neumann, 2008: 3), these concerns are widely set aside.

Congressman Dennis Kucinich, one of only six opponents of the US Violent Radicalization and Homegrown Terrorism Prevention Act, has critiqued this expropriation of radicalism and the way in which it acts to disallow dissenting thought. Speaking in New York before the Act was passed, Kucinich said 'it really sets the stage for further criminalization of protest' (Lee 2007) and shortly after the vote he suggested that the first amendment protecting freedom of speech was 'undercut' by the Act because 'lines like "ideologically based" . . . say government should police ideas, not conduct' (Kucinich cited by Abel 2008). There is also a current of academic research that challenges this expropriation of radicalism. Peter Burgess (2008) argues that within the contemporary discourse of the War on Terror the notion of 'radicalization' comes to mean anything that threatens liberal democracy. This, he suggests, exposes the illiberalism at the heart of liberalism where we are free to critique as long as we do not critique liberal democracy itself, a limit that disallows radical political thinking. Burgess poses the question: 'When does radicalization threaten to harm the liberal democratic order?' and responds that:

> [T]here is an unstable difference between acting in the name of change within the democratic order and acting in the name of change through mechanisms of radicalization. Indeed, one might even say that pursuing change in liberal, democratic societies involves a *structural contradiction* or even *aporia*: The principles of liberal democracy allow change up to, but not including, changes to the principles that authorize change. In this sense the *supporting principles* of liberal democracy are essentially *illiberal*.
>
> (Burgess 2008: 2, original emphasis)

This construction of radicalism is wholly racialized (UKREN n.d.). In the discourse of the War on Terror radicalization is positioned as the indoctrination of simultaneously 'dangerous' and 'at risk' *racial, religious and cultural Others* into an erroneous, 'backward' and anti-democratic ideology and its expression through terrorist acts. Key in these significations is the place of reason and irrationality, civilization and barbarity, truth and ideology: the radical politics (whether real or imagined) of Islam are constituted as irrational, barbaric and ideological against the reason, civility and Truth claimed for the West. This particular racialization of radicalism precludes radical collectivities across minoritized groups as well as radical racial identifications amongst people identified as White and breaks a connection to prior radical traditions. Whiteness is a fundamental feature of this series of resignifying moves. Indeed, as David Gillborn has shown, Whiteness and its interests are at the centre of the 'aggressive majoritarian' policy, media and mainstream responses that come together in the War on Terror (Gillborn 2008: 81). Furthermore, the collapsing of radical thought with violent action effects a shift from the radical as derided to the *radical as dangerous*. This collapsing cements the radical in the barbarism of the racial and religious Other, a constitution of barbarism and radicalism that is doubled-back in further practices of racialization.

Through this expropriation and resignification of radicalism, prior radical traditions are erased and the acceptability, speakability and even thinkability of radicalism is undercut. Indeed, the radical is effectively disallowed and any call to its legitimacy is opened up absolutely to not just the accusation of violent extremism but also to intervention and punishment under the law. Furthermore, the state, media and mass obsession with the actions of 'violent extremists', who are always a priori constituted as Muslim, is also a moment of the singular focus on and constitution of violence as that which is enacted by aberrant Others and is acted on bodies and buildings and tears them apart. This is a focus that renders invisible the systemic and symbolic violences of the social order and the everyday business of society (Zizek 2008), including those that act on the lives, bodies and very humanity of Muslim communities (Butler 2004b; Gillborn 2008).

The racialization of the radical and its subsuming in the War on Terror ensures that radicalism is surveilled, regulated and, at least partially, disallowed. This constitution is situated but it is not unique – the hegemony of liberalism has, it seems, always found disciplinary and coercive strategies through which radicalism can be rendered as not simply erroneous and implausible, but as deluded, undemocratic and dangerous. Perhaps more importantly, this rendering also constitutes liberalism as the ultimate expression of rationalism and democracy. It may be that radicalism is only allowed when it is nothing more than nostalgic reminiscence or melancholic longings – as illustrated by the romanticization of figures such as Che Guevara and Muhammad Ali that plays out in a co-option and commodification of *past* radicalism in the form of the ubiquitous Che t-shirt and the blockbuster film of Muhammad Ali's life (Mann 2001).

In addition to this expropriation of radicalism, radical modes of political thought and action have been subject to extensive criticism from within the political Left itself. These critiques focus on ongoing contestation over the 'proper' sites of and strategies for radical social change; the possibility of effecting such fundamental change; and the ways that these sorts of understandings might inadvertently contribute to the very social systems and inequalities that they aim to change. Neo-Marxist and critical theorists have explored in detail the limits of revolutionary impetus, the results of revolutionary action and the absence in practice of the revolutionary shifts that dialectical thinking predicts (Gramsci 2003; McLaren 1995; Ollman 2003; Rees 1998). One of the ways that the absence of revolutionary waves at a societal level has been responded to has been through problematizations of the claim to the dialectical movement of history itself. Radical political thinking has also been called into question through the take up of understandings of Same/Other relations. These have been used to argue that radical politics are inevitably implicated in the creation, operation and effects of hierarchical binaries such as Right/Left, Capitalist/Communist, Liberal/Radical, binaries whose reliance on their opposite for meaning render them reproductive rather than revolutionary (Laclau and Mouffe 2001; Derrida 1988).

Identity politics

Radical Left politics have run alongside, beneath and against a more mainstream liberal reform tradition throughout the history of modern industrial societies. Movements for liberal reform seek incremental change through legislation and policy inside the existing social and political system and institutions such as schools (Cornell 2000). The movements for the enfranchisement of the lower classes, women and people of colour during the late nineteenth century and through much of the twentieth century provide illustrations of this. Human Rights movements and legislation, including at the international level, are also often instances of this form of politics (Kennedy 2001). In the last two or three decades much of this political action has taken the form of 'identity politics'. As revolutionary radical politics have declined and been critiqued and liberal reform-based politics have come to appear as the only mode of counter-politics available, new social movements and identity politics have foregrounded the abiding material, social and symbolic inequalities that persistently affect or are experienced by particular social groups. These social groups are understood through categories such as race, class, gender, disability, sexuality, religion, nationality and so on; indeed, to identify inequalities is to call up a range of categorizations of identity.

The basic underpinning of identity politics is the claim to recognition of and rights for the people who come under the identity category in question (Cornell 2000). A range of engagements with identity can be found in these politics. Policy reform orientated identity politics tends to accept identity categories, even when these are seen to be socially or culturally constructed. For instance, the UK Department for Children, Schools and Families' 'Gender Agenda' focuses on the relative achievement of boys and girls (DCSF n.d.). In doing this it challenges stereotypical and homogenizing representations of gender and asserts more nuanced accounts of these to be engaged in schools, such as through its 'Myth-buster' resource that was developed in collaboration with feminist scholars (DCSF 2009c). Yet the 'Gender Agenda' does not engage with the more fundamental question of the ways in which gender is *constituted as gender*, or how these processes might be implicated in achievement patterns. In this sense, the existence of gender, its categories and its correspondence to people and lives is taken as self-evident. Identity politics of this sort have been problematized on the grounds that promoting equalities for subjects constituted under a particular identity category is to assert and bolster this category. Such an assertion of the proper place of the category inevitably draws the boundary of a new outside, those subjects who have not quite made the entry criteria, and cites once again the prevailing sense of the unitary, enduring, self-knowing subject. In having these effects the call for equality under a given sign further cements that sign, and the bodies marked by it (Butler 1990, 1991).

In contrast, identity politics that are informed by post-structural, queer or deconstructive theorizations, place the question of the subject and how she/he comes to be perceived and located in and between particular categorical identities at the centre of enquiry. Here the concern is how categories themselves are constituted, how they relate to each other, how these constitutions are made in hierarchical relations and how these relations are implicated in creating intersecting inequalities. The political move then becomes the dismantling of the very categories themselves. In this sense Queer is not an identity but a set of practices that take up post-structural theory in order to conceptualize and enact a politics in which the identities to which subjects are attached are troubled, including in the everyday practices of schools (Butler 1993, 1997a).

The differences between liberal and post-structural forms of identity politics are not simply differences in focus or priority – they are fundamental theoretical differences that are central to thinking about and enacting politics. Identity politics concerned with reform, recognition and the shifting of stereotypes and identity politics underpinned by deconstructive politics that are concerned to unsettle identity categories themselves cannot run alongside one another in any easy way. The meanings of this first form of identity politics are the very meanings that deconstructive identity politics seeks to unsettle. These are not simply different tactics; they are fundamentally different conceptions of the subject and politics. They do not just contradict one another – they undercut one another. Given that identity-based equalities approaches reflect the normative conception of both the subject and political practice, it is these reform orientated identity politics that are likely to foreclose deconstructive identity politics rather than the other way around.

The critique of identity and the assertion that identity is implicated in the very problematics that it is called up to address, has led to new post-structural, queer or deconstructive approaches to politics (Butler 1992; Derrida 1997; Sullivan 2006). One response to the apparent impossibility of a post-structural identity politics has been a shift from the notion of identity to the notion of identification, allowing the focus to move from who a person 'is' to how a person identifies and is identified and to their sense of self or subjectivity. Another has been to jettison identity entirely on the basis that its conceptual problems and reproductive effects make it unhelpful ground for political organization and action. Yet scholars and activists engaging and extending identity politics in a post-structural framework have noted that identity categories are not so easy to give up – they are pressed upon us, are the condition of our recognition and are necessary signs under which to act (Rasmussen 2009). For these reasons, despite the inherent conceptual tensions and political limits, it may be necessary to retain a reconfigured notion of identity and tactically continue to call to and enact a post-structural or queer identity politics. I explore these issues further in later chapters.

Post-structural politics

What comes after revolutionary politics when the dialectical immanence of revolution appears to have failed? And what comes after identity politics when the identity categories that we organize around are seen as simultaneously constraining and enabling? As I have already begun to show, post-structural approaches to politics have critiqued theorizations of change based on revolution, liberal reform and identity-based claims for recognition. This critique is based on the argument that these inadvertently but intrinsically reinscribe the very economic, political and social forms that they aim to overturn or shift (Butler 1990; Kennedy 2001). Calls to socialism invoke the notion of capitalism, indeed, socialism and communism as political philosophies emerged out of the analysis and critique of capitalism and can thus be seen as being inseparable from it. Calls to legislative reform legitimize the political structures and their underpinning principles that the call seeks to change as well as the insider citizen who is extended the 'right' to participate in these. In turn, reform-based politics cement the illegitimacy, or even unspeakability, of any alternative models of social and political organization or change as well as the outsider non-citizen who is denied this participation. And identity politics take up the subject positions of the oppressed and in so doing also inscribe again the subject positions of the privileged and are implicated in constituting a further excluded Other.

In a range of manifestations, post-structural theory has responded to these limits by considering the costs as well as the benefits of legislative reform and identity politics. These theorizations look for further ways of conceptualizing power, knowledge, the subject and politics in order to identify ways of interrupting material conditions through an engagement with language, a decentred subject and an unstable truth. Instead of asking what structures and institutions produce material conditions, this move reconfigures this concern and it asks how power operates across orders and spaces; how knowledge and power are joined together; how the self, or subject, is made and constrained in these conditions; what the place of feeling, the unconscious and identification might be in these processes; and how assemblages of power, discourse, practice, representation and affect come together.

In the remainder of this chapter I set out a series of ideas drawn from post-structural thinking that have the potential to extend our understanding of enacting politics in education. Working with the ideas of Michel Foucault, Judith Butler, Ernesto Laclau and Chantal Mouffe and Gilles Deleuze and Felix Guattari I suggest a series of potential lines for political practice: a politics of discourse, an anti-identity politics, a politics of feeling and a politics of becoming.

A politics of discourse

Foucault explains his political and conceptual work as underpinned by a concern to interrogate the 'nature of the present' (Foucault 1988a: 36). Such an interrogation, for Foucault, seeks to expose the relationship between 'the subject, truth, and the constitution of experience' (Foucault 1988b: 48), focusing on those aspects of the present that are 'intolerable'. In seeking to understand how the present is made, and so how it might be unmade, Foucault follows 'lines of fragility in the present', trajectories that might allow us to '*grasp why and how that-which-is might no longer be that-which-is*' (Foucault 1988a: 37, my emphasis).

In understanding this intolerable present and finding ways of undoing it, a conception of power and how power works is crucial. Foucault (1991) makes an important contribution to this by setting the idea of power that is productive alongside the more usual conception of power as something that is held by the powerful and wielded over the powerless. Foucault argues that as well as understanding the power embedded in the law – 'juridical power' – and the power of the state or monarch to impose their will – 'sovereign power' – we should also take account of the power that circulates in the everyday processes and practices of institutions, communities and persons – 'disciplinary power'. Foucault writes:

> Power is everywhere; not because it embraces everything, but because it comes from everywhere . . . Power is not something that is acquired, seized, or shared, something that one holds on to or allows to slip away; power is exercised from innumerable points, in the interplay of nonegalitarian and mobile relations.
>
> (Foucault 1990a: 93–4)

I explore this understanding of power further in the next chapter. Here I outline it in order to show it is useful for conceptualizing the top-down restrictions and definitions that are imposed on education as well as the ways that the minutiae of practices inside schools are infused with and products of productive power *and* that resistance is integral to power as it is exercised in mobile relations and from innumerable points inside schools.

A key site and tool for such resistance rests in Foucault's understanding of discourse and the way that power and knowledge are tied together through it. In this understanding, discourses are shifting systems of knowledge with varied and potentially porous statuses ranging from what is taken as self-evident and valorized – a 'regime of truth' – through to what is unspeakable or ridiculed – 'disavowed' or 'subjugated' knowledges (Foucault 1990a). As conduits of productive power, *discourses are not descriptive but creative* – they have the potential to produce and regulate the world in their own terms as if they were true. Particular discourses may well be taken as reflecting 'truth', the way things are, but for Foucault these are not reflections but the very moment and means of the *production* of these truths. The circulation of power, then, is inseparable from and an effect of knowledge and the deployment of its 'truths': 'what is said [. . .] must not be analyzed simply as the surface of projection of these power mechanisms. Indeed, it is in discourse that power and knowledge are joined together' (Foucault 1990a: 100).

Yet while certain discourses do become sedimented and some discourses prevail as truth in particular milieux or moments, they are never cemented as irrefutable or unmovable Truth. Discourses are unstable and always open to resistance and change as they run up against alternative discourses. Foucault says:

> [W]e must conceive discourse as a series of discontinuous segments whose tactical function is neither uniform nor stable. . . . we must not imagine a world

of discourse divided between accepted discourse and excluded discourse, or between the dominant discourse and the dominated one; but as a multiplicity of discursive elements that can come into play in various strategies.

(Foucault 1990a: 100)

This notion of discourse offers a lens for understanding how education comes to be understood as a particular sort of activity with particular ends, for understanding the way that particular knowledges are propagated and circulate in education policy as well as in the daily activities of educational institutions and for conceiving of how these discourses are unsettled as subjugated discourses are constantly deployed in practice.

Judith Butler (1997a, 1997b) engages the insights of Foucault in her suggestion of a performative politics. Building on Derrida (1988), Butler understands the performative in a similar way as Foucault understands the operation of productive power in discourse. That is, a performative enacts rather than describes the thing that it names. But this production is never guaranteed because performatives are, in Derrida's terms, always open to misfire. With this underpinning Butler suggests that a performative politics can be pursued through what she calls 'radical public acts' of 'discursive insurrection' and 'misappropriation' (Butler 1997a: 100). These radical deployments of discourse have the potential to make discourses take on new meanings and circulate in contexts from which they have been barred or in which they have been rendered unintelligible (Butler 1997a; Youdell 2006b). This becomes a politics of resignification in which the signified is shifted as its meanings are made differently.

Ernesto Laclau and Chantal Mouffe (2001) bring together the work of both Gramsci and Foucault to make similar moves. They take up Foucault's notion of discourse to develop a politics concerned with the struggle for hegemony. Following Gramsci, they locate hegemony at the centre of the political, but use the notion of discourse to understand how particular ideas and social and political forms come to be hegemonic. Hegemony is regularly understood as those ideas and forms that prevail in a political and social situation and are taken up as common sense even by those whose interests these ideas and forms do not serve. By bringing the idea of hegemony alongside a Foucauldian insight into the inevitably multiple and mobile nature of discourse and its implication in power/knowledge formations, Laclau and Mouffe demonstrate that hegemony cannot simply be seen as ideological duping, but should instead be understood as a fundamental discursive condition of the socio-political: '[T]he terrain of hegemonic practices is constituted out of the fundamental ambiguity of the social, the impossibility of establishing in a definitive manner the meaning of a struggle' (Laclau and Mouffe 2001: 170).

Hegemony is intrinsic to the multiplicity and insolubility of discourses and meanings that shape and circulate within a given social context and for this reason it cannot be 'overcome'. Chantal Mouffe extends this line of thinking when she argues:

[I]f we did not have any kind of hegemony, we would be living in complete schizophrenia. There would not be any form of meaning, any form of order. In other words, the question is not to get rid of power. Power is constitutive for the social; there is no social without power relations. Now, any form of order is a hegemonic order, but of course there are some forms of order that are more democratic than others.

(Mouffe in Carpentier and Cammaerts 2006: 967)

Laclau and Mouffe do not suggest that we endeavour to oust hegemonic ideas and replace these with a 'truth' that is currently repressed or obscured. Rather, they suggest that the political efforts of the Left should be located in a struggle for hegemony, that is, in a struggle over *which ideas might be hegemonic*. Laclau and Mouffe suggest that 'a struggle for hegemony is a struggle to transform the consciousness of individual groups in society so that they see that their interests are tied up with the interests of other groups' (Laclau and Mouffe in Castle n.d.). This thinking opens up the idea of hegemony, positing it as something not simply to be struggled against or countered – although the current hegemonic formations are seen to demand such a response – but instead something to be struggled *over*, to be remade in a wider, pluralistic and democratic form.

An anti-identity politics

While issues of identity and identity politics have been key ground for the development of post-structural thinking and politics, as I have already begun to outline, post-structural theory sees the notion of identity as a site of counter-political mobilization as inherently problematic. This is because it sees identity as a product of 'subjectivation' – the process of being named and made a subject – and therefore an effect of productive power. As productive power circulates in discourse the person is subjected to relations of power and rendered a subject, or *subjectivated*. The sorts of categories that identity and identity politics rest on are constantly either explicitly or implicitly deployed in these processes. This means that a call to an identity or take up of identity politics is already situated in processes of subjectivation and relations of productive power. Furthermore, classification brings with it constraint – naming inevitably excludes other possible grounds for recognition and there are benefits to not being spoken or seen if we are subjectivated in the terms of a vilified or wounded identity. Indeed, identifying subjectivation as an order of the assemblage, Deleuze and Guattari (1983) look to a politics that is 'anti-subjectivation' and that flies from the subjectivities that the assemblage constitutes and deploys. I will return to this idea shortly.

Despite these inherent problems, subjectivation makes us subjects – this constraint is the condition and the price of subject-hood (Butler 1997a, 1997b, 2004a; Foucault 1992). As we are made subject by and subject to these classifications we can also interrogate, resist and attempt to imagine outside them. Post-structural understandings of agency, the capacity to act with intent and influence the social world, emphasize the discursive terrains on which subjects are located and the discursive repertoire they can deploy. We have what Judith Butler calls 'discursive agency' (Butler 1997a: 127). By thinking of agency as discursive we can conceive of a political subject who challenges prevailing constitutions as part of a set of self-conscious discursive practices without assuming a rational self-knowing subject who exists outside subjectivation. By understanding identity categories as performatives, names that *make something happen*, they become the ground and object of the performative politics I sketched earlier. It is important to retain a sense of the limits to discursive agency. Subjectivated subjects have the capacity for intentional action and their practices inevitably have discursive effects. Yet the constitutive force of these discourses exceeds our intentions and performative misfire can work in ways that restrict us as well as in ways that might unsettle the constraints of identity.

Foucault has explored how practice of the self, which we might think about as the flip side of subjectivation, might be taken-up in and as an ethics of care that is itself a practice of politics. In *An Aesthetic of Existence* Foucault says that 'the subject is constituted through practices of subjection, or, in a more autonomous way, through practices of liberation, or liberty' (1988b: 51). In his books *Uses of Pleasure* (Foucault 1992) and *Care of the Self* (Foucault 1990b) the turn to self-care and technologies of self suggest the possibilities for subjects to practice self-consciously, even if these subjects come into being through the condition of subjectivation. These ethics connect to Foucault's consideration of 'fearless speech' (Foucault 2001), that is, the speaking of unpalatable truths despite the risks that accompany such a practice. While these practices of liberation, liberty, self-care and fearless speech are constrained by the particularities of context, the subject – including teachers and students – can act, and these actions can be political.

In an attempt to extend both identity politics and counter-politics enacted at the level of individual lives and practices, Judith Butler suggests that we might conceptualize the 'cross cutting modalities of life' (Butler 1997b), through which we are made meaningful to ourselves and to others and across which political struggles might be pursued. More recently, she has turned her attention to the inability of identity politics predicated on a 'liberal conception of personal freedom' (Butler 2008: 6) to respond to the coercive mechanism of the state, its violence, its constructions of 'subject[s] of cultural difference' and its exclusions from recognition as human. She suggests that reconceptualizing freedom as 'a condition of solidarity among minorities' (ibid.: 21) and orienting politics to a critique of these operations of the state opens up possibilities for new political 'convergences', 'alliances' (ibid.: 6) or 'collectivities' (Butler 2007). These collectivities may be antagonistic and may not result in a unified struggle, but Butler suggests that foregrounding a critique of the state offers the chance of 'finding and acknowledging the already existing alliances and sites of contact' across minoritized groups (Butler 2008: 21). She says:

> The possibility of a political framework that opens up our ideas of cultural norms to contestation and dynamism within a global frame would surely be one way to begin to think a politics that re-engages sexual freedom in the context of allied struggles against racism, nationalism, and the persecution of national and religious minorities.
>
> (Butler 2008: 19–20)

Thinking in terms of the convergence of cross-cutting modalities of life through which seams of inequality run, instead of thinking in terms of identities, may enable a politics that remains concerned with inequalities but which avoids further reifying categorical identity. And simultaneously foregrounding the operations of the state may renew the possibility for counter-political action to be pursued by collectivities that are not undermined by struggles over the primacy of particular identity based claims. Such a politics moves beyond forms of identity politics that call for freedom, recognition and rights; the demand to 'be' who we 'are'. Yet it makes this move without losing sight of the way material and symbolic inequality adheres to subjects constituted in particular ways through particular discursive constellations and the convergence of particular cross-cutting modalities of life. And it keeps sight of the fact that it is subjectivated subjects who are entreated to take up these politics. In this sense these politics might be, borrowing Deleuze and Guattari's formulation, anti-identity.

Ernesto Laclau and Chantal Mouffe's (2001) thinking about political practice also looks to move beyond struggles over the primacy of the political claims made by divergent social groups and movements and find ways of acting politically across these. In doing this they posit a 'politics of agonistic pluralism'. Laclau and Mouffe retain a commitment to the concerns of the neo-Marxist Left but move beyond a revolutionary politics reliant on the conscienticization and mobilization of the working class. Instead, they foreground discourse and the multiplicity of social identities and movements that it constitutes. Laclau and Mouffe argue that the new social movements that have emerged in the later decades of the twentieth century are concerned with 'defending a type of identity under threat' (Laclau and Mouffe 2001: 158) and so are not reducible to the workers' movement. Likewise, the claims made by these new social movements are not reducible to class politics. Furthermore, while many of these movements might be identified as being on the political Left, the form they take is dependent on their discursive constitution and articulation, not on the social identities that underpin them, and as such extreme Right new social movements have also emerged. Emphasizing the potential for new social movements to act in coalition Laclau and Mouffe suggest the need to understand the equivalence and interdependence of divergent political claims in order for these claims to be brought together in a 'chain of equivalence'. The key concern becomes, then, identifying 'the discursive conditions for the emergence of a collective action' (Laclau and Mouffe 2001: 153).

In pursuing such collective action Laclau and Mouffe mobilize the notion of radicalization, looking to the 'radicalization of ideas and values which were already present, although unfulfilled in liberal capitalism' and so defining 'the left-wing project as the radicalization of democracy' (Laclau and Mouffe in Castle n.d.). Such moves to radicalization, however, need to be situated in the specificities of the social and political moment. Speaking in 2006, almost two decades on from the first appearance of *Hegemony and Socialist Strategy*, Chantal Mouffe suggests that '[t]oday, the main task is no longer to radicalize democracy, but to protect the democratic institutions – which we have taken for granted – from being dismantled and demolished' (Mouffe in Carpentier and Cammaerts 2006: 970).

In the contemporary context in which radicalism has been expropriated by the War on Terror to such an extent that radicalism and radicalization are rendered almost unthinkable, this acts as a useful reminder of the situatedness of political practices and the need to identify and pursue tactics that are commensurate with the problematic and moment at hand. It may be that in contemporary schools and classrooms, thinking and practising democratically are themselves radical political moves.

A politics of feeling

The idea of forming new collectivities and pursuing collective action that does not seek to collapse all counter-political claims into class struggle raises the question of how such collectivities might come together, particularly as their claims are not only divergent but also potentially contradictory. Laclau and Mouffe point to the assumption of consensus that underpins not just liberal democratic forms but also the radical Left in which the rational maturation of the working class is anticipated to lead to both solidarity and a unified left-wing movement and ensure consensus in a post-revolutionary society. Laclau and Mouffe replace this assumption of the need for consensus with an acceptance of antagonism. This antagonism reflects not only the competing and contradictory concerns and claims of new social movements, but also the inevitable antagonisms inside the Left. These antagonisms are, according to Laclau and Mouffe, discursively constituted and hence multiple forms of struggle emerge around even a single social identity. For instance, multiple feminisms have been articulated as a 'result of hegemonic struggle' (Laclau and Mouffe 2001: 168). In addition, Laclau and Mouffe see these antagonisms as inseparable from identities – antagonisms and their articulation are constituted around and through particular identities which are themselves constituted through these antagonisms. These antagonisms and identities are discursively and temporarily situated and so cannot be predicted or determined. In this sense, counter-hegemonic struggle is not inevitable, struggle is not necessarily political, and struggle with subordination as its focus is non-necessary:

> [P]olitics as a practice of creation, reproduction and transformation of social relations cannot be located at a determinate level of the social, as the problem of the political is the problem of the institution of the social, that is, of the definition and articulation of social relations in a *field criss-crossed with antagonisms*.
> (Laclau and Mouffe 2001: 153, my emphasis)

In a recent interview Chantal Mouffe has elaborated further on the place of antagonism and the ineradicability of conflict in the political field. She suggests that '[d]emocratic politics should create the conditions for the conflict to find its expression in agonistic terms, avoiding that it becomes antagonistic' (Carpentier and Cammaerts 2006: 973). That is, it is argumentative and competing but avoids hostility and aggression. She also argues that creating public spaces 'for the expression of dissensus, for bringing to the floor what forces attempt to keep concealed' is necessary to guard against authoritarianism. For Mouffe the pressing need is to engage conflict productively:

> The question then becomes how are we going to deal with conflict and what kinds of conflicts you allow for. When a society does not allow this agonistic form of conflict to express itself, you see the emergence of antagonistic forms of conflict.
> (Carpentier and Cammaerts 2006: 974)

Especially generative in Chantal Mouffe's recent account of the centrality of conflict and antagonism in political struggle is her interest in 'the role of what I call "passion" in politics' (Carpentier and Cammaerts 2006: 974). These might be the passions of a reformer for their reform agendas or the passions of radicals for their agenda of transformation and their visions of an alternative social and political order. This emphasis on the passions that underpin the political is particularly useful for thinking about the political feeling within education.

The passion in politics is articulated in another way in Foucault's work through his concern with what he calls the 'intolerable' (Foucault 1988a, 1988b). To find a social or political situation and set of relations intolerable is to be affected by it, and to have an embodied, visceral relationship to it. A political commitment to undo these circumstances or relations is one that is shot through with feeling. It is to feel outrage, disgust and empathy. It is perhaps even to be constituted a political subject through these feelings. Foucault's 'ethics' (1990b) might similarly suggest a feeling subject as might his exploration of *parrhesia* or 'fearless speech' (Foucault 2001).

In Deleuze and Guattari's (1983, 2008) work, affectivity is itself a feature of the political; it is a site and moment of politics. In their 'rhizomatics' they foreground affectivities, intensities and flows of energies that exceed prevailing symbolic orders. A rhizomatic politics is concerned precisely with pursuing the affectivities, intensities, eruptions, and lines of flight of bodies that are anti-subjectivation.

Michalinos Zembylas makes use of Deleuze and Guattari's work in his thinking about the potential for feeling to be at the centre of transformatory pedagogies. He suggests that the 'the theme of politics of emotions focuses on the connection between emotional practices, sociability, bodies and power in everyday school contexts' (Zembylas 2007: xiv). Zembylas insists that feeling is not necessarily emancipatory, a claim that echoes Laclau and Mouffe's insistence that antagonisms expressed in new social movements are not necessarily of the political Left. Nevertheless, he takes up the ideas of affectivity as a source of resistances, lines of flight and deterritorialization and posits the political potential of 'creative affective connections' (ibid.). In doing this, he foregrounds desire suggesting that 'it is desire that is transformed into hope and will for change' (Zembylas 2007: xviii). Zembylas explores the pedagogic possibilities of a series of affects, including passion and desire. His pedagogy of passion builds on Foucauldian ideas to consider 'teachers and students who practice "the art of not being themselves", a "no longer being oneself"', practices that Zembylas suggests has ethical and radical potential (ibid.: xxix). And his pedagogy of desire, following Deleuze and Guattari, suggests that 'through mobilization and release of desiring production, teachers and students make available to themselves the powerful flows of desire, thereby turning themselves into subjects who subvert normalized representations and significations and find access to a radical self' (ibid.).

Zembylas' work not only highlights the significance of affectivities in political practice, importantly he also highlights the promise of affectivities as a ground for political pedagogic practices in schools.

These lines of political theorizing suggest a wholly feeling political terrain, whether or not this is acknowledged by the discourses, institutions and subjects who constitute and struggle within it, and irrespective of the disqualification of feeling within the discourses that define the political. Consider teachers engaged in critical pedagogic work in schools and classrooms that are, globally, defined and constrained by neo-liberal policy frameworks as well as institutional structures. In these circumstances, critical teachers do not act against the grain of dominant policy and accounts of proper (or 'best') practice due solely to contradictory rational judgement, they do it because they *feel strongly* that they should, that this is the right thing to do.

A politics of becoming

The final political tactic that I posit here is a politics of becoming which is based in Deleuze and Guattari's (1983, 2008) 'rhizomatic' method for analysing the social and political moment and for enacting a politics. They suggest that the hierarchical thinking of the orders of the assemblage might be rethought through a shift to rhizomatics that emphasizes a multiplicity of 'dimensions, lines, and directions' (1983: 86). The radical political promise of these rhizomatics rests in the 'line of flight' and its 'becomings'. Here the ideas of rigid molar lines and segmented molecular lines are used to characterize assemblages and the idea of unruly 'lines of flight' is used to imagine ways of escaping this and 'becoming' otherwise. As the line of flight flees from the middle of the rhizome it promises the 'deterritorialization' of the assemblage and, therefore, a new becoming. And as they scatter the assemblage these becomings might even have the potential to escape the power set ups through which individuals are subjectivated, that is, to be anti-subjectivation.

The image of the rhizome and the lines of flight fleeing from multiple points and scattering the assemblage and opening-up becomings-otherwise offers an image of movement beyond the present; in Foucault's terms, it is the image of 'that-which-is no longer being that-which-is'. Becomings are not imagined as systematic or systemic; they replace the ambition to reform or resist the assemblage with an orientation that is anti-assemblage. This orientation looks to becomings that move across and occupy multiple assemblages simultaneously, movements and occupations that are deterritorializations or 'en route to deterritorialization' that are *'assemblage converters'* (Deleuze and Guattari 2008: 358, original emphasis). Likewise a politics of becoming sets aside ambitions for revolution to come in the dialectical movement of history, and thinks of 'the becoming-revolutionary of people everywhere and at every level' (Deleuze and Parnet 1983: 114). This is a way of thinking and acting politically in the present that understands the pursuit of lines of flight as a form of revolutionary practice:

> Why not think that *a new type of revolution is becoming possible*, and that all kinds of mutant machines are alive, engaged in warfare, joining one another, and tracing a plane of consistency that undermines the organizational plan of the World State.
>
> (Deleuze and Parnet 1983: 113, original emphasis)

Deleuze and Parnet's imagining here is for rhizomatics that scramble the institutions, systems, knowledges, practices and subjects of assemblages at a global level. Radicalism, expropriated by the neo-liberal assemblage, might have become a molecular line, segmented but drawn into the assemblage, it may even have been rendered a molar line. But becoming-revolutionary retains the promise of radical political practices as a line of flight. While there is an element of imagination, or futurism here, this imagining invites us to enact the possibility that these revolutionary-becomings might take flight in the next moment, and then in this moment.

Whether becomings are intelligible as a politics in education, when politics so often means at best transformation and at least recognition or reform, is a question that I explore through this book. Likewise, if becomings are intelligible as a politics, then whether these moves are adequate, whether they satisfy, can be seen in their application in practice. Echoing Judith Butler's call to deconstructive politics (Butler 2007) and accounts that do not satisfy (Butler 2005), a move to a politics of becomings may simultaneously be a move to embracing the absence of satisfaction on prevailing registers of politics and resistance.

Radical politics on the move

In the context of the disavowal of radical politics that I have discussed, any ideas concerned with radical social change are at risk of not just being marginalized and derided, but of being constituted as a terrorist threat or even a terrorist act. In the light of the far-reaching expropriation and resignification of radicalism as terrorism, we need to consider what the future of politics named 'radical' might be and what possibilities and risks it might offer. Might we continue or resume using the name radical, insisting on its thinkability and insisting that the critique of the liberal democratic order is legitimate and not inherently despotic, totalitarian or an act of terrorist thought? Conversely, given liberal capitalism's demonstrated capacity to co-opt, commodify and domesticate radicalism and redeploy it to entrench its own rationality and democratic nature, might we act to ensure that radical politics remain radical? Resignification works in multiple directions – we cannot know in advance what work language will be put to and what meanings will be asserted and adhere.

It seems that it is when radical thinking and action is evident in the present, when people are becoming-radical, that it must be disallowed through exclusion, expropriation, resignification and erasure. In this context, disciplinary mechanisms silence any discourse which might signify the radical outside of the confines of 'Islamic terrorism', while the coercive force of sovereign power remains available and ready to be deployed. As Judith Butler (2004a) has argued, the state's capacity to deploy sovereign power is manifest in the USA and UK's military action in Iraq and Afghanistan as well as in the USA's internment camp at Guantanamo Bay, a manifestation that we can also see in the Israeli military action in Gaza. These manifestations of sovereign power might be understood as having the wider effect of simultaneously disciplining potentially unruly subjects and undercutting the possibility of wider dissent and radicalism. That is, the threat of the old power over death continues to resonate in the power over life, undergirding disciplinary power and provoking self-surveillant subjects. This underscores the idea that radical politics must be constantly on the move, in Deleuze and Parnet's (1983) terms, permanently following lines of flight and becoming-revolutionary.

In his book *Violence* (2008), Slavoj Zizek claims that the clatter of concern and the insistence that we 'do something' about what he calls 'visible' violence masks the 'symbolic' violence of dominant meanings and the 'systemic' violence which is an ordinary part of the 'smooth functioning of our economic and political systems' (Zizek, 2008: 1). In the case of inequalities, inside education and beyond, a similar analysis holds true. The failure to reach Millennium Development Goals for universal basic education and girls' participation, or the failure to 'close the gaps' between the education outcomes of the most privileged and most disadvantaged sections of society, provoke demands for renewed efforts to remedy these failures. Yet these concerns eclipse the ways in which education's business as usual constitutes and limits what counts as valid knowledge, valuable culture, acceptable behaviour, thinkable ideas, acknowledgeable feelings, and 'who' counts as a valuable, legitimate and worthwhile teacher, student, learner and person. And in eclipsing these processes it also eclipses the gross exclusions, erasures and denials that they have a part in. In Zizek's (2008) analysis he does not move immediately to a call to action in relation to these symbolic and systemic violences. Instead he argues that 'doing something' is not always the correct course of action, suggesting instead that critical politics should at times properly postpone action in order to ensure that it understands the problem at hand: '[t]here are situations when the only truly "practical" thing to do is to resist the temptation to engage immediately and to "wait and see" by means of a patient critical analysis'. Zizek also reminds us that when action appears to offer a light at the end of the tunnel, this light 'might belong to a train crashing towards us' (Zizek, 2008: 6). Proceeding cautiously, with a mindfulness of unforeseen consequences, misfires, reterritorializations, black holes and micro-fascisms, may well be necessary. And proceeding with an openness in our orientation to 'what' our concerns might be and become, and 'what' we might aim to achieve is also suggested. As Butler writes:

> The notion of equality would proceed undemocratically if we claim to know in advance who might make use of its claim, and what kinds of issues fall within its purview . . . who is included among those who might make the claim to equality? What kinds of issues undermine the very possibility of certain groups making such a claim?
>
> (Butler 1997c cited by Kitching 2009)

Yet in the case of education, its inequalities, its constant reiteration of normative knowledges and social forms and its subjectivating effects, we already know a great deal. Various forms of critical scholarship in education have mapped out many manifestations of these processes, have collaborated with educators in developing and enacting interventions and have engaged in analyses of the effects of these interventions. And in the face of persistent injustices, inequalities and exclusions, action seems pressing. This presents us with something of a dilemma: a call and compulsion to action *and* a need for caution and undecidedness.

What happens to radical politics in education if we take up these ideas and attempt to move rhizomatically? If, after Deleuze and Guattari, we replace the tree with grass, and instead of aiming to transforming the root of the tree we conceive of the tuber working from the middle, finding its way between the terms of binaries, following lines of flight, then what might radical politics in education look like? If we forget cutting down one tree and replacing it with another assemblage of correct knowledges, structures, subjects and affectivities and instead conceive of an endless meadow of shifting forms then what might rhizomatic education look like? I explore these questions in the chapters that follow.

3   Theorizing political subjects

In the previous chapter I detailed a series of political tools for pursuing a new radical politics in education. Drawing on a range of post-structural thinking I posited a politics of discourse, an anti-identity politics, a politics of feeling and a politics of becoming and suggested that we might bring these together to both map the education assemblage and identify tactics for unsettling this assemblage in practice. All of these political possibilities are grounded in wider theorizing about the nature and workings of power, knowledge, discourse, the subject and feeling. In this chapter I offer accounts of key aspects of the theoretical work that underpins these politics. Together these theoretical tools invite us to explore the ways that state and judicial power come together with disciplinary power in the micro-circuits of the everyday; they offer avenues for understanding the way that institutions and their practices are made and constrained; they provide ways into thinking about the people or subjects or education; they help us to conceptualize the inter-relations between apparently disparate levels or orders of intensely varied and variable knowledge, organization, practice and people; and they provide ideas for thinking about how education might be different.

Power

In the previous chapter I explored how Foucault's understanding of power/ knowledge, discourse and the subject brings him to a particular understanding of resistance. For Foucault, because power/knowledge is effected through discourses that are mobile and contingent, the possibility of resistance is intrinsic to it. This situates the resistance of subjugated discourses, their meanings and effects at the centre of Foucault's politics.

Foucault suggests that power takes multiple forms including judicial and sovereign power that include the imposition of constraint by force or repression as well as disciplinary power that deploys disciplinary technologies marked by improvisational borrowing in the face of pressing demands and is effected through and productive of discourses. Disciplinary power simultaneously is produced by and has as one of its effects the management of populations at the micro-level of daily life; it is a form of governance that reaches into the smallest of moments without the need to be exerted – it is 'governmentality' (Foucault 1991b; Rose 1998). Foucault offers the figure of the panopticon – Jeremy Bentham's Victorian design for the ideal prison in which a central observation tower encircled by inward-facing cells creates prisoners who assume constant observation, whether or not the central tower is occupied, and so survey themselves – to illustrate the way that disciplinary power reaches into life without overt force or repression. He suggests:

> It implies an uninterrupted, constant coercion, supervising the processes of the activity rather than its result and it is exercised according to a codification that partitions as closely as possible time, space, movement. These methods, which made possible the meticulous control of the operations of the body, which assured the constant subjection of its forces and imposed upon them a relation of docility-utility, might be called the 'disciplines'.
>
> (Foucault 1991a: 137)

These sorts of arrangements and their effects can be found, according to Foucault, across modern institutions, including schools. Foucault (1991a) identifies a series of 'disciplines' or 'technologies' of disciplinary power. These concern the spaces in which practices are organized; the way that bodies, activities and time are managed; the way that hierarchical classifications are developed and used; and the way that people are created as individuals as they are documented as cases. 'Spatial distributions' are concerned with functional sites, enclosures and partitions, rankings and classifications, and the distribution of bodies in and across these. We can see this in the assembly hall, the classroom and the row of desks. 'The control of activity' is concerned with timetabling and the filling of time as well as the definition of the proper body, gesture and action. We can see this in the school timetable and the student sitting neatly at her/his desk. 'Normalizing judgement' compares, differentiates, categorizes and homogenizes; it corrects the correctable and excludes the irredeemable. We can see this in the 'good' student, the 'gifted' student, the student 'suitable for treatment', the 'hopeless' student and the 'special' student. The 'examination' documents individuals into cases. We can see this in school and government databases of student-by-student performance. 'Hierarchical observation' or 'surveillance' underpins these technologies – the student, teacher and school are each subject to the gaze of the next, and all are subject to the gaze of the state. This provokes 'self-surveillance' as the observed, examined and judged 'individual' turns her/his attention on her/him self and acts in particular ways in order to make her/him self and others particular sorts of persons. We see the student acting the 'good' student, the teacher acting the 'good' teacher and the school acting the 'good' school as accountability mechanisms open each up to assessment, correction and expulsion.

Foucault sees these disciplinary technologies as drawing on those established and emergent organizational forms, knowledges and practices that are available in particular historical circumstances. In the contemporary moment we see the market form, techniques of corporate management and newly available information technologies borrowed and redeployed by governments, education policy makers and schools themselves. As such, schools can be understood as disciplinary institutions in which the practices that constitute school life are shaped and permeated by the localized effects of disciplinary power.

Allied to Foucault's idea of productive power is the idea of knowledge as located and partial (Foucault 2002). For Foucault, knowledge is inseparable from the circulation of power – he posits the notion of power/knowledge to express this and suggests that this is evident and effected in discourse (Foucault 1990a, 1991a) and the disciplinary technologies that constitute, disavow and resist particular knowledges. Distinct from the more common postulation that knowledge is the key to power that exists outside objective knowledge, Foucault's formulation signals the way that productive power constitutes particular regimes of knowledge at the same time as these regimes of knowledge are deployed in the exercise of productive power.

At the heart of the conceptualization of knowledge offered in Foucault's work is an interrogation of knowledge within a Western modernist framework of reason, science and progress (Foucault 2002). This intersects with wider post-structural interrogations of hierarchical binaries, often conceptualized in terms of Same/Other relations, that are at the centre of such thought (see Butler 1990; Cixous and Clement 1986b; Deleuze and Guattari 1983; Derrida 1978, 1988, 1997) and underpin post-structural work in education (see Rasmussen 2006; Youdell 2006a). The principal argument forwarded by these analyses is that meaning is ordered and reproduced in terms of hierarchical binaries: *the Same and the Other*. The pairs that make these hierarchical binaries give each other meaning through their opposition of each other: man/woman. And they are products of and productive of relations of power; one side of the binary is privileged and/or normative while the other side of the binary is subjugated and/or aberrant: White/Black. The terms of these binaries are interdependent – the normative Same is defined against the aberrant Other as *what it is not*: we know what reason is because it is not the reviled manifestation of madness. Hence, the privileged term comes to be meaningful through and in relation to its *difference from* its subjugated other. This means that the subjugated term is always an absent presence in the privileged term: reason cannot escape being haunted by madness. These binary pairs are also caught in chains of meaning. The terms of binary pairs constantly refer on to further binaries for their meaning: man/woman, penis/vagina, masculine/feminine. Terms from one or other side of a chain of binaries are so entangled that they become almost synonymous: man-penis-masculine/woman-vagina-feminine. And terms that seem to challenge a binary are rapidly subsumed into another hierarchical pair. For instance, a White/Black dichotomy that seems to overlook and/or be escaped by further racialized positions, is supplemented by a further binary that draws these terms back into hierarchical relation – Occident/Orient. In this framework meaning is never settled, but it may well become sedimented (Butler 1997a). It is quite common to find a dismissal of or complaint against hierarchical binaries in research on difference and inequality. These complaints, for me, miss the key point of analyses of hierarchical binaries and their operations and effects. That is, work that makes use of this analytic does not promote, adhere to, or only see the world in these terms. Rather, it is concerned precisely with the possibilities for sidestepping or undercutting these hierarchical binaries and thinking *without* these pairs. Yet it is also acutely aware of the pervasiveness, resilience and constitutive force of these hierarchical binaries and sees them in the practices and meanings that constitute the social. We might choose to pursue a tactics of refusal of or flight from these binary forms, but we must choose this in the knowledge of the likelihood of its failure.

Identity

Hierarchical binaries are evident in prevailing constructions of identity: man/woman, White/Black, hetero-/homo- and so on. The problematics of these binaries are key to the critique of identity and the interrogation of its usefulness that I began to map in the previous chapter. Raewyn Connell has been engaged in critique of the notion of identity for some time. Amongst Connell's concerns are the term's embeddedness in the vocabulary of the unique individual of developmental psychology, the fragmentation of the person when s/he is reduced to a series of identity categories and the unitary nature of the person signified in popular usage of the term 'identity'. That these grounds of critique are themselves in tension, Connell suggests, is further demonstration of the limitations of identity as a conceptual tool (Connell n.d.). The relative significance of these 'parts' is another problematic that 'identity' analyses face. Concerns over identities in education have grown out of wider political movements: the labour movement, feminism, anti-racism. Each concerned with the particular identity category that it organizes around, there are longstanding and ongoing debates between feminism, anti-racism and neo-Marxism over whether one identity category and axis of domination/subordination takes primacy over the others and which is at work in any given empirical instance. For many education scholars this conceptualization has proved unsatisfactory because it has not included an account of the *ways* these multiple positions *interact and are implicated by and in one another.*

Intersectional approaches have attempted to engage and move on these problematics. The relationships between multiple categories of identity and multiple inequalities are at the heart of intersectional approaches. Since its development in black feminism by Kimberly Crenshaw (1991) and further popularization through Patricia Hill Collins' work (2000), discussions and analyses of identities and inequalities have drawn heavily on the idea of intersectionality. Patricia Hill Collins is popularly cited as asserting that, in the context of a 'matrix of domination': '[c]ultural patterns of oppression are not only interrelated, but are bound together and influenced by the intersectional systems of society. Examples of this include race, gender, class, and ethnicity' (Collins 2000: 42).

The notion is often used when education researchers and increasingly policy makers attempt to explain the connections *between* not just race, class and gender but also between sexuality, disability, religion and nationality, and how these relate to inequalities. For some who take up the concept of intersectionality this is built on a notion of standpoint, the array of identity categories – and their lessons and limits – that come together to create the lens or lenses that we bring to any situation, idea, experience as well as to our engagement with and sense of ourselves (Mirza 1997). This can be the end-point of a discussion of the nature of the person to whom this standpoint belongs – leaving the conscious intents and dis-conscious limitations that are inferred by a standpoint ultimately belonging to unitary agents. More often the person of intersectionality is problematized and understood as constrained. Constraint here is a product of the very intersectioning positions that create a given standpoint *as well as* a result of the material conditions that are themselves a product of the 'matrix of domination' that intersectionality attempts to speak of and decipher.

To suggest that singular categories intersect and to say that in their intersecting something new, more or further is done to the categories, the identities and the inequalities is not necessarily to move past these categories in any fundamental way. Identit*ies* suggest a person made up of a collection of identity categories, whether these are discrete or intersectional. Furthermore, pluralization, a turn to *identities*, does not get us any closer to the nature of the connections *between* categories, especially as these are lived. Nor does it bring us any closer to understanding the subject about whom these identity categories speak. Asserting the intersectionality of these multiple identities risks a postponement of the encounter with the subjects about whom it attempts to speak, a risk that is reminiscent of the postponements of the encounter with embodiment and essence that critics of the move to constructionism offered (Rich 1980; Grosz 1995). As a way of speaking and thinking about the nature of these categories and their relationships, intersectionality remains limited. Despite efforts to move beyond this it retains an abiding sense of the separateness of categories that then intersect – the building blocks and raw materials that have been at the heart of essentialist/constructivist debates (Fuss 1990; Grosz 1995), the series of *pre-existing* parts that have led critics such as Judith Butler to express their misgivings over the term (Butler 2007). Intersectional thinking does not intend to speak about a sum of parts, a chain, a crossing, and yet there remains a sense of junctions, overlapping elements, common points that in turn suggest discrete elements.

At its richest, intersectionality has attempted to tease out how multiple identities intersect and interact with each other, the subjectivities that are constituted and foreclosed at/by these intersections, and how these are then implicated in or tied to particular inequalities through processes that operate at a range of levels of political and social life (see Ahmed *et al.* 2003; Ali 2003; Yuval-Davis 2007). Avtar Brah and Ann Phoenix offer a useful account of intersectionality that captures this complexity:

> We regard the concept of 'intersectionality' as signifying the complex, irreducible, varied, and variable effects which ensue when multiple axis of differentiation – economic, political, cultural, psychic, subjective and experiential – intersect in historically specific contexts. The concept emphasizes that different dimensions of social life cannot be separated out into discrete and pure strands.
>
> (Brah and Phoenix 2004: 76)

If we understand intersectionality in the way suggested by Brah and Phoenix, it offers us a shared language to talk about the complex connections that we are grappling with. In this sense it is particularly useful as an orientating notion that points us towards particular sorts of questions and substantive concerns. Brah and Phoenix's account also underscored the need to bring together a set of theorizations of the economic, political, cultural, psychic, subjective and experiential in order to develop an analytical framework for making sense of the categories that intersectionality calls up, the inequalities that particular groups face and the processes through which these are created and sustained, and the possibilities for intervening in these. This invites an engagement with the materiality of experience and inequality, with 'real life' as well as with the discursive, the symbolic, the psychic and the affective. In turn, this requires that we account for the relationships across the material, the discursive, the symbolic, the psychic and the affective and that we also keep multiple identity categories in play.

Michel Foucault's ideas about power, knowledge and discourse underpin key post-structural approaches to understanding the subjects of education and the subjects of politics. While the repressive or coercive powers of a ruling monarch, class or state and its military and legal apparatus remain, an analysis of disciplinary power foregrounds the way that institutionalized practices, or technologies, regulate populations and people. It does this by establishing normative criteria for judgement and subjecting populations and people to these through technologies of individuation and visibility. In turn, these hyper-visible subjects come to regulate themselves according to the normative criteria of disciplinary power (Foucault 1991a).

Foucault suggests that the subject is subjectivated through her/his constitution in and by discourse. Notions of subjectivation and the performative constitution of the subject and the question of intelligibility that these bring with them help us to understand the nature of the subject, the limits of 'who' this subject might be and the constraints and disavowals that are intrinsic to particular subject positions. 'Subjectivation', sometimes also referred to as 'subjectivization' or 'subjectification', builds on Althusser's (1971) idea of 'subjection' through being named or 'interpellated'. This idea suggests that we are 'called' or 'hailed' and as we turn to the call we accept it, allowing ourselves to be recognized in its terms in order to be recognized at all. In this acceptance and recognition we become a subject within the terms of the call. These are processes that are shot through with relations of power. This simultaneous being made subject to power *and* being made a subject means that subject-hood is always situated in and constrained by relations of power. Judith Butler says:

> 'subjectivation' . . . denotes both the becoming of the subject and the process of subjection – one inhabits the figure of autonomy only by becoming subjected to a power, a subjection which implies a radical dependency. [. . .] Subjection is, literally, the *making* of a subject, the principle of regulation according to which a subject is formulated or produced. Such subjection is a kind of power that not only unilaterally *acts on* a given individual as a form of domination, but also *activates* or forms the subject. Hence, subjection is neither simply the domination of a subject nor its production, but designates a certain kind of restriction *in* production.
>
> (Butler 1997b: 83–4, original emphasis)

A key way in which subjectivation works is by calling up the sorts of categories of identity that I have discussed above. Judith Butler suggests that these categories can be understood as performatives. That is, they are names that *make something happen*. Judith Butler defines the performative as: 'that discursive practice that enacts or produces that which it names' (1993: 13) and '[d]iscursive performativity appears to produce that which it names, to enact its own referent, to name and to do, to name and to make. . . . [g]enerally speaking, a performative functions to produce that which it declares' (ibid.: 107).

Performatives make subjects through their deployment in the classificatory systems, categories and names that are used to designate, differentiate and sort people. The performative, then, can be understood as being an aspect of or culpable in processes of subjectivation. The notions of 'intelligibility' or 'recognizability' help to further demonstrate how performative constitutions are constrained and why they are necessarily embroiled in processes of subjectivation. This is because processes of subjectivation and the performatives involved in these processes have to make sense to work – they have to be *'recognizable'* (Butler 1997a: 5, original emphasis) in the discourses that are circulating in the settings and moments in which they are deployed. Subject-hood and intelligibility, then, are bound together. If practices do not cite an intelligible discourse then their performatives and subjectivations will fail. While this failure might be seen as 'freeing' the subject from subjectivation, if this is a freedom from subject-hood then the question of whether we can 'be' anyone or anything if we are not subjects becomes pressing.

Notions of recognition and intelligibility come together with the ideas of identification and subjectivity to help make sense of the subject's conscious sense of self and the unconscious processes that contribute to this. Mary-Lou Rasmussen (2006) offers a useful account of the relationships between identity, identification, subjectivity and subjectivation. She argues that identity indicates categories of classification and spaces of identification; subjectivation indicates how the subject is made a subject; and subjectivity indicates the subject's capacity for self-recognition and (constrained) action. Subjectivity, then, is a subject's sense of their own subject-hood, their recognizability to themselves as well as their constitution and recognition as a subject in and to the social world. Furthermore, psychoanalytic accounts of the unconscious suggest that the dependence on and desire for the recognition of the other is fundamental to the fragmented subject (Benjamin 1998).

The importance of recognition and identification is made clear when we turn to the consequences of not being recognized. One tool for thinking about the subject who is not recognizable within the terms of the prevailing subjectivating discourses is the concept of 'abjection'. The abject subject is the subject who is both outside the terms of recognizability and conceived of as threatening to contaminate those within its terms. The abject subject is a risk, a threat, and so must be expelled. Kenway *et al.* (2006) build on Julia Kristeva and Elizabeth Grosz in describing the abject as:

> [T]hose bodily fluids, people, objects and places that are couched as unclean, impure and even immoral. [It] provokes the desire to expel the unclean to an outside, to create boundaries in order to establish the certainty of self. . . . Insofar as the abject challenges notions of identity and social order it 'must' be cast out. Abjection involves the processes whereby that or those named unclean are reviled, repelled, resisted. But the 'abject' does not respect such expulsions and boundaries and so constantly threatens to move across boundaries and contaminate.
>
> (Kenway *et al.* 2006: 120)

Identity, subjects and education

What to do about identity categories and the selves they delineate? The conceptual framework I have mapped here convinces me of the utility of thinking of the subject as discursively constituted through multiple discourses which establish lines of identification and recognition and so subjectivities and spaces for practice. Yet constituted in this way, the subject experiences her/himself, and is experienced by others, as unitary and abiding, as a complete whole and not as an amalgam of intersecting categories that might rupture and shift at any moment. Indeed, how ever much the place of our experience of ourselves, others and the social is problematized (Scott 1992), the contemporary subject remains individualized, entreated to work on her/him self reflexively in order to achieve self-knowledge and through this wholeness (Davies 2003; Hey 2005; Youdell 2004a). While the injunction to reflexive individuality might belie the fact that the subject is not this already, it is an injunction that, as it is lived out, is lived as if one 'ought' to be this already. Subject-hood, our subjectivity and our projections and constitutions of others, our lived lives, are perhaps not easily felt as the product of discourse and its categories.

In a Foucauldian analysis categorization is a disciplinary technology, a key to the constitution of the individual as a unit of discipline and self-discipline. It is at the centre of contemporary processes of subjectivation. These categories cannot simply be rejected; the discursive regimes through which subjects become intelligible through categories of identity are deeply sedimented and our status as human rests on our recognizability – livable lives depend on this recognition (Butler 1999, 2004b). Some categories are intransigent while others are continuously erased. For instance, the persistent residues of visual economies of race leave bodies raced in ways that, except at the (heavily policed) boundaries of classification, are all but immobile. Similar arguments are made for gender, for disability. Conversely, the persistent invisibility and silencing of non-normative sexualities renders 'lesbian' almost unspeakable in many discursive fields, while a new sanitized, Americanized, speakability emerges in the 'gay girl' acting her proper place in gender discourse as she is chaperoned by her gay brother. But as some categories press upon us and others are elided, any notion of 'wholeness' that is not a return to unitary subjects or essences remains elusive. Indeed, engaging with psychoanalytic thinking identifies a fragmented subject and a fundamental loss (loss of the mother and of the real, lack of the phallus, or the symbolic) and the persistent desire for the impossible restoration of the lost object. Indeed, finding ourselves cleaving to 'wholeness' might be read as this loss and desire for return (Benjamin 1998; Britzman 1998).

As I noted in the previous chapter, Judith Butler (2008) has suggested that we might think about 'convergence' in order to conceptualize the 'cross cutting modalities of life' (Butler 1997b) that are the sites of livable lives, agency and politics, rather than the intersections of identities. In suggesting a merging or coming together it may be that convergence goes some way to indicate the inseparability of these 'cross cutting modalities' which constitute not categories but the lived lives of subjects. In my previous work (Youdell 2003, 2006a), I have worked with the notion of constellations of discourses and the identity categories they constitute in an attempt to tease out the nuanced processes of subjectivization. The notion of constellation has been useful to me because it asks how classificatory systems (e.g. gender or race) and their categories (boy/girl, White/Black) come to be meaningful through their relationships to other classifications and categories within particular constellations. And it asks whether these constellations might be necessary for apparently singular categories to be meaningful. This suggests that intrinsic to the meaning of the set of identity categories within a classificatory system is its intersections and interactions with the terms of further sets of identity categories, such that the markers from within each classification (boy; White; Social, Emotional and Behavioural Difficulties (SEBD)) form a 'constellation' that comes to 'be' the apparently 'whole' person.

Intersection, convergence, constellation. Take the Russian dolls, imagine there are tendrils inside each doll connecting one to the next, take the game of Misfits, see the intelligible subjects and the unintelligible, the ridiculous, the absurd, the impossible, the demand for coherence and continuity. Can I conjure a notion that doesn't infer a priori ingredients? Wine, perfume, scent: not seen or held but experienced; fragile, fleeting, changing but with meaning. Yet these too include individual, identifiable ingredients, whether bacteria or floral oils, the collapse into singularities seems unavoidable.

Politics

What are the implications of the disjuncture between theory, experience and feeling for conceptualizing a politics in education that can challenge the connections between subjects marked in particular ways and educational inequalities as well as for the intentionality of the discursively constituted and constrained subject who might take up these politics?

Building on Foucault's understanding of discourse and the way in which it is always open to resistance within the circuits of productive power, Butler offers the notion of discursive agency (Butler 1997a) to think about how the subjectivated subject might act politically. In this conceptual framework agency is discursive because it is derived from productive power and is enacted in the take up and deployment of discourse, rather than the possession of a self-knowing unitary subject. Butler writes:

> Because the agency of the subject is not a property of the subject, an inherent will or freedom, but an effect of power, it is constrained but not determined in advance. . . . As the agency of a postsovereign subject, its discursive operation is delimited in advance but also open to a further unexpected delimitation.
>
> (Butler 1997a: 139–40)

This discursive agency is itself the product of subjectivation; having been constituted as a recognizable subject in discourse, this subject can deploy discourse to call up her/him self again or to call up another:

> [T]he one who names, who works within language to find a name for another, is presumed to be already named, positioned within language as one who is already

subject to the founding or inaugurating address. This suggests that such a subject in language is positioned as both addressed and addressing, and that the very possibility of naming another requires that one first be named. The subject of speech who is named becomes, potentially, one who might well name another in time.

(Butler 1997a: 29)

These new meanings and meaningfulness in new spaces is the key to resistant political practice: 'the possibility for the speech act to take on a non-ordinary meaning, to function in contexts where it has not belonged, is precisely the political promise of the performative' (Butler 1997a: 161).

While subject-hood depends on subjectivation and the intelligibility of the performatives deployed in a given discursive terrain, discursive agency means these can also be resisted. The sedimented meanings of enduring discourses might be unsettled and *re*signified or *re*inscribed and subjugated or silenced discourses might be deployed in, and made meaningful in, spaces from which they have been barred. This understanding of discursive agency allows Butler to imagine collective and public insurrectionary practices that amount to a performative politics. These involve 'decontextualizing and recontextualizing . . . terms through radical acts of public misappropriation such that the conventional relation between [naming and meaning] might become tenuous and even broken over time' (Butler 1997a: 100).

Butler's performative politics imagines discourses taking on new meanings and circulating in contexts from which they have been barred or in which they have been rendered unintelligible. It envisages subjectivated subjects engaged in a deconstructive politics that intervenes and unsettles normative meanings. This is how subjects who have been impossible and lives that have been unlivable might be rendered viable, recognizable and livable (Butler 2004b).

Butler's discursive agency and performative politics can be seen as expressions of Foucault's concern with interrogating the 'nature of the present' (Foucault 1988a: 36) and intervening into those aspects of the present that are *intolerable*. They might be grounds for following Foucault's lines of fragility to understand how the present is made and tactics for moving towards its unmaking. It is the unending adherence of material and symbolic subjugation and inequalities to particular subjects, the symbolic valorization and material privileging of certain subjects, and the disavowal and erasure of yet other subjects that is intolerable in the present of education. And it is these subjects and these subjugations that these lines of fragility might help us to undo. These lines of fragility may be a point at which Foucault meets the 'rhizomatics' and 'lines of flight' of Deleuze and Guattari (1983).

Assemblages and rhizomatics

As I began to explore in the previous chapters Deleuze and Guattari's (1983) understanding of assemblages and rhizomatics (1983) is having an increasing influence on scholarship in education. These ideas are relatively new to the field of education so I will explore them in some detail here. Deleuze and Guattari use notions of 'ensembles', 'arrangements' and 'assemblages' to think about the multiplicity of diverse elements that combine to form a field of understanding and activity. The key insight offered by this idea is the recognition that the economic, political, institutional, social, linguistic, semiotic, representational, discursive, subjective and affective are all potentially implicated in the assemblage, and so all are potentially significant in our analysis. That these different orders are also potentially incoherent or contradictory does not undermine analysis in terms of the assemblage. Rather, analysis of assemblages might well be concerned with the ways that apparently inchoate elements come together to form a particular whole. Thinking about an 'education assemblage', then, is useful as it helps us to keep in play the significance of this variety of orders and how they frame education and offers a conceptual terrain on which to interrogate these orders and their interconnections. Importantly, the multiplicity of elements that come together to create assemblages are understood by Deleuze and Guattari as cutting across orders that are often treated as separate or of differential significance in much social and political thinking. For instance, while structural social theory has contested the relative significance of structure and agency, and much post-structural theory has been charged with privileging Foucauldian discourse and disciplinary power over the material and other forms of power, Deleuze and Guattari insist on the inseparability of all of these orders. They argue that:

> An arrangement in its multiplicity necessarily works at once on semiotic, material, and social flows [. . .] There is no longer a tripartite division between a field of reality (the world), a field of representation (a book), and a field of subjectivity (the author). Rather, an arrangement connects together certain multiplicities caught up in each of these orders.
>
> (Deleuze and Guattari, 1983: 52)

Taking up this understanding, Maria Tamboukou suggests that in analyses of education we consider 'a complex assemblage of interrelations between social structures, economic conditions, power/knowledge relations, architectural and spatial arrangements, forces of desire and pleasure seductions' (Tamboukou, 2008: 369). The orders and multiplicities that come together to make the assemblage that makes up education are reminiscent of and might include the discursive matrices and disciplinary technologies found in Foucauldian work. Yet the notion of the assemblage helps us to bring into analysis a series of further orders and elements that are potentially present but often not foregrounded in Foucauldian work.

In order to understand assemblages Deleuze and Guattari move away from hierarchical tree-like or 'arborescent' forms of thinking and analysis; forms which they see as dominating and constraining knowledge, social orders and social subjects through their rigid and linear hierarchical relations. Deleuze and Guattari look to scramble the arborescent with the rhizome and the image of the grasses that grow endlessly from it. They suggest that this image allows us to think about the horizontal, multi-directional and never ending: '[t]here are no points or positions in a rhizome, as one finds in a structure, tree or root. There are only lines' (Deleuze and Guattari 1983: 14). One key promise of the rhizome, both for interrogating existing assemblages and for conceptualizing new lines of thinking and activity, lies in its absence of super-ordinate and subordinate components, meanings or relations. The rhizome is always in the middle, moving in and from the middle 'through which it pushes and overflows' (ibid.: 47). Another is its connectivity, its bringing together of apparently divergent elements: 'a rhizome never ceases to connect semiotic chains, organizations of power, and events in the arts, sciences, and social struggles' (ibid.: 12).

Rather than an analysis that proceeds from the macro to the micro or takes these elements as separate or hierarchically arranged – for instance, from education policy, to institutions, to teachers' practices – these elements are taken together as hetero-geneous parts of the education assemblage. An instance on the interrelations and interplay of these various aspects of education is not all together new, but rhizomatics offers a new set of tools for thinking about and analysing this complexity.

A further promise of the rhizome is the 'lines of flight' that its connectivities and movements from the middle offers. Deleuze and Guattari use the notion of the 'line' to think about the multiplicities that the assemblage brings together and rhizomatic thinking open up to movement from. They consider the molar line, which they describe as a rigid and segmented line that is a 'plane of organization' (Deleuze and Guattari 1983: 80); the molecular line, a supple and segmented line of thresholds, flows and flux; and a line of flight, which is described as a line of 'becoming' (ibid.: 81). This image of the rhizome pushing through its middle and overflowing in any and all directions, following any lines, invites us to imagine the immediacy and indeterminacy of these movements and ruptures, movements which are Deleuze and Guattari's 'lines of flight'. The image of rigid molar lines might help us to understand the endurance and fixity of notions of intelligence in education and the selection and setting practices that flow from these; molecular lines might help us to make sense of schools and teachers trying to find ways of working with a notion of 'multiple intelligences', or 'abilities' that are not generalized across all areas of learning, or strategies for organizing schools, classrooms and pedagogies that are not predicated on prior assessments of 'ability'; and lines of flight might help us to imagine the practices that might ensue if schools and teachers discarded 'intelligence' and its associated practices altogether.

The shift from the arborescent to the rhizomatic in Deleuze and Guattari's work resonates with the shift from a focus on sovereign, top-down power and dominant and subordinate knowledge to disciplinary power and power/knowledge effected through discourse in Foucault. Indeed, Gilles Deleuze and Catherine Parnet's (1983) consideration of the place of the state and its apparatus and their relationship to knowledge and meaning is reminiscent of the conceptual work achieved by Foucault's distinction between judicial, sovereign and disciplinary power. Deleuze and Parnet write:

> Not that the State apparatus has no meaning: it has a very particular function, insofar as it overcodes all segments, simultaneously both those it takes for itself at a particular moment and those it leaves outside itself. Or rather, the State apparatus is a concrete arrangement that puts society's overcoding machine into effect. This machine in its turn is thus not the State itself, but the abstract

machine that organizes the dominant statements and the established order of a society, the languages and dominant forms of knowledge, and the segments that win over the others.

(Deleuze and Parnet 1983: 78–9)

Knowledges, meanings and social practices are therefore not of or reducible to the state and its apparatus, but they are effects of the state and its apparatus and so are not wholly separate from it. The assemblage of knowledges, meanings and practices that Deleuze and Parnet refers to here as the 'abstract machine' operates to delineate the social as well as what is excluded from it – in their terms it 'overcodes' the social. Various manifestations of power, or 'power set ups' (Deleuze and Parnet 1983: 80), their institutions and their abstract machines are inseparable and are key to understanding a given assemblage.

The point, then, is not to determine the relative force and influence of the power of the state and its apparatus versus the diffuse power effects of discourses, representations and meanings. The point is to understand the flows, operations and effects of these various manifestations of power and their relations to each other as they circulate in and define the political, economic, social, representational and affective. In this sense they provide an analytic device that enables us to encounter Foucault's judicial, sovereign and disciplinary powers simultaneously and in their interrelation, maintaining the significance of the discursive without rendering everything in the analytical frame *as* discourse. I begin to demonstrate this approach in the following chapters.

Affectivities are central to Deleuze and Guattari's rhizomatics. In thinking about affectivities the question of the relationship between affect and emotion is central. One approach to this is to understand affect as bodily sensation and emotion as the naming of these sensations through discourse; mediation that makes affect meaningful and mean particular things. In this sense the affective might be thought of as extra-discursive, as something that is not already in discourse. Whether affect and emotion can be separated in this way, however, is unclear. The possibility that the affective might not *already* be *in* discourse, that it is extra-discursive, allows us to think about productive possibilities that exceed the reach of discourse. Yet bodily sensation and its meanings may not be separable from emotion, sensation may only be accessible to the subject through discursive registers of emotion (Ahmed 2004). A similar debate surrounds the body more broadly – a body that exceeds discourse may suggest new potentialities, but while the body is not simply discourse, even its materiality may not be accessible or understood outside discourse – discourses might be needed to make material bodies meaningful (Butler 1993) That this argument is irresolvable is a clue to the potential that is seen in affect by those theorists who pursue it.

Deleuze and Guattari (2008) understand affectivities as eruptions and flows of bodily sensation and intensities, and the encounters between these eruptions and flows, between bodies, as being beyond or before subjectivation. In this sense, their thinking is anti-subjectivation, offering ways of thinking and feeling that might escape the bounds of subjectivation. Affect and affectivity is central to Deleuze and Guattari's thinking about anti-subjectivation politics and about other ways of being, or in their terminology, 'becoming'. Anna Hickey-Moody and Peta Malins explain Deleuze and Guattari's understanding of affect in the following way:

> Affect is that which is felt before it is thought; it has visceral impact on the body before it gives subjective or emotive meaning. [. . .] Affect is . . . very different from emotion: it is an *a*-subjective bodily response to an encounter. Emotion comes later, a classifying or *stratifying* of affect.
>
> (Hickey-Moody and Malins 2007: 9, original emphasis)

And Brian Massumi, in his notes to his translation of Deleuze and Guattari's *A Thousand Plateaus* describes affect as: '[A]n ability to affect and be affected. It is a prepersonal intensity corresponding to the passage from one experiential state of the body to another implying an augmentation or diminution in that body's capacity to act' (Massumi in Deleuze and Guattari 2008: xvii).

The focus on affectivity invites a focus on bodies rather than subjects. Affects are not the property of a subject, but constitute a body and a body's capacities and limits.

> We know nothing about a body until we know what it can do, in other words, what its affects are, and how they can or cannot enter into composition with other affects, with the affects of another body, either to destroy that body or be destroyed by it, either to exchange actions and passions with it or to join with it in composing a more powerful body.
>
> (Deleuze and Guattari 2008: 284)

Deleuze and Guttari understand these relations between bodies as symbiotic, as mutually constituting and sustaining, not as a moment of identification between discrete bodies. And they also insist that this thinking is not an analogy or invention but is the 'composition of speeds and affects on the plane of consistency' (Deleuze and Guattari 2008: 285). They also think of affectivity and flows of intensities by using the notion of 'haecceity', or 'this thing', or 'ecceity', or 'here is' (ibid.: 599). These notions suggest for Deleuze and Gattari individuation that is not a subject or a person but rather a passage from subject to event. As such, 'affects are becomings' (ibid.: 283) and haecceity is rhizomatic. They suggest:

> For you will yield nothing to haecceity unless you realize that that is what you are and that you are nothing but that. [. . .] You are longitude and latitude, a set of speeds and slownesses between unformed particles, a set of nonsubjectified affects. You have the individuality of a day, a season, a year, a life (regardless of its duration) – a climate, a wind, a fog, a swarm, a pack (regardless of its regularity). Or at least you can have it, you can reach it.
>
> (Deleuze and Guttari 2008: 289)

Is feeling that of a subject or prior to subjectivation? Emotion is the translation of affective intensity into a symbolic framework of understanding, interpretation and regulation and it is here that the subjectivating force of emotion is located. She's a worrier, a hysteric; he's a rock, a tower of strength. The binary of rationality/emotionality is a molar line that scores deep striations in the education assemblage. Even if affect is outside meaning for only a moment, a second, a pulse, it might still be productive. Meaning may not have to reside in discourse, the intellect. Instead the body's experience of affect and of other bodies might register its own meanings without these having to be 'decoded', which may well be an 'overcoding', in discourse or symbolic registers.

These rhizomatics look to a politics that pursues becomings, deterritorializations and assemblage conversions. I began to discuss these ideas in the previous chapters and I demonstrate them inside school practices in the chapters that follow. As a politics the task is 'the study of these lines, in groups or in individuals' (Deleuze and Guattari 1983: 72). While the possibility of change or 'becoming-otherwise' that the 'line of flight' offers might seem abstract, imaginary or a utopian impossibility, it is fully a part of the social:

> Far from being a flight outside the social, or from being utopian or even ideological, these lines actually constitute the social field, tracing its shapes and borders, its entire state of becoming. [. . .] in a society everything flees and . . . society is defined by its lines of flight.
>
> (Deleuze and Parnet 1983: 91)

Deleuze and Parnet suggest that in escaping binaries we can look 'between' terms in order to find 'a narrow pass like a border or frontier which will make of the ensemble a multiplicity' (1983: 85). Deleuze and Guattari suggest that:

> An element of intensity begins to work on its own behalf, an hallucinatory perception, a perverse mutation, a play of images stands out, and the hegemony of the signifier is suddenly put into doubt. The semiotics of gesture, of mimicry, of game-playing regain their liberty in the child's activities, are disengaged from the 'trace', that is, from the dominant competence of the schoolteacher's language, and a microscopic event disrupts the equilibrium of local power.
>
> (Deleuze and Guattari 1983: 32–3)

Deleuze and Parnet remind us that 'we don't know in advance what will function as a line of inclination, nor the form an obstacle to it will take' (1983: 87). Becomings, then, are not without risk. Deleuze and Parnet speak of the prudence, precaution and labour needed when pursuing a line of flight: '[t]he prudence required to guide this line, the precautions needed to soften, suspend, divert or undermine it, all point to a long process of labor directed not only against the State, but against itself as well' (ibid.: 96).

Without prudence and precautions those who pursue the line of flight risk 'turning into abolition and destruction, both of others and of themselves' (ibid.: 99) and so, rather than a becoming-otherwise, it becomes a 'line of death' (ibid.: 105). Furthermore, lines of flight might collapse into 'black holes' when intensities are 'no longer bearable' and thresholds are 'crossed too quickly' (ibid.: 97). When we fly along these lines '[w]e have left the shores of rigid segmentation, and entered a realm no less organized, where each one plumbs his own black hole, thereby becoming dangerous, confident about his own situation, his role and his mission' (ibid.: 97).

Becoming-otherwise is a rejection of the subjectivations of a given assemblage that segment us and let us know 'what' and 'who' we must be. Becomings fly from subjectivations but, even if escaping these is possible, Deleuze and Parnet ask: 'even if we had the power to get rid of [subjectivation], could we do so without destroying ourselves, so much is it part of the conditions of life' (Deleuze and Parnet 1983: 96). Deleuze and Parnet use the idea of the 'marginals' and 'men of the line' to think about the subjects who pursue these lines of flight and run these risks of annihilation. They say:

> The marginals are not the ones who create the lines; they install themselves on them, and make of them their property. It's perfect when they have the curious modesty of 'men of the line', and the prudence of an experimenter, but a catastrophe when they slide into a black hole, from which emerges only the microfascist speech of their eddying dependency: 'we are the avante-garde!' or 'we are the marginals!'
>
> (Deleuze and Parnet 1983: 98)

This account of the risks of becoming-otherwise offer insights into the retreats, recuperations and failures of a politics of resignification and begins to illuminate a potential limit of a performative politics. If the rejection of subjectivation that is involved in becomings also risks the annihilating threat of the black hole, then the lure of the retreat or compulsion to the subject-self and so identity politics, and the arborescent thinking and molar lines that underpin them, begins to make sense. Butler's demonstration of the force of the desire for/necessity of recognizability and so intelligibility is another way of understanding this; here the risk is subject-hood. In both of these accounts the incredible force of the hail of the subject, and the subject's turn to the hail is underscored. Deleuze and Parnet ask, then, 'which are your lines, as an individual or group, and what are their dangers?' (1983: 106). They ask us to consider the sum of our deterritorializations and the costs and risks of reterritorializations. They invite us to identify the locus of black holes and their contents, which, they suggest, might be 'a little beast' or a 'growing micro-facism' (ibid: 107). Furthermore, Deleuze and Parnet's account of the micro-fascisms that may emerge from the black hole in the form of confident and self-congratulatory certainties insist further on the prudence and curious modesty of the men (and women) of the line – a significant degree of openness and circumspection is called for.

Rhizomatics in education

The philosophical work of Deleuze and Guattari, and Deleuze's work with Parnet, often feels abstract and impenetrable to new readers. As they shift between thinking in terms of the arborescent, the rhizomatic, the molecular and molar, lines of rupture, flight, becoming, they keep their ideas moving – like the rhizome itself – but they also challenge those of us engaging with their writing in the search for useful analytic tools to keep up and to envisage their ideas at work in our worlds. Nevertheless, the perpetual movement in their work demonstrates a conceptual and writing strategy that is itself rhizomatic; constantly moving it avoids cementing, capture, recuperation, reterritorialization within the assemblage. Rhizomatics includes the multiplicity of ideas and ways of thinking; lines of flight. It keeps becoming.

Rhizomatics seems to offer a generative conceptual framework for thinking about power and of the place of the state, its institutions, its structures and systems, its legislative and policy frameworks and formulations, its knowledges and its subjects in intimate inter-relation with the meanings and practices that delineate the social, the material conditions of social life, the minutiae of the day-to-day and the identifications and affectivities of social subjects. This is a tremendously complex and multi-faceted field to attempt to encounter, one which haunts us but whose shape and form slips away perhaps as much as Deleuze and Guattari's tools for thinking it. In making use of these tools to engage with the real world of education in this book, I want to reveal some of this slipperiness, this movement, this ghost-like quality that holds the promise of rhizomatics and the assemblages it invites us to struggle to map and the lines of flight it suggests we take.

Rhizomatics also helps us to move beyond criticisms of the limits of disciplinary power, governmentality and a person subjected in and to relations of power. Inside post-structural thinking this has seen a tendency towards reading power as only disciplinary, resistance as necessarily curtailed in advance, and subjection as foreclosing agency and political action. For instance, Devine (1996) has called into question the usefulness of a notion of disciplinary power and a self-surveillant subject in contexts where active surveillance by the state or its institution marks the failure of disciplinary power self-surveillance. Yet this critique seems to imagine a move *from* sovereign or repressive power *to* disciplinary power rather than an augmentation, movement between and simultaneity of these modes of power. Scholars such as Judith Butler, and Michel Foucault himself, have continually asserted the layering of disciplinary power and governmental forms over sovereign power and placed a political subject, albeit radically re-theorized, at the centre of their work (Butler 1997a, 1997b, 2004a; Foucault 1990a, 1990b, 1992). Judith Butler's work on the US and UK military operations in Iraq and the detentions at Guantanamo Bay (Butler 2004b) is illustrative of Foucault's abiding insistence that disciplinary power augments sovereign/judicial, and that the oppressive force of the state is brought into play in the very moments when the reach of disciplinary power appears to fail. The interplay and inseparability of these modes of power – improvised and deployed strategically (and no doubt reactively and in panic) by states and in the moment of brute force between one body and another – that Foucault insists on and that Butler illustrates is usefully thought about as a network of lines in the assemblage. Foucauldian understandings of power and discourse have also been drawn on to enrich analyses of state policy and social movements, for instance, Said's analysis of Orientalism (Said 2003); Apple's work on 'why the Right is winning' (Apple 2006); Ball's analysis of policy tendencies (Ball

1994, 2006); and other recent work on educational inequalities and school practices (Gillborn and Youdell 2000).

Nicolas Rose, well known for his development of Foucault's writing on governmentality, has used the work of Deleuze and Guattari to think about contemporary governmental practice in terms of assemblages (Rose 2000 in Leahy 2009). Deana Leahy (2009) has taken up this development offered by Rose to extend analysis of the governmental project of school-based health education by understanding this as a 'pedagogic assemblage' whose 'bio-pedagogies' 'contribute to the classroom assemblage' and are part of a 'wider governmental assemblage' (Leahy 2009: 176) concerned with the control of obesity. This move, she suggests, enables us to engage and map 'the messiness that characterizes contemporary projects of governance' (ibid.: 177). Leahy suggests that the Deleuzo-Guattarian notion of the assemblage provokes us to engage factors and forces that are beyond the expert knowledges, or prevailing discourses, that are usually analysed as central in analyses of health education as a governmental project. She suggests that this line of analysis brings into play 'other dynamics and affects' (ibid.: 180), exposing the convergences, hybridizing and morphing of knowledges in the classroom as well as processes of subjectivation and the provocation and recruitment of affectivities into the pedagogical assemblage. In the case of health education interventions concerned with obesity, this involves eliciting bodily responses of disgust, shame and pride that 'interweave and fold expert knowledges into and onto the body' (ibid.: 181). Leahy argues, then, that the conceptual framework of the pedagogic assemblage enriches Foucauldian analyses of governmentality:

> Classrooms are indeed complex spaces, made up of a vast assemblage of objects, bodies, curriculum imperatives, and pedagogic practices that are connected to broader assemblages. There is much value I suggest in conceptualizing the field as a governmental assemblage and, in so doing, considering all of what is going on in that assemblage.
>
> (Leahy 2009: 181)

Maria Tamboukou (2008) too has made use of the work of Deleuze and Guattari in her analysis of the 'art education assemblage'. Considering the biography of a particular nineteenth-century woman art educator and artist, Tamboukou argues that within this Deleuzo-Guattarrian rhizomatic framing:

> Becoming an artist cannot be pinned down within a specific space/time block, it would rather be seen as a continuum that needs to be mapped on a grid of intelligibility, a machinic rather than a linear model of transformations, that allows for rhizomatic connections to be seen working together.
>
> (Tamboukou 2008: 365–6)

In this art education assemblage, the artist 'emerges as an effect of disparate, coexisting elements, producing the real: subjects and their social milieus' (Tamboukou 2008: 369). Tamboukou argues that the becoming-artist of the woman art educator whose biography she reconstructs suggests the deterritorialization of the art education assemblage that would foreclose the possibility of artist for this woman educator:

> [I]ts mission and its students had opened up fields of forces for lines of flight to be released and new subjectivities to emerge, irrespective of the fact that these new women would soon be reterritorialized within the segmentarities of the social formations and cultural institutions of the elite.
>
> (Tamboukou 2008: 369)

Michaelinos Zembylas (2007) has taken up the idea of affect developed by Deleuze and Guattari for thinking about pedagogy. Zembylas suggests that affect should be understood as autonomous and not as mirror of intent and, after Butler, that affect creates the surfaces and boundaries of the body, effecting the body's materialization (Butler 1993). He suggests that an 'affective terrain is unavoidably political' (Zembylas 2007: xiii), 'in that power is an inextricable aspect of how bodies come together, move and dwell' (ibid.: xiv) and stressing that emotional investments, however ambivalent, are embroiled in relations of power. As such he is critical of the erasure of feeling in education, suggesting that this erasure is dangerous and that the positioning of this erasure as 'objective' is indicative of the manipulation of emotion by educational institutions.

Using Deleuze and Guattari's rhizomatics to think in terms of an education assemblage invites us to consider the nature, operations and effects of state structures, or apparatus, that is, the power of the state to demarcate the border of the education assemblage. As the discussion in Chapter 1 suggested, states internationally, allied to particular notions of the proper relationship between the modern state and society and between the public and the private sectors, have pursued vigorously forms of privatization in and of education. The legislative and policy frameworks at national and trans-national levels that have made these moves possible, and the institutions and institutional forms that these have provoked, might be understood as moments, apparatus and artifacts of state power.

At the same time, the notion of the education assemblage also insists on an analysis of further power setups, including the productive force of disciplinary technologies and power/knowledges. The markets, competition, accountability, choice, performance management, effectiveness, efficiency, individualism and instrumentalism embedded in and emanating from these legislative and policy frameworks might be understood as combining to create the 'abstract machine' that overcodes the education assemblage, marking its surfaces and delineating what is inside it and what remains outside. Practices of performance management; the deployment of performance indicators, high-stakes national testing and benchmark grades; diversification of provision; delegated budgets determined by performance through per-capita funding; National Curriculum; regimes of school inspection and intervention; provision and requirements for selection, sorting and setting; practices of educational triage; measurements of 'ability' and diagnoses of 'special needs'; 'behaviour management'; school exclusions; and the use of special schools and other alternative provision outside the education mainstream might all be understood as lines, whether molar or molecular, complete with their rank of disciplinary technologies, that make up the education assemblage. The discourses of education's economic imperative; education as commodity and private good; ability; giftedness; special needs; meritocracy; deprivation; social exclusion; social capital; and cultural capital that make meaningful and so possible these practices and technologies can all be understood as further lines in the tangled network of lines in this assemblage. Furthermore, the subjectivities and identifications that are effected through these discourses, practices and power setup, and the recognitions and identifications that these make possible, provoke and exclude, are further lines in the assemblage. Finally, the affectivities that flow through education and its spaces, those that are called up as pedagogic devices and those that erupt, overflow and collide unbidden or despite censure or prohibition, can also be understood in these terms.

This rhizomatic approach to what education is, how it moves and mutates, how it defines and patrols its borders, how it renders particular educational subjects and how it provokes and corrals affectivities suggests a complex map of education that brings together forces, orders, discourses, technologies, practices and bodies; from the legislative functions of the state to the affective eruptions of the playground. The account offered in this book is not an exhaustive mapping of the contemporary education assemblage in England, let alone elsewhere, but it goes some way to demonstrate how thinking in terms of the assemblage invites us to think across the diverse activities of the state, institutions and subjects and to begin to draw these together. As we begin to map the education assemblage we can decipher how its elements interact, how they are bricolaged, improvised, borrowed and remade. We can begin to see how the elements in the machine rub up against each other, how cog-teeth intersect smoothly or grind against each other, synapses firing, programmes crashing, outputs churning, distorting, jamming, creating a hybrid machine that is education and its effects. This assemblage is irreducible to its component parts; it is a vast plane formed of dense igneous, unexpected metamorphic and crumbling sedimentary strata inseparably enfolded in each other. Yet it is also an undulating plain of moving grass from whose rhizome new lines constantly fly.

Deleuze and Guattari suggest that in taking-up rhizomatics as a method we should:

> Always follow the rhizome by rupturing, lengthening, prolonging, taking up the line of flight, make it vary, until it produces the most abstract and tortuous line in *n* dimensions and scattered directions. Combine the deterritorializing flows. Follow the plants: begin by fixing the limits of a first line according to circles of convergence around successive singularities; next see if new circles of convergence are established along the interior of this line, with new points situated outside its limits and other directions. To write, form rhizomes, expand your own territory by deterritorialization, extend the line of flight to the point where it covers the whole plane of consistency in an abstract machine.
>
> (Deleuze and Guattari, 1983: 23)

This book does not take up this injunction as though it were a systematic model to be followed in linear form to a final analytic certainty, a thoroughly arborescent way to proceed. Rather, it responds to the call for a rhizomatic analysis that moves from the middle and in many directions, that trips, that gets tied up in the lines it pursues, that finds and takes lines of flight, that deterritorializes and is reterritorialized.

Part II

Troubling schools

Places, people, feelings

4 Troubling school knowledges

In this chapter I explore possibilities for engaging in a counter-politics in education in relation to school knowledges. I consider the nature and place of knowledges in education and the ways these knowledges are implicated in demarcating not just 'what' is knowable, but also 'who' is knowable. As I do this I examine the possibilities and limits for troubling approved knowledges and enabling knowledges that have been barred from education to be meaningful and legitimate in these spaces. Thinking about a political pedagogy means engaging with the multiple traditions of critical pedagogies that have been developed through a range of lenses and undergone notable revisions over the last 30 to 40 years. If we take Paulo Freire's (1970) neo-Marxist critical pedagogy of class conscientization and social transformation as a starting point, we can trace moves through feminist and critical race concerns with gender and race empowerment, emancipation and cultural politics, to post-structurally informed approaches to critical and deconstructive reading, queer politics and resignification. I explore these in more detail in Chapter 6. For the purposes of this chapter it is useful to note the key concerns shared across these divergent pedagogies. One is the recognition and interrogation of inequalities with a view to interrupting these. A second is the critique of the status of prevailing knowledge, the interrogation of its effects, and the introduction of alternative ways of knowing. Underpinned by differing conceptual and political frameworks, all invite scrutiny of privilege and its reproduction and problematize knowledge and its connection to social relations and subjectivities. These pedagogies hope to change the way students, educators and others think about and see themselves as well as wider social structures, relations, practices and meanings.

Underpinning the concerns and ambitions of critical pedagogies is a set of readings of education's culpability in producing and reproducing inequalities inside education and in wider society. At their heart, critical pedagogies reject the presentation of differential locations, experiences or outcomes in education as the 'natural' result of abilities, talents or pre-dispositions or the inevitable products of identity, culture or personal circumstances. Instead, critical pedagogies invite scrutiny of such ideas and move from the assertion that students are differentially and hierarchically positioned in terms of social class, race, gender, sexuality, religion, nationality, (dis)ability, first language; that education is constitutive of these hierarchical positionings; and that while the prevailing discourse of meritocratic individualism and the business as usual of education are implicated in rewarding and reproducing these hierarchical positionings, schooling is also a significant site in which these are struggled against (Apple 2000; Apple and Beane 2007). Within education systems, institutional procedures, classrooms, pedagogies and approved knowledges it is White, elite, upper middle class, masculine, heterosexual, able-bodied and rational-minded forms that are privileged and normalized (Walkerdine 1989, 1990; Paechter 2001). These are often silent and implicit and they shift and mutate as they and their meanings are struggled over, as might be suggested by girls' recent outperformance of boys in national tests. It is the approved knowledges of education, and our capacity to expand, contest or shift these that I focus on in this chapter.

I do this by engaging with aspects of work undertaken as part of an Economic and Social Research Council (ESRC) funded project that used a practitioner action research approach with early years and primary educators (children aged 3 to 11) in English schools between September 2006 and December 2008, to develop and try out ways of including issues of sexualities equalities in the classroom (see Atkinson and DePalma 2009). The project was led by Elizabeth Atkinson and Renee DePalma and I was a regional academic lead. Describing even the aims of the project is complex because more than 30 university and school educators as well as policy workers and activists were involved in the project. Conceptualizations of the project's concerns and goals shifted across people and over time, and the goals of team members were not necessarily those of the project leaders.

These complexities of the project's multiple goals are exemplified in its naming. The project's main title was 'No Outsiders', a citation of Desmond Tutu's assertion '[e]veryone is an insider, there are no outsiders whatever their belief, whatever their colour, gender or sexuality' (Tutu 2004 cited by No Outsiders 2009). This citation is an appropriation that has the effect of claiming a high status and relatively conservative legitimacy for the project at the same time as claiming something that the project knows not to be the case – that there are no outsiders. The website offers the project's position that the Tutu citation was an:

> inspiration to work toward a society where his words are true. At the same time, these words remind us that continuing discrimination, whether in relation to 'race', class, gender, disability, sexuality or other features of identity, still conveys a message to 'outsiders' that they have no place in 'our' society.
>
> (No Outsiders 2009)

The project concerned itself with questions of discrimination in relation to a range of sexual and gender identities. In its action research it explored approaches and responses to a variety of practical issues that arise when addressing sexualities issues in primary school; parental concern, staff discomfort and student resistances amongst these. Alongside this identity politics-based equalities approach to the project's work there was also a commitment to taking up queer theory in the project, particularly in relation to deconstructing sexuality and gender binaries and their undergirding of heteronormativity. This dual framing of the project was also reflected in the articulation of its accomplishments. The project 'developed strategies and resources to address lesbian, gay, bisexual and transgender equality in their own primary education settings'. And, it has been involved in 'exploring and challenging how normal-deviant, us-Other categories are socially constructed and maintained' (No Outsiders 2009).

The conceptual framing and outcomes of the project suggest that it pursued equalities for multiply positioned subjects *and* sought to unsettle and undo the sexualized and gendered subject positions for which it pursues equality. This pair of goals is clearly in tension; as I explored in detail in Chapter 2, to seek to promote equalities for subjects constituted under a particular identity category is to assert and bolster this category. Such an assertion of the proper place of the category inevitably draws the boundary of a new outside, those subjects who have not quite made the entry criteria, and cites once again the prevailing sense of the unitary, enduring, self-knowing subject. The No Outsiders website argues that taking these dual approaches 'is a kind of social activism that goes beyond a simplistic tolerance model of inclusion' (No Outsiders 2009). This is certainly the case in particular moments and instances. Yet as I explored in detail in previous chapters, identity politics and queer or deconstructive politics cannot easily run alongside one another and it is queer politics that is likely to be foreclosed by the normative conception of the subject and politics at the centre of equalities approaches to identity politics.

Perhaps inevitably, then, this equalities-based form of identity politics came increasingly to dominate the efforts of the project. This is reflected in the project's shifting sub-title. On the website the project leaders assert that it was 'researching approaches to sexualities equalities in primary schools', a series of pluralizations that leaves open the possibility of the dual conceptual framings that I have sketched, despite their tensions. At the project's press launch, however, the sub-title had mutated into 'challenging homophobia in primary schools', an assertion of a singular identity-based equalities approach that appears to suggest the 'answer' to the more open-ended question of the sub-title's earlier incarnation. The project has no doubt made significant inroads into developing ways of representing gay and lesbian families in primary school settings and using these representations to posit the 'normalcy' of these families and as an avenue for challenging homophobic sentiment and practice. Yet the shift from multiple approaches to a more singular identity politics does not reflect a consensus that the multiple approaches have been researched and a 'solution' – challenging homophobia – has been found. Rather it demonstrates the persistent reach of this way of knowing subjects and knowing political action. It illustrates the way that reform and recognition pursued by rational, unitary, self-knowing (but diverse) subjects operates as a regime of truth of political practice. And it demonstrates the unsettling effects of deconstructive or queer politics; not just on the normative majority but also on those who might be positioned as the Other and towards whom the entreaty to queer practice might be directed.

The ideas of subjectivation, recognizability, identification and abjection that I have already discussed help to make sense of the alignment with identity politics of the project's 'lesbian', 'gay', 'bisexual', 'transgender' (LGBT) and 'LGBT-friendly' straight educators. LGBT identity politics offers recognizability and viability to subjects who have been subjectivated as Other or even abject. It offers a point of identification and a subjectivity that, rather than being 'wounded' (Rasmussen and Crowley 2004), is promised new legitimacy. Alongside its familiarity and acceptability as a proper political mode of engagement, and the widespread belief in the 'advances' won by such politics historically – from women's suffrage to desegregation – this recognition is a powerful 'hail' to which many of the project's LGBT-identified members readily turn. At the same time, this identity politics allows the LGBT-friendly straight educator to offer recognition and authorization to LGBT team members while not opening-up their own heterosexuality to the troubling that queer politics threatens. In this sense we might follow Critical Race Theory's understanding of Whiteness and White Supremacy in order to think of the operations of the supremacy of Straightness. Straight people, then, might learn lessons from the race traitors of CRT and Critical Whiteness studies and, rather than bestowing recognition and rights, they might endeavour to practise as 'straight traitors' – 'what makes you think I'm straight?'.

I am convinced by post-structural politics and an anti-identity position. I am also convinced that the successes of identity politics simultaneously shore up the classificatory systems and categories, and so hierarchies that post-structural politics endeavours to undermine. And that identity-based politics can be, and have been, deployed in ways that are extremely damaging, for instance, in nationalist claims against migrants and minoritized ethnic communities. Yet I am ambivalent about jettisoning once and for all the sorts of identity politics that have formed the major thread of the No Outsiders project's work. The project's participants are agreed, on the whole, that they have achieved a great deal in these terms. For instance, mainstream media coverage of the project's representation of gay and lesbian families in schools, whilst also giving air-time to counter-positions, does show that the project has enabled a significant wave of age-appropriate, liberal identity politics work in schools that almost certainly could not have happened on this scale and with this profile without the project (BBC1 2009). That this could not have happened without the commitment and work of the project's 'teacher-researchers' is reflected in their being awarded the 2008 British Educational Research Association/Sage Publishers award for practitioner research.

As I struggle to hold my ambivalence over the continued place of identity politics despite its problematics, I wonder whether its 'gains' are necessary to make lives survivable, even if these are achieved by further cementing subjugation and supremacy. I wonder whether the political subject needs these subjectivating subjectivities in order to be intelligible, to act meaningfully within discourse. I wonder when I will next need identity politics. But I also wonder about a politics that is post-identitarian (Butler 2007), or a politics of anti-subjectivation (Deleuze and Guattari 1983) or of unintelligibility. The analysis that I offer in this chapter underscores, for me, the urgency of these questions. I return to the question of what these politics might look like in the chapters that follow.

In my interrogation of the possibilities and constraints for doing critical pedagogic work in primary classrooms around sexualized and gendered subjectivities I focus on some of the storybooks that the No Outsiders project distributed to all participating schools. These books were a heavily used resource but also came to be emblematic of the project and its commitments, particularly after they were targeted in hostile media coverage of the project (Youdell 2009). This interrogation raises fundamental questions about what it is possible to know in school settings, the varied status of the divergent knowledges that circulate in schools, whether knowledges that exist at or beyond the fringes of acceptability in schools might be made admissible in the formal school curriculum and what the implications of such movements of knowledge might be.

Social and political theorizing and empirical research have treated the status of knowledge and the disconnection of knowledge from enlightenment notions of truth and progress as a significant concern for some time. In the sociology of education the idea that disciplinary knowledge and curriculum are constructions that reflect and constitute particular world-views, values and normative frameworks for thinking and knowing is longstanding (see Apple 1990, 2000, 2003; Giroux 1981; McLaren 1994; Riddell 1992; Whitty 1985; Yates 1990; Young 1971, 1977). While these knowledges are identified as being tightly demarcated and stratified, changing global economic contexts have precipitated shifts in official knowledges and seen these further specialized, instrumentalized and hierarchized as differentiated students are taught what 'they' 'need' to know. Indeed, accurately predicating the knowledge needs of the global economy has become one of the fundamental goals of education policy makers, especially those hoping to deploy education instrumentally to secure the future of the wealthiest nations (Brown and Lauder 2006; Guile 2006). Formal curriculum knowledges, then, are temporally and contextually situated, they may well be contradictory and in moments incoherent, and they are subject to change through contestation, tactical practices and policy reform. These knowledges may at times reflect and/or be mobilized in order to serve the interests of some over the interests of others, even as they appear to be neutral and disinterested, but there is no direct correspondence between particular knowledges and the interests of particular groups and so knowledge – both prevailing and subjugated – can be deployed to multiple and shifting ends and is the site of struggle.

The conceptual framing of these readings of school knowledge is not undisputed. Arguing the partiality of school knowledge may be part of a claim to the ideological nature of formal curriculum knowledges in which the truth, including or especially of class exploitation, is distorted allowing false and partial accounts of knowledge and its worth to become dominant (Althusser 1971; Apple 2003). This conception of the status and nature of school knowledge can be found in many Left critical accounts, where much use has been made of Gramsci's idea of 'hegemony' and the notion of hegemonic knowledge – knowledge that comes to be widely accepted as true but which serves the interests of a dominant social group (Gramsci 2003). Feminist accounts emphasize the divisions between dominant and subjugated knowledges to explain how school knowledges that are presented as neutral are, in fact, masculine, male-orientated or patriarchal (Paechter 2001; Walkerdine 1989, 1990). This involves a move from a truth/ideology distinction to a concern with the relative visibility and value of knowledges. Feminist readings that have insisted that school knowledges are masculine and so orientated towards male learners to the exclusion of girls, have been challenged in many highly industrialized nations by claims that improvement in girls' educational performance reflects a 'feminization' of the curriculum, pedagogy and assessment. These claims are countered by an insistence on intersectional analysis that asks 'which girls and which boys?', a question that demonstrates that girls' successes and boys' failures are marked heavily by social class, race and geographic location and by the ways these intersect with constitutions of ideal, acceptable and impossible student and learner subjectivities (Collins *et al.* 2000; Epstein *et al.* 1998; Younger and Warrington 2007; Youdell 2006a). Likewise, anti-racist and multicultural readings have indicated the partiality of curriculum and its erasure of the knowledges and cultures of black and minority ethnic groups (Grande 2004; Nieto and Bode 2008) and work informed by Critical Race Theory has underscored the way that knowledge and curriculum are marked by Whiteness and its privilege (Allen 2004).

This shift from a foregrounding of a truth/ideology distinction to a focus on the relative status of socially constructed knowledges, evident in contemporary feminist and critical engagements, is inflected by a wider post-modern turn. This is marked by what Lyotard (1984) calls incredulity to Truth involving a rejection of the grand narratives that characterize the enlightenment tradition and are manifest in modern sciences. Yet despite the conceptual rejection or apparent practical collapse of master narratives, knowledges that have the status of abiding truth and worth do endure and continue to have force (Deleuze and Guattari 1983; Foucault 1990a, 2002, 2007). What remains, then, is a terrain of contestation over knowledge, its nature and status and the claim that knowledge is fundamentally implicated in relations of power.

As I discussed in the previous chapters, Michel Foucault's work is central to contemporary understandings of the relationship between knowledge and power. A Foucauldian account of discourse and disciplinary power identifies the constituted and productive nature of knowledge at the same time as it underscores the indivisibility of power and knowledge (Foucault 1990a, 1991a). Central to this understanding is the inquiry into how a particular set of ideas comes to attain the status of truth in a given context and moment; Foucault does not ask 'is this true?' or 'is this more or less true that that?', but 'how does this come to operate as a "regime of truth" here and now?' (Foucault 1990a, 2002, 2007). This orientation to thinking about knowledge and its relationship to disciplinary power makes the central point that these knowledges are productive, they create the world in their own terms as they set out the boundaries of what is knowable. It also brings with it the expectation that multiple orientations to knowledge, and multiple knowledges, will circulate simultaneously, that some of these knowledges will be subjugated while some will be so self-evident as to operate as regimes of truth, and that the status of knowledges will be open to contestation.

Deleuze and Guattari's (1983) idea of assemblages that operate across orders, from the political and social to the affective is useful for thinking about knowledges. Deleuze and Guattari (1983) use the notion of the binary machine to think about the way that hierarchical binary relations impose meaning in, or overcode, these assemblages, creating arborescent knowledge that is tree-like in the solidity of its hierarchical structure. They also use the idea of molar lines that are rigid and territorializing, imposing their structures and meanings. This offers a further way of conceptualizing the constitution and constitutive force of knowledges and the ways that these are part of wider assemblages of structures, practices and subjectivities. The pressing question that emerges from these ideas, then, is what can we know here (and what else might it be possible to know)?

In the rest of this chapter I consider this question in relation to two key empirical examples, both of which come out of the No Outsiders project. First, I examine a series of storybooks taken up in the work of the No Outsiders project and consider the knowledges that are embedded in these and so their potential meanings and effects. Second, I examine a plan for a series of lessons that make use of a selection of these storybooks. Developed and shared by Laura, one of the teachers participating in the project, I consider the spaces that the lessons might open up for contesting normative knowledges about gender, sexualities and the classroom as well as the ways the lessons might risk reinscribing these.

Gay fairy tales and other everyday meanings

Literature is an established site where dominant accounts of social life are contested and where radical politics are developed and deployed (Dollimore and Sinfield 1985; Eagleton 1983; Sinfield 2005; Wray 1997). This often takes the form of asserting stories of the oppressed or the disavowed – a practice that can be found across literatures and historical moments. Late mediaeval and reformation literatures offer contestations of women's responsibility for original sin, such as Aemilia Lanyar's *Salve Deus, Rex Judeorum* (Purkiss 1994; Rowse 1976) and assertions of women's intimate connection to Christ, such as Julian of Norwich's *Revelations* (Glasscoe 1976). Nineteenth- and early twentieth-century fiction offers refutations of women's confinement and subordination, such as Charlotte Perkins-Gilman's *Yellow Wallpaper* (1992) and Virginia Woolf's *A Room of One's Own* (2005). And the collection of black folk tales, such as the stories of Uncle Remus (Chandler Harris 2002), and slave narratives such as Harriet Jacobs' *Incidents in the Life of a Slave Girl* (1987) undercut the erasure of Black experience. Since the 1960s we have seen burgeoning politicized insider-representations of the lives of men and women of colour, the enslaved and the colonized such as the autobiography of Malcolm X (1965) and the work of Alice Walker (1982), Toni Morrison (1999), Arundhati Roy (1998), Monica Ali (2004) and Andrea Levy (2004); the lives of lesbians, such as the work Jeanette Winterson (1991), Pat Califia (1996) and Sarah Waters (1998), and of gay men such as the work of Armistead Maupin (1993) and Pierre Seel (1995). Science fiction has been a site where contemporary social forms have been critiqued through explorations of dystopias of gender and reproductive relations, such as the work of Marge Piercy (1991) and Margaret Atwood (1990), and modes of state power and control, such as the work of George Orwell (2000), Aldous Huxley (2007), Ray Bradbury (2008) and Philip K. Dick (1991). In addition, fairy tales, from E.T.A. Hoffmann (1992) and the Brothers Grimm (Owens 2006) to feminist re-writing of these and contemporary tales in the genre (Carter 1992), have been sites where the incredible can happen, where boundaries can be breached and where the uncanny of the repressed familiar can re-emerge (Britzman 1998; Freud 1990).

These traditions have been extended to the production and reading of children's literature and have become a site of critical pedagogic intervention. Bronwyn Davies' (2003) ground-breaking research worked with children and young people to develop deconstructive readings of children's literature with a view to enabling them to deploy this analytic technique and encounter troubled gender. While these interventions and readings were by no means unproblematic, they demonstrate that such approaches to reading and troubling meaning can be used with children as a deconstructive pedagogy. In Australia this deconstructive reading made its way onto official English curricula having such an impact that it has been the focus of criticism by the previous Liberal Prime Minister John Howard and the conservative press who have deployed what Jane Kenway calls a 'discourse of derision' (Kenway 1987) in their ongoing attacks on this work (Freesmith 2006; Maiden 2007). This may well be a mark of their success. A wider critical literacy movement has been established, especially in primary school literature, and has promoted approaches that push against the technical approaches to literacy as skills acquisition embedded in formal policy (Desai and Marsh 2005; Keddie 2008; Luke 1997; Moss 1999).

Children's literature has been taken up as a site for the representation of intelligible gay and lesbian subjects and lives and there is an extensive children's literature representing the lives of families headed by gay and lesbian parents and the lives of children whose gender enactments are non-normative. Since the controversial appearance of *Jenny Lives with Eric and Martin* (Bosche 1983), a number of these books have been published. Many of these are populated by human characters and take place in the real world, and there are sub-genres that introduce science fiction elements into the everyday or where animals take on leading anthropomorphized roles.

Key to recognize here is that gay and lesbian literature for children is not necessarily in itself critical, an act of deconstruction or a challenge to the heteronormative. And educators who make use of this literature in their classrooms will not necessarily interrogate it through a deconstructive or critical lens. Indeed, text of this sort may, in fact, reinforce the heteronormative, and educators may engage them as a 'corrective' through an identity politics frame to represent diversity without subjecting to critical scrutiny either these representations or the dominant representations they offer to augment. As I engage with a selection of the texts that were drawn on in the No Outsiders project schools, I explore the connections and disconnections between the discourses that these texts deploy and critical or deconstructive representations and readings. The focus here is not on the form of the texts, although this is a potentially useful line of analysis, but on the discourses cited and silenced in the texts; the potential subjectivating effects of these discourses; and the possibilities for these to be interrogated as part of a radical pedagogic practice.

And Tango Makes Three (Richardson *et al.* 2005) is the story of two male penguins in New York Zoo who form a relationship and together incubate an abandoned egg and rear the chick. While this is a tale about penguins, in the tradition of such stories these are anthropomorphized, with human characters, emotions and engagements and so it is a story about penguins and about people. The male penguins are not explicitly named, or 'hailed', in terms of sexual identity but the story does locate the male penguin couple in contrast to the rest of the penguins' male–female pairs and as unnatural in as much as the egg they hatch is donated to them by the Keeper after it is abandoned. In this series of contrasts the male-pair are implicitly rendered recognizable as homosexual, at least to adult readers, even as their incubation of the egg and rearing of the chick cites and inscribes the normative status of heterosexuality, monogamous adult coupling, homemaking and the rearing of young as the coveted prize of couplings entered into by enduring, self-evident, natural subjects. It is a tale of heterosexual, reproductive sex in the context of emotional attachment and normative family relations.

In this sense the book can be read as a relatively conservative inscription of enduring unitary subjects, romantic love, fidelity and restraint (Reiss 2009), and the normative heterosexual nuclear family, even as it asserts the legitimacy of a homosexual emulation of it. This representation of gay life as 'just like' heterosexual life constitutes this heterosexual life as the ideal and risks disavowing lives that do not look like this idealized hetero-monogamous nuclear family. Yet the exceptional nature of the penguins in the tale insists that they are not 'just like' the others, the homosexual is the necessary Other of the heterosexual norm and so its emulation of it will always fail (Butler 1991). At the same time, the book renders intimate same-sex relationships and same-sex parents and families visible, intelligible and legitimate. And used in primary classrooms it has the potential to make homosexual subjects – even if only those that are derivative of the heterosexual ideal – visible, intelligible and legitimate in a place where they have been invisible, unintelligible and illegitimate. Neither one nor the other of these readings of *And Tango Makes Three* is correct, or more compelling or worthwhile. One reading cannot be made to erase the other; the first reading cannot simply be extracted from the second. The book is part of a citational chain that inscribes heteronormativity and it is part of a resistant performative politics.

A similar series of simultaneously conservative and reinscriptive meanings are evident in *King and King* (De Haan and Nijland 2002), a fairy tale with a gay twist. *King and King* is the story of a prince who 'never cared much for princesses' and who could not choose a princess to marry despite his parents' best efforts and multiple introductions. The story's happy ending comes, however, when a princess offered in marriage is escorted by her brother and the prince immediately falls in love with him. The feeling is reciprocated and the two princes are married with the blessing of the Kings and Queens becoming, together, King and King. The tale cites the standard format of fairy tale Kings and Queens, princes and princesses, arranged marriages, hurdles to be overcome, eventual romantic love and happily ever after. In this sense it is wholly recognizable to children already familiar with the genre and its narrative conventions. And it is this recognizability that offers the story its intelligibility – like *And Tango Makes Three* it cites normative discourse and constitutes the gay-replica of heterosexual romantic love and gay subjects 'just like us'. As I suggested in relation to *And Tango Makes Three*, this citation inscribes hetero-normative romantic love and marriage, a citation that rests on an impossible replica *at the same time* as it insists on the legitimacy of particular sorts of homosexual subjects and relationships.

In *King and King and Family* (De Haan and Nijland 2004) this citation of the normative conventions of heterosexual marriage is continued when the two newly-wed Kings go on honeymoon to the Jungle. The tale cites and inscribes conventional notions of the White-Anglo-Western marriage and honeymoon package; the neo-colonialism of the 'dark continent' once claimed by the colonial explorer now turned holiday destination; and the reduction of gay masculinity to a pair of butch/camp opposites that once again are impossible emulations of the masculine/feminine of the hetero-sexual 'original'. These may well be parodies that offer in-jokes to the adult reader. But they are parodies that rest on and inscribe a neo-colonial, gender-normative, hetero-normative, Western, White, elite. And they confirm these as the site of desirability and inculcate the child-audience into these ways of knowing at the same time as they demarcate the limits of intelligibility.

The final illustration in the book demonstrates these constitutive effects. The picture shows the two White Kings and a White Queen, the mother of one, each with a large 'O'-shaped mouth along with a White princess, goofy and bespectacled. All four royals wear crowns askew. Before them is an open suitcase and above it a brown child with mid-length brown hair, half the size of the Kings, perhaps aged 6 or 7, wearing a skirt, t-shirt and sandals, all decorated with flowers, leaping frog-like into the air, arms extended, legs wide, knees bent, a big smile spread across her face. Stars, swirls, large leaves and flowers, a snake and an up-ended cat give chaos to the scene. 'All at once the suitcase burst open', says the text, ' "Oh my, it's a little girl from the jungle" said the Queen', it goes on. Above the girl's head, in large letters, but not indicated as speech, the text reads 'surprise'. In this neo-colonial narrative the elite White homosexual couple's family is 'completed' by the addition of the brown child, a child 'saved' by this adoption from the uncivilized and undeveloped Other place to the palaces of the civilized world. Rather than being a tale of 'rescue' from the uncivilized life of the jungle, however, here the child takes her relocation upon herself and gifts herself to the Kings with whom she has fallen in love. Those children of the world's poorest nations who are adopted in desperation, with uncertain consent and legality and with money exchanged, are silenced here. The brown body of this child springs full of life and joy from the suitcase. And the bodies, lives and deaths of asylum seekers crammed desperately into containers and holds are erased. There is an unavoidable and deeply discomforting incommensurability here: White, Western, elite gay rights and rights to international adoption simply cannot be reconciled with post-colonial feminist readings of the forced mobility of minoritized women of colour and their consumption in the West (Bulbeck 1998; Lewis and Mills 2003); an incommensurability that underscores the pressing significance of a politics of decolonization (Grande 2004).

Despite the significant problematics in these and other storybooks in the genre that were circulated and used by the project, members of the No Outsiders team have rightly suggested that in contexts of compulsory heterosexuality and ambivalence or even hostility towards homosexuality, 'simply opening the box containing the project books in the staff room becomes a risky political act' (DePalma and Atkinson 2009: 850). It is to enact an identity politics that demands recognition and a post-structural politics that unsettles normative meanings and insists on the intelligibility of lives and meanings in a context in which they have been disallowed. This unsettling is, of course, open to recuperation and one of the ways this might be effected is through the deployment of discourses of the neutrality of 'proper' school knowledge in opposition to the partiality of 'improper' knowledges. In such conditions, providing a set of books of the sort examined here, 'position[s] teachers as experts with resources rather than individuals with a personal agenda' (DePalma and Atkinson 2009: 850). I will explore such agendas, and the feelings that might underpin them, in Chapter 7.

In moments such as these it may be that truth claims are made tactically for subjugated knowledges – the viability of gay and lesbian lives. In making such tactical claims it might be recognized that such tactics contribute both to these subjugated knowledges and the prevailing knowledges they counter and inevitably cite being constituted as 'truth' through their circulation as true. This is not to try to move from one 'truth' to another, to argue that all claims are of equal value even if they are irreconcilable, to argue that some sort of reconciliation should be sought, or that one set of ideas should be prioritized over others. It is a reminder that within a Foucauldian frame ideas are indivisible from power, that all ideas are positioned, and that we can move tactically between these orientations keeping sight of their promises and costs and the implications of these movements.

In primary school classrooms the acceptability of even sanitized and heterosexualized versions of homosexuality is fragile and transient. In these contexts the inclusion of such texts can be seen as a powerful practice of troubling simply in speaking the legitimacy of same-sex relationships and parenting. The take up of a sexuality-focused diversity discourse that foregrounds recognition, equal opportunities and equal treatment – even when these calls for recognition and equality inevitably inscribe the sorts of natural, abiding, self-knowing LGBT subjects that post-structural accounts have challenged and queer politics have troubled – may be an important tactical option. This is perhaps especially the case when the alternative is the erasure of these subjects. Indeed, given the need to be recognizable in order to act (Butler 1997a, 1999), these unitary subjects might not be escapable. Nevertheless, these books are simultaneously implicated in the further inscription of heteronormativity, idealized family forms, Whiteness and elite Western forms of culture. These simultaneous inscriptions demand that we ask whether and more importantly *how* texts of this sort can have a place in a critical or deconstructive pedagogic politics. We cannot simply 'weigh up' the advantages of representing and inscribing gay and lesbian lives and subjects against the disadvantages of representing and inscribing Whiteness, elite Western culture, heteronormativity and an idealized family while erasing other lives and subjects who are minoritized along lines of race, geographical location, cultural practice or relationship and/or family forms. We have to go further and interrogate the constitutive work that these texts do: the subjects that these texts render intelligible and the subjects that they render unintelligible.

The analyses of the texts I have offered here underscores the importance of educators' awareness of what their practices and their curriculum resources might do, including those that, on the surface, are counter-hegemonic and/or inclusive. Following Judith Butler this suggests that educators must think tactically about the multiple effects of texts and classroom engagements with them and devise pedagogic approaches that draw out and make visible subjugated meanings and unsettle and open up to troubling those meanings that inscribe the normative. Borrowing from Deleuze and Guattari, the multiple and simultaneous effects of the books suggests that we might engage the texts and their effects as assemblages that are overcoded by binary machines and run through with molar lines which fix normative meanings and effects. At the same time they offer the promise of lines of flight which have the potential to shift meaning, effects and so the assemblages themselves. Educators working with resources of this sort – the texts and critical analyses of them – might look for ways to act as assemblage convertors (Hickey-Moody 2009), recognizing the binary machines and molar lines in play and finding spaces between these through which they might follow other lines, moves which have the potential to shift, or convert, the assemblage itself.

An example of a pedagogic intervention that might be understood in this way is a plan for a series of lessons and their enactment that was developed, deployed and shared by Laura, one of the No Outsiders teachers. During this first year of the No Outsiders project Laura was a newly qualified teacher leading a class of 7- and 8-year-old students in an inner London primary school, which I will call Uplands. The school had recently been the subject of formal intervention by the government department responsible for schools after a series of negative school inspection reports. There was concern and disquiet amongst the school staff, who Laura described as unionized and relatively left-wing, over this process but they were giving support to the new headteacher who had been appointed and was developing previously absent school policy. Laura reported that the school population was predominantly made up of students from minoritized racialized and ethnicized backgrounds and, while there was no single majority population in the school, there was a significant Turkish population. She also felt that the White British students in the school were from more middle class backgrounds than their minoritized classmates. The profile of her own class was, she felt, representative of this wider school population.

In the English education context, the National Curriculum for Subject English and the 'National Literacy Strategy' that accompanies it operate to impose rigid knowledge (curriculum content); mandate organizational structures (the grouping and teaching of children by 'ability'); mandate pedagogic approaches (phonics); tightly bind and monitor teaching (the formal documentation and auditing of teaching activity); and strictly demarcate what counts as literacy (specified competencies, hierarchically arranged into 'levels' on a 'normal' developmental trajectory). In the gaps in this assemblage of systems, processes and meanings, this teacher identified spaces in which work with gay and lesbian children's literature could be undertaken.

Table 4.1 offers an extract of the documentation, which would subsequently be open to audit, of the sequence of lessons developed by Laura to introduce these texts into the formal curriculum and pedagogy of her classroom. She identifies the mandated area of the 'National Literacy Strategy' – 'Narrative Themes' – that the sequence of lessons relates to; the various mandated targets that it contributes to; and a day-by-day, lesson-by-lesson series of teaching and learning activities through which these targets will be achieved. The plan for the lesson offered in Table 4.1 shows the teacher deploying games, props, role-play and popular cultural forms to explore the gay subjectivities introduced through the reading and engagement with the children's book *King and King*. The ideas about legitimate relationships and subjectivities introduced by *King and King* are well beyond those anticipated by the National Curriculum for Subject English in England and the associated 'National Literacy Strategy'. As such these ideas can be seen to trouble both the boundaries of formal curriculum knowledge and the subjectivities ordinarily recognizable in the classroom. Yet at the same time Table 4.1 shows Laura's take up and mobilization of 'ability' groupings –

Table 4.1 Scheme of work on alternative traditional tales, year 3 narrative themes National Literacy Strategy Unit

Year: 3 Classes: Term: Spring 1 Week: 5 [5/2/07]

Outcomes: To write a plan for an alternative version of Cinderella which can be used to write a story.

Text Level Focus	Sentence and Word Level Focus	Speaking and Listening Opportunities
/T7: to describe and sequence key incidents in a variety of ways, e.g. by listing, charting, mapping, making simple storyboards /T9: to write a story plan for own myth, fable or traditional tale, using story theme from reading but substituting different characters or changing the setting	/S2: the function of adjectives within sentences. /W1: the spelling of words containing each of the long vowel phonemes from KS1. /W6: to spell by analogy with other known key words e.g.: light/fright.	/Talk partners (TPs) /Mixed ability group work /Drama /Hotseating

	Whole Class Shared Session	Guided Session	Independent / Group Activities	Plenary	ICT
Mon.	[. . .]				
Tues.	[. . .]				
Wed.	Play 'look, cover, write, check' game with long vowel phoneme words 1) Give children scroll tied with ribbon on which is written a letter from Prince Bertie asking yr 3 for advice – his mother says everyone his age has been married at least twice, he's had to meet lots of princesses but doesn't want to marry them, etc. 2) In TP pairs children thought shower words (adjectives and verbs) to describe Bertie and what he likes doing – give 2 minutes to come up with words. 3) Model writing lonely hearts ad from Bertie. Remind children about varying sentence structure – beginning sentences with adverbs etc.	Class teacher (CT) to work with yellows. Use thesauruses with them to generate good vocabulary.	CT to write word on board then cover it up, children spell it on whiteboards. 1) Discuss why Prince Bertie may not want to marry the princesses. What could he do? 2) CT scribe suggestions around picture of Bertie on A3 sheet. Red group have thesauruses so they can help us to improve vocabulary we are using. 3) Children write ad from Bertie to other Princes using adjectives and adverbs. Give blue group sentence starters on table. *TA to work with green group	Check whether it is correct 1) Read *King and King*. 2) Children tell TPs what Prince Bertie is like. 3) Share superstar sentences and assess against targets.	Interactive wipe board
		CT Yellow Group	Red Group Yellow Group TA Green Group Blue Group		
Thurs.	[. . .]				
Fri.	[. . .]				

popularly disguised by colour-coding – which are a standard feature of literacy policy and practice in primary schools in England (Moss 2007, 2009). And while the sequence of lessons deploys the 'National Literacy Strategy' to make a space for these ideas in the classroom, they remain immersed in the normative concerns of the strategy and 'good' literacy teaching through their focus on word types, sentence structures, the-saurus, 'right' and 'wrong' answers, spelling checks and 'superstar' sentences.

The sequence of lessons, then, appears to be wholly inside the assemblage of the English primary classroom with its mandated processes, approved knowledges and normative practices *and* it introduces into this classroom discourses which have not previously belonged there, validating subjectivities that have been disallowed and perhaps even making these intelligible to the 7- and 8-year-old children in this class. The sequence of lessons is an instance of a previously disallowed knowledge being tactically relocated and resignified so that it encroaches on the terrain of the approved knowledge of the classroom, masquerading as and perhaps even becoming approved knowledge, a becoming that necessarily transforms what counts as knowable in the classroom, even if it is only in this classroom at this moment. This might even be a molecular line that takes flight and becomes a momentary deterritorialization of the classroom, one that promises further deterritorializations in other moments and spaces.

The teacher who pursues this line of flight confronts the contradiction of subjec-tivation as the 'good teacher' and subjectivation as the 'critical or queer pedagogue'. Laura is faced with navigating the tensions between trying to open up spaces to assert non-normative sexuality/gender (and other) subjectivities; asserting these in ways that trouble, rather than simply name an Other to normative subjectivities; fulfilling the demands of the frameworks, targets, accountability and management structures in which she works; and abiding by the normative discourses and practices of the con-temporary primary school, such as notions of natural 'ability' and colour-coded ability groupings. This teacher, it seems may have converted the assemblage, at least for a flicker, but she also got stuck in the grooves of its molar lines. This suggests that in order to devise political pedagogies a radical education politics needs to move beyond 'either/or' assessments of good/bad, resignifying/recuperating and any acceptance that we are perpetually 'stuck' with the simultaneity of these.

The analysis offered in this chapter also underscores the fundamental importance of thinking through what it means to pursue anti-identity politics and what these might look like. This is not to claim that we have 'reached' a moment when we are beyond subjectivation, identification or subjectivity, whether socially, discursively, materially, psychically or affectively. It is to suggest that the limits and the further injuries that an identity politics brings with it have been thoroughly demonstrated. The inscription of the brown child springing full of joy from the suitcase, not human, perhaps not even animal, just luggage, underscores the fundamental importance of not just moving beyond single identity politics based on single classificatory systems (e.g. race) or single categories (e.g. African, Asian, Latina) to an intersectional approach that complexifies this politics by understanding the relationality of these categories and their effects. It insists that we move beyond a politics that places identification and identity at its centre. This suggests that readings of the resources, practices and knowledges that might be deployed in all manner of 'inclusive' curriculum that are underpinned by discourses of diversity and rights and which take up an identity politics predicated on particular subjectivities are likely to throw up the sorts of problematics I have identified here. That is, they will be part of subjectivating chains that constitute the Same and the Other, the intelligible and the unintelligible, viable lives and those that are not survivable. They will not trouble normative knowledge or normative subjects, they may augment these, they may render other knowledges or subjects a little 'less' subjugated in the assemblages in which they are made and located. A strategy of deterritorialization looks to find or open up spaces for lines of flight and becomings that are not additional, but less valid, forms that are then incorporated into the molar lines of the dominant assemblage. Rather, it looks to scatter the assemblage. I will return to this in subsequent chapters.

5 Schooling's unruly subjects

The interplay of identification and recognition, and the ways that recognizability is both constrained within the education assemblage and struggled over inside schools is the central concern of this chapter. In the previous chapter I argued that the education assemblage imposes limits on what is knowable and known inside schools and demonstrated how these limits might be resisted and shifted as well as inadvertently reinscribed by educators taking up a politics of knowledge in a range of ways. In this chapter I engage with the subjects of schooling – the ways in which students and teachers are constituted as recognizable and legitimate subjects inside the education assemblage. As I have argued in the preceding chapters, the identifications and recognitions that are intrinsic to processes of subjectivation are made available both by the educational discourses that frame schooling and by those wider discourses that permeate the school, circulate inside it and are deployed and foreclosed through the practices of institutions, teachers and students. This understanding allows us to explore the multiplicity, contingency and malleability of students' and teachers' identifications and recognitions and show how struggles over subjectivities are a part of the politics of education. In engaging with the issue of student and teacher 'identity' in this way and by asserting the politics intrinsic to these I am engaging with those debates about identity politics that I explored in Chapter 2 and the theorizations of subjectivation and performative politics that I posited as a part of an anti-identity politics.

In this chapter I take as my particular focus a school formally designated as catering for students identified as having 'Social, Emotional and Behavioural Difficulties', or 'SEBD' as it is regularly abbreviated in the UK education system. While this terminology is particular to the UK system, it resonates with the 'Emotional and Behavioural Difficulties' or 'EBD' of the US system, the 'Emotional Difficulty and Behavioural Disorder' or 'EDBD' of the Australian system and similar formal designations that can be found in education systems elsewhere. These are particular sorts of designation of 'difficulty' and 'disorder' that are distinct from other forms of learning difficulty or disability – dyslexia, for instance – and which work to constitute students in particular ways (Corbett 1996; Harwood 2006). Considering the constitution, identification and recognition of students who have been designated in such ways and, often, removed from mainstream schooling into a 'special' provision brings into view the costs to those unruly or even abject subjects who are rendered unrecognizable by these designations and the educational discourses that they circulate in. It also foregrounds these students' struggles over identification and recognition, as well as the struggles of their teachers.

The primary data that I draw on here were generated through my most recent ethnographic research in a 'special' school for boys aged 5 to 16 and who are designated as having 'Social, Emotional and Behavioural Difficulties' ('SEBD'). I spent around two days each week during the 2008 Summer term in the school, which I call Bay Tree, which is located on the edge of a village in an area of rural England where industrial agriculture is key to the regional economy. Many of the boys at Bay Tree have education histories of rejection in and by mainstream schooling and personal histories of disrupted family life and social care. Almost all of the boys and staff in the school are White, reflecting the regional population. All of the boys who attend Bay Tree have been removed from mainstream schooling and most will never return to it. In this chapter I offer one episode of data generated in Bay Tree, but I return to the school and my study there throughout the book.

Ethnography is a well-established approach to education research drawing on a range of methods – from observation and interview to the collection of documentary data and surveys – to develop detailed accounts of life inside the context of study. Ethnography, and those data generated through it and the sorts of analyses it makes possible are extremely useful for understanding the way that identity, power and politics might work at the level of everyday life inside school. Ethnography, however, is not straightforward. The nature and status of ethnographic representations, what is included and what is left out, and the inclusions and silences as the author speaks have all been the subject of feminist methodological consideration (Stanley 1989; Stanley and Wise 1993). And ethnography underpinned by the sorts of post-structural theory I have explored earlier has moved away from a concern with authenticity and reciprocity to foreground the circulation of discourses and their constitutive force, including the ways they constitute particular sorts of subjects, in research encounters, representations and analyses (Harwood 2006; Lather 1991; Maclure 2004; St. Pierre and Pillow 2000; Youdell 2006a). The status of ethnographic writing as a genre has also been underscored (Atkinson 1990). Ethnography does not produce, then, transparent representations of an objective, observed reality. Rather, its representations are shot through with the researcher's judgements about what was going on, who was engaging with who, what was and was not important, and 'who' people are. Nevertheless, ethnography continues to offer detailed present-tense representations of 'real life' that allow us to interrogate discursive practices, the subjectivating force of these, and the minutiae of their interruption.

One of the ways that education researchers have responded to the recognition of the way we are embroiled in ethnography and its products has been a turn to reflexivity (Delamont and Atkinson 1995; Silverman 1997). Reflection on relations and practices in the field that focuses on the individual researcher has been critiqued as failing to understand the way the researcher is situated, relational and constituted. Instead, a reflexivity that locates this individual in historical contexts and social relations has been emphasized (Moore 2004; Pillow 2003). Wanda Pillow (2003) offers a particularly helpful intervention, suggesting that reflexivity usefully sets out how/ where a researcher is located in the discursive field of the research and demonstrates the constitutive effects of this and so helps us to see into processes of knowledge production. Yet she also shows that when reflexivity is concerned with the recognition of self and Other, it inadvertently imagines a transcendence of this self and so a 'better' reading of data. In order to avoid this, Pillow advocates vigilance over practices and their effects – what she calls an 'uncomfortable reflexivity' that is concerned with unfamiliar and uncomfortable accounts and accounts that escape representation (2003: 188). This account of ethnography, ethnographic representation and uncomfortable reflexivity does not undermine ethnographic research or the insights that it makes available. Rather, my aim is to recognize that we are always 'in' our data and interpretation discursively, psychically and affectively and that we cannot, nor should we want to, weed ourselves out of the field, representation or analysis.

Discomfort, the limits of what is speakable and what is silenced and the constraints of representation were recurrent in my fieldwork and in my later engagement with the data I generated in Bay Tree School. One of the reasons for this is that the practices of both students and teachers in Bay Tree often did not correspond to those that might be found in a mainstream school – Bay Tree at once was and was not recognizable as 'school'. Another reason for this is the nature of my research concerns – exploring processes of subjectivation and its resistance and looking for moments of radical politics or moments which seem to offer radical political potential means focusing on that which does not easily conform to the terms of the education assemblage and so is in some sense discomforting. Another space of uncomfortable reflexivity and locus of discomfort has been the process of sharing my representations and analyses with the teachers whose classrooms and practices they refer to. All of the chapters in this book have been shared with those concerned, a sharing that had the potential to discomfort both the teachers' perception of their practice and my perception of my research practice and representation and analysis. Teachers were invited to consider whether they recognized themselves, their classrooms, students and practices; whether my representations felt plausible and fair; and whether my analyses were useful. I engaged in extended discussions with two of the teachers and revisited my representations and analyses in the light of these discussions. The discomfort, as well as the shared excitement, that this process provoked was no doubt enriching to both the analysis and the politics pursued in the book.

Troubling 'social, emotional and behavioural difficulties'

The organization, concerns and practices of 'special schools' may on the surface seem tangential to wider educational issues. Yet while only a small proportion of students in England attend special schools and other forms of alternative provision, over 17 per cent of all students – in the region of 1.4 million students – are identified as having some sort of 'Special Educational Need' (DCSF 2008). In this sense, the notion of 'special needs' permeates the whole of the educational assemblage in England, its institutions, discourses and practices. The 'special educational needs' of a proportion of these students – around 3 per cent of all students and a figure of over 220,000 – are deemed to be such that a formal 'statement' of 'special educational needs' is required (DCSF 2008). Of this group of students, just over half are officially recorded as attending mainstream schools. However, many of these students are formally acknowledged by the government education department as in fact being placed in 'resourced provision/units/special classes' or 'SEN units' located in mainstream schools (DCSF 2008: 2). Boys in England are three times more likely than girls to be identified as having special educational needs, and students eligible for free school meals – a common proxy for poverty – are twice as likely to be identified in this way than their peers. The education department for England and Wales, at the time the Department for Children, Schools and Families, offers research into 'deprivation' (DCSF 2009a) which shows that students eligible for free school meals are disproportionately represented amongst students designated as having 'behavioural, emotional and social difficulty' – the cohort who Bay Tree School caters for – as well as 'moderate learning difficulty' and 'severe learning difficulty', with around a third of students designated as having one of these forms of SEN also eligible for FSM. Indeed, the Department itself notes that these are forms of special educational need that are *socially* defined rather than based on an impairment of some sort (DCSF 2009a: 10).

Those students who are not in mainstream school, or in a provision attached to a mainstream school, are distributed across a range of alternative provisions. These are predominantly state maintained and independent 'special schools' but also include 'Pupil Referral Units' (PRUs), hospital schools and home provision. In 2007 a total of 89,410 students attended special schools, of whom 62,770 were boys and 26,640 were girls (DCFS 2008). There is, then, a sizable population of students in England who are designated as having special educational needs and who are being educated outside mainstream education in 'special schools'. These students are massively disproportionately deprived, from minoritized ethnic backgrounds, boys and in foster or residential care under the formal guardianship of the state. As Table 5.1 shows, the educational outcomes attained by this group of students – as measured by the key benchmark that I discussed in Chapter 1 – are extremely poor.

While the national average attainment of the national benchmark is 60.9 for boys and 69.9 for girls, in state special schools attainment at this level is less than 1 per cent

Table 5.1 Attainment in GCSE exams taken at age 16 amongst students in special schools in England 2007/8

	5+ GCSE entries		National benchmark: 5+A–C GCSE passes		Any entries		Any passes	
	boys	*girls*	*boys*	*girls*	*boys*	*girls*	*boys*	*girls*
State maintained special schools	8.1	4.7	**0.5**	**0.6**	70.0	70.0	71.7	66.7
Independent special schools	59.3	47.9	**7.6**	**6.2**	81.0	72.7	80.8	73.7
All Schools	*92.4*	*95.3*	**60.9**	**69.9**	*98.6*	*99.5*	*82.7*	*88.6*

Adapted from: Statistical First Release GCSE and Equivalent Examination Results in England 2007/8 (Revised) DCFS (DCSF 2009d).

and in independent special schools attainment at the benchmark does not come close to double figures.

A commonsense encounter with these figures might lead to the suggestion that they simply reflect the 'special educational needs' of the students and the various forms of social and economic deprivation that they face. Yet as my discussion of 'ability' and 'deprivation' in Chapter 1 showed, this is by no means straightforward. Furthermore, schools have a role in constituting both these students and their experiences in and of education. A number of scholars working in the field of inclusive education have noted that the designations and diagnoses attached to these students, such as 'Attention Deficit Hyperactivity Disorder', 'Conduct Disorder', broader terms such as 'Social Emotional and Behavioural Difficulties' and its international equivalents or the common umbrella 'Special Educational Needs' itself, are not simply descriptive but act to constitute and limit who these students are and contribute to the ongoing making of these students in these terms (Corbett 1996; Graham 2007; Harwood 2006; Youdell 2006a). Students who finish their compulsory education in special school, facing outcomes of this sort, have an educational trajectory that has almost certainly begun in mainstream education. *How* these students come to be in special school is, then, a process in which *all* educational institutions and educators are implicated. And 'who' the students of special schools come to be tells us much about 'who' the students of mainstream education *may not be*.

Recognizing the subjects of Bay Tree School

In the rest of this chapter I explore the struggles over 'who' the students and teachers of Bay Tree School can be by interrogating ethnographic data that represent a small moment in the daily lives of these students and teachers. The episode I offer here draws on fieldnotes that I wrote at the end of this day of observation in this school. It is not intended as a neutral observation of events, but is a re-making of these few minutes. In the episode, one of the boys is mixed race, all other students as well as the teachers are White.

This is one of two classes of boys in this year group. The official principle of allocation to each of the classes is unclear, however, teachers confirm that the make-up of the two classes is quite distinct. The class in 'Hungover' includes boys/young men with developed masculine bodies; youth sub-cultural affiliations; a degree of sporting prowess and youth cultural 'cool'; who regularly engage in hetero-masculine banter and smart (and funny) back-chat; and who are likely to get GCSE exams, the English end-of-compulsory-schooling qualification (although not at the benchmark grades). The other class includes boys whose bodies are small-framed and frail, or soft and uncoordinated, or oversized and cumbersome; their sub-cultural affiliations, if they have them, are outmoded, or relentlessly singular, or 'un-cool' – metal music, horror films, the occult, adult-organized groups; and their banter too often seems to miss the joke or wander off track. They are talkative, but for some of these boys enunciation runs together making it difficult to follow, or is stammering, or a high-pitch sing-song. One of these boys, Anth, with a degree of sub-cultural cool and a skill for smart back-chat, seems to mark the boundary between the two groups. Already, then, these

Hungover

It's the morning tutor group session at Bay Tree School. I'm following Miss Groves around. She recently joined the school as IT teacher and still smells of the real world. We go into the tutor room of seven 14-year-old boys to give the teacher a pile of completed tests along with the answer book. The tutor, one of the English teachers, exudes a belief that things can and will be good.

The two teachers exchange a pair of 'Hi Miss' greetings, the absurdity of the address underscored by its cheerful gloss.

A half-meant groan emanates from the boys at Miss Groves' entry and she offsets it with an assurance that: It's ok, this 'isn't another test. It's the answers, so you can see how you did'. Another half-groan ripples around.

The boys sit around, not so much in conversation as throwing out one-liners that bounce around the room. The focus is on Justin who's got his head down on his arms: 'I was drunk last night, I'm gonna get drunk again tonight' he offers resignedly. Rhys responds 'And if you don't get drunk you'll get high'. 'Drunk' and 'high' pop laughing around the room. Justin leans across to the desk next to him and pushes Jed who falls off his seat sideways onto the floor. Jed chuckles as he hits the ground, stretches out on his back as if reclining on a comfortable sofa and says 'I'll stay down here'. Rhys jumps out of his chair and mimes putting the boot in, provoking Jed to quickly get back into his seat. More high-energy laughing.

The bundle of booklets is smilingly presented to Miss Appleton as 'a free lesson', who welcomes the generosity of the offering and, warm-up over, the two sort the papers together.

Mr Newton the popular deputy headteacher comes in and joins the teacher huddle but shifts it by reminding Miss Groves to put a copy of the answer book on file.

As the boy's game registers Mr Newton offers a soft but firm 'boys' to the class, and again, 'erm, boys'. Game over.

I hang just inside the classroom playing the part of audience.

(from DY fieldnotes Summer 2008)

are particular *sorts* of students and particular *sorts* of teachers. But what *sorts* are these, and how does this come to be the case?

Research in the sociology of education has often engaged with such questions through the lens of 'identity'. Such an approach would be likely to analyse these data by considering the gender, race, social class and learner 'identities' of the boys and, perhaps the gender, race, social class and professional 'identities' of the teachers. It might look to know 'which' of the boys' multiple positionings is significant here – are their practices in the scene the product of their gender, their social class position, their failure as learners? These lines of enquiry recognize multiple markers of identity and points of identification, however, they do not open up a space to understand the inter-play between these categories, demonstrating, as I argued in Chapter 2, the limits of categorical identity as an analytic tool and as the basis for political claims and actions. Education research has attempted to respond to these limits and address the various identities a person might be associated with and the layers of associated disadvantage they might face. These concerns were at the centre of what are often referred to as 'additive' notions of multiple subordination or disadvantage that were regular features of work concerned with understanding inequalities in the 1980s and 1990s. These understandings of double, triple, multiple subordination and/or disadvantage were extremely important in that they insisted on the importance of engaging with an array of positions in which individuals and groups might be located. A notion of 'nested inequalities' and the identity categories these invoke or reflect has also been offered (Weis 2007), conjuring images of Russian dolls stacked inside one another and ques-tions of which identity or inequality sits within which. Such approaches might suggest that the boys in 'Hungover' are multiply disadvantaged as low socio-economic posi-tion and low educational performance come together.

As I discussed in Chapter 3, the notion of intersectionality has made a significant contribution to focusing attention on the complexity of the intersections and interre-lations between multiple axes of inequalities and sites of identification. Understanding the 'Hungover' classroom scene through an intersectional lens might suggest that the boys' social class and gender identities intersect to create a particular working class form of masculinity, a form that they play out in the scene. But this is a working class masculinity that is unwelcome in mainstream schools and at odds with dominant notions of proper student behaviour, a 'lack of fit' that may well underpin the boys' trajectory into an 'SEBD' school. In turn the teachers' delayed intervention might be read as a reflection of an assumption that these 'SEBD'-diagnosed boys are inca-pable of behaving in more student-appropriate ways, an assumption that reflects the mismatch between the boys' and teachers' social class positions and which cements the boys' positioning as 'SEBD'. This intersectional analysis, then, pays attention to more than one axis of subordination and inequality and more than one category of identity and attempts to tease out the relationships between these and the constraints that they infer.

Coupling the idea of intersectionality with post-structural notions of subjectivation and the performative constitution of the subject and the question of intelligibility that these bring with them advances this analysis further. It does this by offering concep-tual tools for understanding the nature of the subject, the limits of 'who' this subject might be and the constraints and disavowals that are intrinsic to particular subject positions. In addition, post-structurally inflected engagements with psychoanalytic concepts such as identification, recognition and abjection help us to tease out why we might be attached to forms of subjectivity that appear to injure us. And the ideas of discursive agency and performative politics show the potential for subject positions to be resisted or mean something else.

Thinking of the students and teachers in 'Hungover' as subjectivated suggests that we understand them as made as subjects through the discursive matrices that make the practices in this classroom meaningful and as situated in the relations of power that are enacted through these discursive matrices. The boys are subjectivated as particular sorts of boys and particular sorts of students and the teachers are subjectivated as particular sorts of teachers and particular sorts of women and men. The boys' practices cite coalesced discourses of classed masculinity, risky and illegal youth sub-culture, as well as youth 'at risk', failed learning and unacceptable student behaviour. The citation of these discourses calls up the boys as 'at risk', 'bad' and 'failed' school boys *at the same time* as it calls them up as 'cool' and 'successful' anti-authoritarian/establishment working class boys and proto-men. And in this simultaneous subjectivation (bad) 'school subjects' and (good) 'street subjects' are tethered together in their incommensurability. These, then, are the terms in which these boys are made subjects here.

The teachers' practices can also be seen as calling up these 'bad' students and 'good' street subjects. By ignoring practices that are wholly inappropriate within the normative terms of schooling the teachers can be seen as subjectivating the boys as impossible students or, as the designation of 'Social Emotional and Behavioural Difficulties' comes to be tied to and describe and constitute subjects, as 'SEBD'. But the teachers do (almost) act their place in the discourse of teacher behaviour: they 'hail' each other teacher in their 'Hi Miss', although the irony of the delivery unsettles this subjectivation of the women as 'teacher' and so the boys as 'student'. The teachers are engaged with the boys' tests; testing and teaching the boys subjectivates them 'student'. But, as with the 'Hi Miss', the teachers' suggestion of a 'free lesson' might undercut the women's 'teacher' and so the boys' 'student'. The third teacher's 'proper' intervention into the boys' practices subjectivates him within the terms of the good teacher, and the intervention subjectivates the boys as 'student', albeit as 'bad' students in need of correction. The hail of subjectivation, then, is ongoing and potentially multiple and even contradictory – a subject can be hailed in multiple ways at once, but if these are incompatible there are likely to be consequences.

Designations such as 'boy' and 'SEBD' that are at play in the 'Hungover' scene can be understood as performative – they *create* the gendered and diagnosed subject that they name, and they do this while appearing to be just *descriptive*. By appearing to be descriptive they create the *illusion* of the *prior* existence of gender and of educational disorders. So while it appears that the subject *expresses* a gender or a disorder, this is actually a performative *effect* of the respective categorizations and their use (Butler 1990, 1993, 1997a, 2004a). Suturing this idea to Bourdieu's notion of *habitus* Butler also offers an account of the performative force of forms of embodiment and bodily practice, suggesting that 'the bodily *habitus* constitutes a tacit form of performativity, a citational chain lived and believed at the level of the body' (Butler 1997a: 155). One boy's torso and outstretched arm as it pushes the body of another boy, a body slid-ing to the floor and stretching out can be understood as practices of a performative *habitus*, tacit bodily citations that constitute the playful physicality of masculinity and subjectivate subjects in these terms.

These are bodies that make sense in this moment in this setting. As they talk about illegal alcohol and drug use, the boys in 'Hungover' are intelligible as 'naughty boys', 'bad students', even impossible students – being hungover in class renders a sub-ject who is unintelligible as 'school student'. As they act out pushing over, resting on the classroom floor they are intelligible as 'bad students', as bringing with them 'Social, Emotional and Behavioural Difficulties', as 'being' 'SEBD'. As they succumb to Mr Newton's intervention they are intelligible as 'just-good-enough students'. These constitutions are all intelligible through the normative discourses of schools and classrooms. But these are not the only discourses that circulate in the classroom. On the walkways of the shopping centre, on the recreation ground, in the boys' bed-rooms, these practices would be intelligible through another set of discourses – anti-authoritarian classed masculinity, risky and illegal youth sub-culture – that have cur-rency in those spaces and that constitute these boys as smart, cool, masculine. These discourses reverberate in the classroom, they are called up in the boys' practices and it is these constitutions that circulate between the boys themselves. In 'Hungover' the subjectivations of one set of discourses and one set of spaces (risk taking, law break-ing, disputed spaces, illicit spaces) bleed into the subjectivations of another set of discourses and spaces (at-risk, 'SEBD', bad-student, school space).

We might also use the notion of abjection to understand the boys in 'Hungover' as the education assemblage's abject others. Literally expelled from mainstream education to an out-of-the-way site, these boys are designated as having 'Social, Emotional and Behavioural Difficulties' – the disturbing potential contaminants of proper schooling and proper school subjects which must be kept away from good students and main-stream schools. These abject 'SEBD' boys cannot be erased by the education assem-blage, rather it must continue to contain them, continue to correct them and, indeed, continue to educate them. The abject student, then, hovers at the edge of education.

These processes of subjectivation and abjection, and the spaces and subject posi-tions into which these subjects are constituted, raise the question of who these subjects are to themselves. Located on the edge of education and constituted at the borders of student-hood, the boys in 'Hungover' face a recurring threat of abjection. Their practices of self, their identifications and self-recognition are likely to shift between desire for recognition as a student and self-recognition as a failed or impossible stu-dent and desire for recognition and self-recognition as a cool, anti-school boy. As failed student and anti-school boy are tied together as commensurable, recognition as both of these – 'failed student anti-school boy' – may well be available to these boys. However, the designation 'SEBD' undercuts anti-school cool, threatening the boys with recognition as 'aberrant-mad' rather than 'cool-bad'. As the boys laugh-ingly throw 'drunk' and 'high' around the classroom they engage in a tacit practice of mutual recognition in terms that might stick: their practices suggest that they are the cool naughty boys who are outside mainstream school, who drink and take drugs not as an exceptional event but as an ordinary nightly activity, who don't care about hiding it from teachers and who don't even need to brag about it. These constitutions may well be experienced by the boys as much more life-affirming than the failed-student-stupid-child that their unwanted test results threatens.

Earlier I suggested that Miss Groves and Miss Appleton's ignoring of the boys' practices might cite a discourse of impossible students and so subjectivate the boys in these terms. But the teachers' apparent disregard might also be understood as a peda-gogic practice. That is, in allowing the boys' practices of identification and recognition to play out, the teachers may offer the boys recognition in these terms, they might give them the 'cool' that they desire and so buffer them against the failed student that their location in this school and their test results constitutes. Mr Newton's interven-tion could be seen as refusing this recognition. Or it might be seen as another move in this pedagogic game; 'cool' has been recognized, so 'good-enough student' can be asserted. The playfulness of the teachers' greetings and positioning of the test papers might be read similarly: rather than constituting them as not-teachers, these practices might constitute them as skilled pedagogues deploying practices that render them just recognizable as teachers, but not as the authoritarians or pathology-spotters that no doubt saw the boys on their way to Bay Tree School. And the boys and the teachers might be fully or partially aware of these moments of identification and recognition, or not aware of them at all. And the teachers may be fully or partially aware of the pedagogic possibilities of their practices, or not aware of them at all.

A politics of the performative or an anti-identity politics?

These analyses of the possible identifications and recognitions of students and teach-ers and the extent to which these might be self-aware, if at all, lead to questions of the place of agency or intentional action in practices of self and whether these might be thought of as practices of performative politics or of a politics that is anti-identity.

The students and teachers in 'Hungover' can be thought of as being engaged in practices of self that have a degree of intentionality. The boys bring discourses of cool, anti-authoritarian masculinity, including talk of habitual alcohol and drug use, into the classroom – a space where such discourses do not belong – and in doing so they constitute themselves against the school failure that is their normative position-ing. And the delayed teacherly intervention gives the discourse and its constitutive force some purchase at the same time as it leaves open the possibility of the boys' rec-ognition as 'student', a student-hood that stretches the normative bounds of this sub-jectivity. The fact that the boys' practices are perhaps all too readily recuperated into prevailing school discourses of risk, failure and 'Social, Emotional and Behavioural Difficulties' does not wholly negate their effects. These might be boys at risk, school failures, 'SEBD' boys, but they are also cool, anti-authoritarian, masculine.

It seems uncertain whether the tacitly understood playful constitutions of a group of boys in a classroom or the interpersonal and pedagogic practices of their teachers can be understood as radical acts of public misappropriation that are practices of per-formative politics. We might argue that the classroom is a public space, that these are collective practices, that they shift or stretch the bounds of normative constitutions of the student and that they exemplify, after de Certeau (1988), the political tactics of everyday life. In this sense, whether the effects of these practices are intentional or not, they may be understood as performative politics. Yet these practices and their effects inside this setting and in this moment do not necessarily shift or stretch meaning and recognizability more widely. While the repetition of such practices and their effects might lead such non-normative meanings to become sedimented over time, the recuperative capacities of the discourses that prevail in the education assemblage suggest that the cumulative effect of many such instances in this classroom, in this school and in schools elsewhere is likely to cement the universal pathology of students who bear the weight of designations such as 'Social, Emotional and Behavioural Difficulties'. We act our place in the discourses through which we are made recognizable as we struggle to choose where we stand.

We might also look to these practices as anti-identity – the boys' practices find the gaps in the discourses, regimes and practices of the education assemblage and follow lines of flight from their 'SEBD' subjectivation, lines of flight that might deterritorialize the 'SEBD'- and student-subject. That these deterritorializing lines fly into other subjectivations (anti-authoritatian cool masculinity) that are themselves territorializing and open to rapid reterritorialization (youth 'at risk' and so 'SEBD' or abject student once again) does not negate their unsettling, anti-identity effects. Just as thinking about these practices as performative politics does not fundamentally require that this be the self-conscious intent of the boys, so these anti-identity deterritorializations do not require intent. Indeed the absence of the self-conscious intent of self-knowing and self-reflective subjects might be a key to understanding these practices, bodies and flows of energy and feelings and their effects as a moment of anti-identity politics.

Ultimately in the scene and the politics that might be read within it, the constraints inherent in the subjectivation of recognition remain. The seemingly simultaneous flight from and foreclosure of one subjectivity (student) opens up the possibility of another subjectivity (cool boy) as well as installing the constraints of this subjectivation. Recognizability is at the centre of subjectivation and the possibility of lives that are viable or livable (Butler 2005). Considering the extent to which these boys are socially and educationally marginalized, it may well be that we should both recognize these subjects and their lives and be cautious about accepting these lives as sufficiently viable or livable. The call to and for viable lives may seem to be in tension with an anti-identity politics that eschews subjectivation because it constantly refuses the subject-hood that underpins recognition and action. Yet anti-identity politics might be understood as rejecting subjectivation as the site from which to act, rather than as rejecting wholly the subject who acts from a position of subjectivation. In Deleuze and Parnet's terms these boys and their teachers might be considered 'people of the line', that is, they are the 'marginals' whose politics practices are lines of flight. Having been propelled into this school and these subjectivities through the operations of the educational assemblage, these boys and their practices might be understood as those of people of the line. Their teachers have moved purposefully into this space and for some this might implicitly include the purpose of practising as people of the line. In the following chapter I turn to the everyday pedagogies of teachers and ask whether these pedagogies can be understood as forms of radical politics, including those that might be thought of as the practices of the people of the line.

6   Everyday political pedagogy

Pedagogy is central to what educators do. It is the act and the art of engaging learners in learning, opening up new possibilities and ideas, and, perhaps, changing the learner and the teacher through this process. It is influenced by how educators think about and engage with educational systems, structures, spaces and processes. It involves how they think about what it means to learn and to teach, and how they think about and engage with students. The encounter between the educator and the student, then, is a pedagogic encounter. But inserting a radical politics into pedagogy is not the 'normal' state of affairs. As Chapters 4 and 5 demonstrated, this is not a straightforward ambition or practice for either a well-supported national project like the No Outsiders research, even at the relatively 'simple' level of identifying potential resources and inserting these into the curriculum, or for teachers engaging with students in the day-to-day life of schools. In this chapter I explore what engaging radical politics in education settings might look like in the classroom. I consider some of the forms that the practices of critical pedagogies have taken, what else might be possible, and what the effects of such pedagogies might be. And I explore the ways in which critical pedagogic interventions might be resisted and recuperated.

As I discussed in Chapter 4, the notion of critical pedagogy is often connected to pedagogic approaches that aim to open up students' and educators' understanding of their social and political context, understandings that are seen to underpin social and political transformations. This version of critical pedagogy is most often associated with the practices developed by Paulo Freire in Brazil in the second part of the last century, where his techniques of dialogic education sought to conscientize – to bring to consciousness of their location in the social hierarchy – the peasant classes, a conscientization that, he anticipated, would lead to social transformation (Freire 1970). This groundbreaking educational work was taken up in the USA by neo-Marxist and critical educators, scholars and activists such as Michael Apple (1996, 2000), Henry Giroux and Peter McLaren (1994). These critical scholars were looking for tools to interrupt education systems' and institutions' reproductive forces and pursuing the goal of making the school a site in which criticality would be enabled and fostered and, reflecting the Freireian tradition, in turn lay the foundations for movements for critical social change.

The work of Freire and subsequent critical work is located in time and space and is the product of and reflects particular forms of political thinking. From these beginnings a diversity of pedagogies concerned with enabling social and political change have been developed and explored in practice. As feminist, anti-racist, disabilities and sexualities movements have been pursued in education, questions have been raised about the extent to which a critical pedagogy resting on neo-Marxist underpinnings can be helpful for political pedagogies that foreground a range of social identities and their concerns. At the same time, the proliferation of identity politics and allied conceptual frameworks as well as a broad engagement with post-structural theories of the social, the subject and power, have extended the conceptual tools that political pedagogic forms draw on. This has seen the development of feminist pedagogy (Luke and Gore 1992), critical multicultural pedagogy (Nieto 2004), critical race pedagogy (Allen 2004; Leonardo 2005), red pedagogy (Grande 2004), inclusive pedagogy (Corbett 2001; Nind 2005), and queer and deconstructive pedagogies (Talburt and Steinburg 2000; Youdell 2006a, 2006c). The proliferation and diversification of what might count as critical pedagogy mean that no singular account of what it is can be offered. This does not suggest, however, that critical pedagogies have been discarded or superseded. The pluralization of critical pedago*gies* might be inadequate in that it suggests an artificial commensurability across these. Nevertheless, it is useful in indicating the way that critical pedagogies have come to incorporate a broad range of practices, goals and political and intellectual underpinnings and been inflected with new conceptual lenses and reworked for new contexts. What is common across these is their concern to pursue radical politics in and through pedagogic practice.

Radical political practices and the insertion and legitimation of previously subjugated or disallowed knowledges may seem unlikely in classrooms that are tightly framed and constrained by the education assemblage and its demands. And this may be exaggerated by a macro-political and economic climate of instability and policy dead ends that might compel educators to 'play safe'. Furthermore, the effectiveness with which Left alternatives have been rendered almost unintelligible, and radical stances tethered to extremism and terrorism and so disqualified that I explored in Chapter 2, means educators may feel there is little space to think, let alone act, in radical ways. Yet as my discussion in Chapter 4 of the constitution of gay and lesbian children's fiction as educational resources for primary schools and the incorporation of these into the formal curriculum shows, gaps can be found into which disallowed knowledges can be inserted and critical pedagogies pursued. Indeed, the macro-political, economic and policy moment might be taken up by critical educators as a moment in which these counter-knowledges and pedagogies are all the more pressing and promising. In this chapter I explore further what critical pedagogies can look like, and examine the potential gaps in the educational assemblage through which these critical pedagogies might work.

Contemporary critical pedagogies

An often-cited instance of critical pedagogy in action is the Citizens' Schools of Porto Alegre, Brazil (Gandin 2003). Luis Gandin's accounts of education in this city map a curriculum that takes the form of thematic blocks that are decided through dialogic processes involving the people of the city. These curricula reflect the self-expressed concerns and needs of the people and are returned to and renegotiated through what Apple (1990) calls thick democratic processes. At the heart of this approach to education has been a concern to interrogate and destabilize the normative privileged/subjugated locations of knowledges after the tradition of Freire's pedagogy. As such, the Citizen's Schools in Porto Alegre offer a glimpse of a wholesale move to a critical pedagogy and demonstrates that such a shift is possible.

Articulating critical pedagogy with critical anti-racist and critical race scholarship has seen the development of critical multicultural and critical race pedagogies. For instance, Sonia Nieto (2004) offers accounts of alternative schools in the US that serve communities of excluded African American and Hispanic students where the curriculum is relevant to (but not necessarily an account of) the lives of the students; where pedagogy is dialogic and respectful; and where students are encouraged to develop critical understandings of their trajectories from high school to alternative school, their wider social location, and the racialized structural and material forces that are involved in these personal journeys. While these critical pedagogic forms are offered to students who are outside mainstream education, and may not offer immediate access to the same pathways to college available to 'successful' high school students, the critical multicultural pedagogy pursued in these alternative schools does re-engage these students with learning and enable them to develop both critical insight and experiences of educational success. Similar moves have been seen in the pedagogy of Erin Gruwell, whose work with disadvantaged urban youth has been made widely known through the film *Freedom Writers* (LaGravenese 2007). Critical Whiteness Studies has developed approaches to curriculum and pedagogy inspired and underpinned by thinking developed by Critical Race Theory. This work has called on critical pedagogy and critical educators to interrogate investments in Whiteness and to foreground White supremacy in analyses and interventions. Ricky Lee Allen usefully sets out how we might locate Freire's analysis of the oppressor and call to love, humanization and dialogue in a radical race framework, positioning the White teacher and student as 'humble learner' in a cross-race dialogue, creating 'dissonance' in Whiteness, and offering White students and educators 'other ways of being white' (Allen 2005: 65). And in the field of indigenous education, critical theory and pedagogy have been brought together with indigenous knowledges and ways of being to develop Red Pedagogy that pursues a politics and pedagogy of decolonization (Grande 2004).

Post-structural engagements with critical pedagogy take up deconstructive and performative politics suggesting that constraining, normative subjectivities can be resisted and alternative subject positions made possible through pedagogic practices (Britzman 1995; Burns 2005; Rasmussen 2001; Youdell 2006a, 2006c). Many educationists who have taken up these approaches have earlier commitments to critical theory. These interconnections are evident in their thinking about/attempts to transform curriculum, pedagogic and institutional approaches as well as students' and educators' perspectives on the identifications and subjectivities of themselves and others and the way practices and meaning are bound up in these.

A prominent example of a post-structural feminist pedagogic intervention that endeavoured to open up spaces where teachers could engage students in critical analysis of curriculum texts as well as the 'texts' of everyday life is found in the work of Bronwyn Davies (2003) and the subsequent wider take up of this. As I discussed in Chapter 4, Davies' research involving adult-led deconstruction with students of the hetero-gender narratives of fairy tales broke the ground for a range of critical literacy interventions. Another significant example of deconstructive pedagogy is the work undertaken by Cath Laws, in collaboration with Bronwyn Davies, in her school for students who have been excluded from mainstream schools (Laws and Davies 2000). In her pedagogic practices Laws engages students in explicit interrogations of the construction of 'normal', exploring how this might be self-consciously 'performed' by these students despite their having been previously diagnosed as having 'emotional and behavioural disorders'. That is, she works with students on 'doing normal'. This is not a straightforward incorporation, however, as Laws works to unsettle the very construction of a normal/abnormal binary, an unsettling that has the potential to extend the intelligibility of the students with whom she works. I have argued that it is moves such as these – that turn to the potential of the performative to reinscribe meanings and subjects and the capacity of deconstruction, after Derrida (1978, 1988), to expose, unpick, reverse and displace hegemonic discourses – that offer promise and possibility for political pedagogy (Youdell 2006a, 2006c). In my previous work I have indicated a series of specific goals that a post-structural political pedagogy might pursue. I have suggested that this pedagogy might attempt to trouble normative constitutions of schooling, students and learners and, through this troubling, create conditions of possibility in which the borders of intelligibility, and/or the meanings of these borders, might be shifted. These shifts might, in turn, allow students who are currently excluded from schooling to be 'someone' and 'somewhere' else. Following the Freireian tradition and building on the work of Davies, I have suggested that this troubling might be pursued through educators mobilizing the resistances and rein-scriptions that students enact every day inside schools and by creating spaces where students' practices of self are not simply recuperated in the constitution of educational and social margins, and that offering students conceptual tools for deconstructing their social and educational locations and redeploying the discourses that locate them might proliferate these everyday resistances and reinscriptions. Making these spaces, resisting these recuperations and proliferating these resistances and reinscriptions foregrounds relationality in the classroom and the recognition that educators can offer (or refuse) through their own practices (Youdell 2006a). These practices are evident in the analysis of practices that follows, both as tactics that successfully trouble the normative student/teacher/school and as tactics that might be recuperated or bring with them further unforeseen or unstoppable constitutions.

Everyday political pedagogies

In the rest of this chapter I engage with a series of examples of educators' interventions inside contemporary classrooms and schools focusing in on pedagogic encounters between teachers and students. In doing this I take up a Butlerian framework and explore the possibilities for critical pedagogic intervention to make 'classroom trouble', to unsettle the normative knowledges, meanings, practices and subjectivities that ordinarily circulate unquestioned in the classroom. As I do this I consider the possibilities for teachers' practices to re-make schooled subjects by opening up 'who' they and their students can be. While I do this I simultaneously interrogate the limits or traps that might be integral to pedagogic moves that foreground subjectivity. I also borrow tools from Deleuze and Guattari (1983) to consider whether teachers' critical practices might act as molecular lines that cross-cut the molar assemblages of the classroom, offering glimpses of lines of flight along which schools and schooled subjects might be deterritorialized. In doing this I begin to consider the significance of bodies and their affectivities.

The pedagogic moments that I consider here include interventions that have been designed and enacted by teachers in a knowing and purposeful attempt to trouble the classroom alongside a series of impromptu interventions into the apparent mundane events of everyday school life. These apparently impromptu interventions seem to be more and less self-consciously enacted to particular ends, whether or not these ends are met. Each of the pedagogic encounters that I interrogate can be read as intervening into both meaning and subjectivities, promising and threatening to shift meaning and to shift 'who' and 'how' subjects are recognized. The teachers make these moves along a series of distinct lines, targeting particular sorts of meanings and subjectivities and employing distinct tactics. These distinctions, I argue, expose the different frames that guide teachers' practices and have particular possible effects and likely limits while being constantly open to recuperation, further misfire and unintelligibility. These pedagogic interventions and my readings of them, then, offer a messy counterpoint to the certainty of policy-focused campaigning and identity politics in the classroom.

Ground-hold

Bay Tree School for boys with 'Social, Emotional and Behaviour Difficulties'. Assembly Hall, before the Friday afternoon sessions begin. The boys are being allocated to their 'options' groups: self-selected activities such as football, music, cookery and canoeing earned by accumulating a threshold of conduct and effort 'points' over the course of the week. Boys who have not reached the threshold spend the afternoon working with senior teachers. The boys sit in year group lines on the hall floor while the headteacher, Mr Parsons, stands at the front of the hall accompanied by the teachers who will lead the options groups.

During morning lesson time and the lunch break I have seen Matthew, a smallish 12-year-old White boy, being closely supervised and at times restrained by several different male members of staff. These restraints have ranged from Matthew appearing to be held loosely by the wrist while sitting on a bench in the quad to appearing to be held tightly from behind by twisted arms thrust up and together. As Mr Parsons is beginning to address the hall of assembled boys and announce who has 'made' options, a male teacher escorts Matthew in, holding him loosely by the arm. In an instant Matthew slips free of the teacher and dashes out of his reach, the teacher rushes to grab Matthew who dodges and evades the teacher but in doing so backs himself against a locked door. Almost

immediately another male teacher, Mr Newton (the popular deputy who intervenes in 'Hungover' in Chapter 5), moves in and intercepts Matthew. While
Matthew writhes and struggles against Mr Newton's hold, he is quickly moved
onto his stomach on the floor. It appears that Mr Newton uses pressure and
leverage on Matthew's arm joints to move him to the ground with minimum
struggle or force. Once he is down, Mr Newton maintains Matthew there by
holding one of his arms straight up behind his back. The escorted entry, the
slipping free and dodging away, the interception and restraint on the floor all
happen in just a couple of minutes, and draw the attention of all in the hall. The
headteacher responds by addressing the assembled boys:

> There's not a boy here who hasn't had a problem so if another boy's got
> a problem just respect that and don't wind him up, just get on with what
> you're doing and let him get on with it. I'm just going to stand here and
> pretend that I'm not looking at Matthew.

As Mr Newton continues the restraint, Matthew alternates between lying his
cheek on the parquet wood of the hall floor and closing his eyes and lifting his
head and grinning out at those boys who turn to look at him.

(From DY fieldnotes, Bay Tree SEBD School, Summer 2008)

Physical restraints of students are a constant feature of life in many, although not
all, special schools for students identified as having emotional or behavioural difficulties or disorders. This particular scene of restraint, with a boy pinned to the
ground, is the only one of its kind that I observed over the course of the term that
I visited Bay Tree School and, based on my time in the school and conversations
with teachers, my sense is that this 'ground-hold' was an exceptional restraint in a
context where other less dramatic but equally effective physical restraints happened
many times a day. I was disturbed in the moment and beyond it, and the headteacher's intervention perhaps suggests that others, teachers and students alike, were
also disturbed. Nevertheless, such restraints take place in special schools, are in
line with policy and legislation and use techniques which the teachers are trained in
and approved to use (Allen 2003; DCSF 2007; Hayden and Pike 2005; Team-Teach
2003).

The handling and restraint of Matthew has constitutive force, but this is subject to
significant contestation, indeed, it is perhaps 'what' and 'who' is constituted in this
moment that is at stake here. In the tightly defined space of the 'Social, Emotional
and Behavioural Difficulties' school, a teacher's physical restraint of a student cites
the normative knowledges, meanings and subjects of this space. As Matthew is corralled into a space at the back of the hall and separated from the bodies and removed
from the eye-line of the assembled students, the restraint cites and constitutes the
pathology or disturbance of the child-student who is not in 'control' of himself emotionally, psychically or bodily. This pathology, disturbance and absence of control
constitute Matthew at the border of student-subject as the other bodies seated on the
hall floor are potentially constituted student. This border-location and the treatment
that it is invoked through threaten to constitute Matthew as schooling's abject, an
abjection that puts his recognizibility as human at risk. And as the restraint constitutes

Matthew in these ways it constitutes the teacher-professional engaged in the proper imposition of control through necessary physical restraint. These constitutions of this student and teacher also threaten and promise to constitute the other students and teachers in this space in similar ways. And as the tightly defined space demarcates the meanings of these practices and so their constitutions, these practices and constitutions flow back and constitute the space, affirming and inscribing the assemblage of the 'SEBD' school.

However, this tightly demarcated and defined space and its knowledges, practices and subjects are not made once and for all and these constitutions are not singular or guaranteed. Borrowing from Deleuze and Guattari (2008), the molar lines and striations of the 'special school' assemblage overcode the meanings of its practices and subjects. But there are other lines that run through this school as well as polished surfaces on which its meanings do not easily adhere. These other meanings bleed into the 'SEBD school', bringing with them constitutive potentials that unsettle the certainties of the 'SEBD' student and the teacher-professional. Outside the school in public and private spaces from the family to the mainstream school to the shopping mall, the physical restraint of a boy by a man is potentially an assault on an innocent and not a correction of a delinquent. Indeed, such physical dominance of a child by an adult man threatens to constitute the man as uncivilized, as savage, as, potentially, sub-human.

As Matthew moves between passive submission and active resistance to restraint, whether through his physical struggle or grinning to the other boys, I can almost see him flicker between dual constitutions – the pathological child subdued or the bad-boy un-invested in and so untouched by the school and its meanings. Matthew's struggle constitutes his refusal of his reduction to the pathological, deviant, the abject, the not-human, inserting instead other meanings that insist that his practices and the restraint constitute his recognizability as anti-authoritarian masculine. Subjectivation in these terms catches Matthew in the molar lines of class and gender and offers recognition as the bad-boy respected by his peers. This constitution mobilizes and undercuts his abjection at the same time as it also promises this recognizability to the other boys. Lines of class and gender run alongside those of pathology and deviance and readily veer and run back into these, rendering them component parts of this constitution. The practices of the bad-boy – grinning at your mates when you are being held down on the floor by a teacher – are also the practices of the pathological boy who is beyond self-control and, perhaps, beyond correction.

The headteacher's intervention seems to attempt to step past these constitutions of Matthew and the other boys, calling up another set of subjectivities in the place of the pathological or the abject. By referring to Mr Newton's restraint of Matthew in terms of a boy having 'a problem', the event and the way that Matthew is understood are transformed. Matthew is no longer pathological, disturbed and out of control, rather, he 'has a problem', a problem that may well be shared and should be understood by all the other boys in the room. Matthew is not pathological and so the other boys 'like' him are not pathological either. It is almost as if the disturbing physical restraint is not occurring – perhaps Mr Newton is simply 'assisting' Matthew with his 'problem'. Mr Parsons' commentary also constructs a narrative of the event in which it is entirely reasonable, rational and humane; a narrative through which both the adults and the children are tutored in their respective roles. Mr Parsons' intervention, then, is a normalizing one; it normalizes these subjects, their practices and the school. This normalization entreats us all to 'act normal'; maintaining the possibility of 'normal' here involves acting as if everything is normal and so 'politely' pretending that the physical restraint is not happening. This normalizing move undercuts the pathologizing meanings of 'Social, Emotional and Behavioural Difficulties' and the 'SEBD' student and school. Yet the remaking of meaning here may not be so straightforward. In asserting that he will 'pretend he cannot see', and by extension entreating others in the hall to 'not see', the risk of pathology seems to be replaced by the risk of invisibility, and invisibility is surely not-human-ness. In this sense the evocation of 'normalcy' here is distinct from the 'doing normal' that includes a querying of the self-evident nature of 'normal' found in Cath Laws' work. It may be that Mr Parsons' intervention only succeeds in protecting Matthew and the other boys from the pathology of 'SEBD' by rendering them invisible, not human. Could it be that invisible not-human-ness is favourable to pathological subject-hood? As I reflect on this moment, it seems to me that it called less for a normalizing intervention that erased the practice of physical restraint, and more for an interruption by a risky truth telling; what Foucault calls 'fearless speech' (Foucault 2001). Yet such an interruption is all but unimaginable – what would one of the students, a teaching assistant or the headteacher himself say or do to interrupt this encounter and expose and unsettle the regimes of truth, the rigid molar lines and the subjectivations of this education assemblage?

Mr Parsons' intervention into the pathologizing effects of the physical restraint and the inadvertent erasure of subject-hood that it risks resonates with the intervention made by Miss Carter into the classroom outburst of an 'Emotional Difficulty, Behavioural Disorder' or 'EDBD' designated student at Plains High in Sydney, Australia. In that incident the boy, Paul, repeatedly shouts out in a silent classroom 'Hands up who agrees Ian's gay', an outburst that Miss Carter responds to by firmly informing the class that 'you can't hear Paul'. I wrote about this episode in *Impossible Bodies, Impossible Selves* (Youdell 2006a) where I considered its various constitutive effects. The effect that I want to draw attention to here concerns the teacher's statement 'you can't hear Paul' which seems to do similar work to Mr Parsons' 'I can't see him'. Like Mr Parsons, Miss Carter is attempting to step past the constitution of Paul as pathological and undercut his homophobic constitution of Ian as the reviled and ridiculed homosexual. But stepping past this pathological constitution is achieved at the expense of Paul's subject-hood; he speaks but he cannot be heard, he is silenced, he is not-human. There appears to be a further limit to the interventions of Mr Parsons and Miss Carter. That is, their interventions can be read as refusing recognition of the pathological where this refusal is impossible. The meanings and practices of the education assemblage insist that the pathology and disturbance of Matthew and Paul are recognized and delineate the terms of this recognition, and so this border-subjectivity is constituted despite the teachers' attempts to veer away from it.

These attempts to reconstitute Matthew and Paul, however limited, mark a significant shift in normative teacher practices. For example, when Paul fidgeted so much in his English class that he got out of his seat and stood against the wall, Miss Ellis did not allow this to be a recognizable student practice; she sent him out of the room (Youdell 2006a). Yet Mr Parsons' and Miss Carter's interventions do not have the reconstitutive effects achieved by the deconstructive pedagogic practices of Cath Laws that I sketched earlier in this chapter (Laws and Davies 2000). Laws does not attempt to avoid the constitution of students as pathological, disturbed, abnormal through refusing to recognize their practices. On the contrary, she explicitly engages their practices, taking them out of their prevailing meanings and reframing them in order to offer different forms of recognition that are neither pathological nor less-than-human. The point of Laws' practices is that they reconfigure the boys' practices as recognizable in regimes of meaning that render these legitimate and 'normal'. For instance, a boy is upset because something upsetting has happened, not because he is emotionally out-of-control. A boy flees to the school roof not because he is both mad and bad but because he is responding to a legitimate need to escape the classroom and its events. Roof-sitting is reconstituted as 'normal' in this context and in this moment.

The teachers' practices in 'Ground-hold', then, might be understood as attempts to step past the normative discourses of proper student conduct at the same time as they seek to draw 'aberrant' student conduct (and perhaps even unrecognizable adult-teacher conduct) back into this normative register. Yet the pathology and abjection effected by these practices remains. 'Ground-hold' reverberates with variously valorized adult as well as child and youth masculinities, and the unspoken contestation of which forms of masculinity will be recognized, which will be approved, and which will be disallowed.

In the following analysis, I return to Laura, whose work on the No Outsiders project I introduced in Chapter 4. In this chapter I engage with Laura's accounts of pedagogic interventions that she made during the second year of the project while working at Prices Common Primary School. Located in a more suburban part of London than the school she was at during the first year of the project, Prices Common School had an established senior management team, strong inspection reports and the requisite school-level planning and policy was in place. Prices Common was again an ethnically mixed school, with notable Turkish and Somali populations and more than half of the students spoke English as an additional language. The accounts I explore here were authored by Laura herself and posted by her on the No Outsiders project website which was used as a repository and discussion space.

Muscles/boobies

Prices Common Primary School, Laura: As we were walking to lunch on our school trip to an environmental centre, Tomas (boy, aged 8) said, for no apparent reason and to no one in particular, 'boys have muscles and girls have boobies'. Both myself and a teaching assistant, Jenny, overheard him. Jenny is very sporty. She does karate and rides her bike everywhere. She rolled up her sleeves and tensed her muscles. 'Look Tomas, I'm a girl and I have muscles!' she said. 'Do you still think it's true that only boys have muscles?' I asked. Tomas scuffed his feet on the ground, hung his head and murmured, 'no' before running off to a different place in the line.

(Laura, No Outsiders teacher, Prices Common Primary School,
web-posting July 2008)

The pedagogic interventions that I explored in relation to 'Ground-hold' attempt to transform the abnormal into the normal, the aberrant into the recognizable. The pedagogic intervention in 'Muscles/Boobies' intervenes into a manifestation of normative masculinity that, while wholly recognizable, is disapproved of in this educational context and moment. Tomas' statement cites and inscribes hetero-masculinity marked by the strength of a hard muscular male body and distinct from and physically dominant to the weak, soft and sexualized bodies of women. Laura and Jenny's intervention troubles this embodied hyper-masculinity and its relationship to the feminine. Muscular masculinity is not refuted. Nor is the sexualization of the female body through its reduction to breast. But the muscular woman (although perhaps not muscular femininity) is made recognizable and Tomas' recognition of this muscular woman is insisted upon. Tomas concedes the recognizability of the muscular woman, but he does not want to do so and resists this recognition with his body, his murmured 'no', and his quick departure. Laura and Jenny's intervention, then, does appear to effect a momentary troubling of sex-gender that demands rigid, hierarchical demarcations of male and female bodies. But it may not trouble the masculine/feminine binary. A muscular female body is presented. But girl, woman, femininity are not fundamentally resignified by this presentation. This body remains exceptional, and is open to ready recuperation by the charge of un-femininity. Furthermore, while these educators might disapprove of the physical masculinity into which they intervene here, the discourses of schooling seem to be somewhat ambivalent about this as evidenced by the contradictory arguments that the 'what about the boys?' debate has deployed (Epstein *et al.* 1998). In addition, this physical masculinity intersects a series of further binary arrangements run through the education assemblage: rational/irrational, cerebral/bodily, advanced/backward, civilized/savage, White/Black, high class/low class. Laura and Jenny's intervention into this particular gender arrangement deploys these further normative hierarchical arrangements and cites another masculinity. The masculinity with which Tomas identified and in which he is invested is refused recognition and he is temporarily silenced. And while it is particular attributes of the female body (muscles-not-breasts) that the teaching assistant calls up and displays, another valorized and prevailing masculinity is implicitly asserted. This masculinity – marked by rationality, civility and even post-feminist equality – is one that the claim that Tomas makes locates him outside and to which he does not have access. The effect of these constitutions, resignifications and bars are perhaps played out in Tomas' scuffed feet, hung head and murmured 'no'.

Similar effects can be seen in Mr Newton's intervention in 'Hungover' from Chapter 5. The boys' practices offer recognition and status to a form of masculinity which offers them a site of identification, which they are invested in and which is available to them. The form of rational, controlled, establishment, middle class, White masculinity that is silently asserted by Mr Newton's 'Err, boys' is not available to these boys, they cannot be recognized as such a man-boy. Mr Newton's intervention might render the boys student-subjects, but it simultaneously subjugates or erases the masculinity through which they are recognized as meaningful gendered subjects. Their subject-hood, their being human, is dependent on this gendered subjectivity and so their investment in it can be understood as their investment in subject-hood itself.

Matthew in 'Ground-hold', Paul at Plains High, Tomas in 'Muscles/Boobies', and the boys in 'Hungover' are stilled, gagged and erased in order to make them recognizable as student-learners and to conceal their challenge from other students and teachers. But this comes at the cost of subjectivities in which the boys are invested, even if this investment only reflects the absence of other possibilities. And this price renders any new planes of recognition extremely fragile and poses the fundamental question of whether a subject can be subjectivated *differently* if this new subjectivation relies on the erase of a prior subjectivity.

In the remainder of this chapter I consider two further interventions made by this teacher, Laura, into the sex-gender regime that prevails in primary school classrooms. A teacher-researcher in the No Outsiders project, Laura has an academic background in queer theory and a political commitment to mobilizing this in her classroom. At the same time she recognizes the apparent irrefutability of sex-gender regimes and the likely limits of post-structural pedagogies. In her everyday pedagogic practice she explores these possibilities and limits as she attempts persistently to do something that has queer hopes. Laura's accounts of her practice are thick with interventions of the sort seen in 'Muscles/Boobies' and these are illustrated in the two interventions I offer below. The first of these, 'Lipstick', is an intervention made impromptu into a conversation that emerged between the children, and the second, 'Bow-ties', is a purposefully designed intervention that Laura inserted into her mathematics teaching.

Lipstick

> *Prices Common Primary School, Laura:* This is from my journal – scribbled quickly after school on Mon.
>
> We were on the carpet during the plenary to an art lesson, looking at some group portraits when I heard A (Muslim, Somali boy) say loudly 'boys can't wear lipstick.' This was said in response to a conversation he was having with another pupil when I asked them to talk in talk partners. The following conversation went along these lines . . .

Laura:	Can't they?
	Lots of children laugh and shout out 'No'.
Laura:	Who says they can't?
A (black girl):	Some can.
Laura:	I know lots of men who wear lipstick (this isn't really true but I was trying to make a case for the okay-ness of it!!).

A (boy who made original comment):	That's wrong.
Laura:	Why? I thought anyone could wear lipstick.
A (black girl):	My dad wears lipstick.
Laura:	Yes, that's ok.
A (black girl):	He mixes his lip balm with my mum's lipstick.
C (white girl):	My dad wears lip balm but he doesn't wear lipstick.
L:	Men can't wear lipstick.
Laura:	Who's told you that?
L [shrugging]:	Nobody.
Laura:	So do you think it's ok?
A (boy who made the original comment):	No.
Laura:	Well, some boys and men wear lipstick and some girls and women do – some don't. It's just what people feel like doing. There are no rules about who can and who can't wear what.

During this exchange, most of the class seems incredulous at the idea that boys can wear lipstick.

I then began reading them the *Sissy Duckling*. Interestingly, all the children except for M (white boy with 'SEN') were defending Elmer's right to be different and were commenting that it was unfair that he was bullied.

(Laura, No Outsiders teacher, Prices Common Primary School, web-posting November 2007)

The sex-gender regime circulating in this classroom as the children insist on the proper gendered use of lipstick is as an economy of difference that is embodied as well as marked on the body through social practice. This sex-gender regime is constituted as a dichotomous line of differentiation, in Deleuzo-Guttarian terms a binary machine, that is not only irrefutable, but also heavily invested in and vigorously patrolled by young children (Blaise 2005; Renold 2005). In 'Lipstick', like many other interventions that Laura has pursued, she attempts to intervene not only into normative sex-gender constitutions, but into sex-gender forms that are ordinarily *valorized and approved* by children, adults and education institutions. In this sense Laura intervenes in hegemonic forms of normative sex-gender that are seldom opened up to question or critique. That is, she is troubling 'proper' sex-gender as she endeavours to make Other subjects recognizable.

In 'Lipstick' she does this by picking up on a sex-gender prohibition asserted by a child and refuting it, insisting that this prohibition does not, in fact, exist. The initial outburst 'boys can't wear lipstick' that opens up the space for this discussion implies that another child had already suggested that it is possible for boys to wear lipstick. It may be that some children in the classroom do believe this to be the case, although such a belief would be likely to be considered erroneous outside 'age-appropriate' dressing-up by many educators as well as by other children. For some of these seven-

and eight-year-old children, in particular some of the boys, this is wholly unintelligible – they reject Laura's refutation and reassert the sex-gender prohibition. Some girls appear to try to work with Laura; they do not accept her assertion that the sex-gender prohibition does not exist and themselves struggle over the proper boundaries of the prohibition. One demarcates lip*balm*, not lip*stick* as the proper boundary. Another perhaps partially accepts Laura's assertion as she exposes men's 'secret' use of lipstick (when it is mixed with lipbalm). Both of these girls' interventions appear to offer Laura routes back from her impossible claim. But Laura does not take either of these routes back and lets her assertion hang, even as the incredulous children reject it. Yet the children's very incredulity, and the work they do to restore sex-gender practices to their 'proper' place and to draw Laura herself back into proper sex-gender, may well go to the sex-gender trouble that Laura has caused. She has unsettled the taken-for-granted-ness of who can and cannot wear lipstick and called on the children to consider this, even provoking them to identify the boundaries of the prohibition against men wearing lipstick: lip balm, or even the private (subtle?) use of mum's lipstick.

The children resist and recuperate Laura's claims and reinstate normative sex-gender practice. But the trouble remains, and Laura will make trouble like this again tomorrow and next week and next term. It seems unlikely, and Laura's own accounts of her practices confirm, that she does not hope to change sex-gender once and for all or even imagine that such practices might provoke new sex-gender to sediment over time. Laura is not trying to move from 'this' sex-gender to 'that' sex-gender, from a start point to an end point. In Deleuzo-Guttarian terms she is acting from the middle, taking a rhizomatic line of flight that finds a gap in the rigid lines of sex-gender (here lipbalm?) and pursues this in a move that might be the promise of a deterritorialization. Similar moves can be seen in her deployment of troubling teaching materials.

Bow-ties

Prices Common Primary School, Laura: Thought I should quickly write up about last week's numeracy lessons.

We were doing addition and subtraction and I was getting my higher ability kids to try to prove or disprove various statements (such as 'when you add 7 units to a number ending in 5 units, the answer always ends in 2 units' etc). I was making up some sheets with these statements on in the morning before the lesson and I was intending to draw some people with speech bubbles and a Fred thinks … and then have the person saying the statement – just to make it perhaps mildly more interesting for the kids.

As I was beginning to draw a boy with spiky hair I decided to make it into a girl. I think the main difference between making the person male or female was the eyelashes (and the name). When the kids got the sheet they did comment on the person I had drawn. O, a Somali Muslim girl, asked me 'Did you draw that Miss T?' but after that they got on with the work without any further references that I was aware of.

So, then the next day came and we were repeating the activity but this time with subtraction statements. This time I drew a person that looked, I would say unmistakably if we're talking in terms of what is conventional, like a girl. But I called the person James. The kids could not get their heads around it. A, a Muslim boy from Egypt (?), asked if he could cross the name out and change it to a girl's name. I asked why he wanted to do that. 'Because it's not a boy!' he replied. 'How do you know?' I asked. 'Because he is wearing a bow in his hair.' 'But can't boys wear bows in their hair?' I asked. At this point the group of six children all laughed and told me 'no, boys can't wear bows in their hair.' Of course, I asked 'Why not?' A told me 'boys wear bows around their necks not on their heads.' I commented that I had never heard of anything like that and that I thought anyone could wear a bow wherever they liked! At this point I had to go to attend to another group doing a different activity. At the end of the lesson, I noticed that O had crossed out the name James on her sheet and written her own name (although the person I had drawn looked nothing like her). I didn't have a chance to speak more to the kids about this. . . .

(Laura, No Outsiders teacher, Prices Common Primary School,
web-posting January 2008)

Here Laura makes a move from intervening in the impromptu practices of children as she does in 'Muscles/Boobies' and 'Lipstick' and inserts her sex-gender trouble into a mathematics worksheet. Moves as small as extending the eyelashes on a drawing of a spiky haired child and giving this drawing a name conventionally recognized as belonging to a girl are sufficient to provoke a girl into checking authorship of the picture with Laura: there is something wrong with this picture, and so Laura, the teacher, 'shouldn't' be its author. When Laura goes further and offers a picture of a child who is wearing a bow in its (I am compelled by convention to say 'her') hair and the name James, the children openly and absolutely reject it. Striking once again is the children's incredulity and their efforts to 'help' Laura back into a proper understanding of sex-gender embodiment. Ultimately they correct her 'error', a correction that may well simultaneously be a rejection of her as 'teacher'. In her efforts to trouble normative sex-gender Laura forfeits her position as the knowing teacher, indeed, her authority as teacher is subordinate to the children's authority as 'properly' sexed and gendered subjects. As in 'Lipstick', girls and boys are involved in these recuperations and while it seems that a number of children involved in the questioning of Laura's gender representations are identified as Muslim, it is not only Muslim children who are troubled by them. Indeed, it is important to be wary of allowing the children's collective efforts to shore up sex-gender to be erased by a silent citation of an Orientalist discourse that constitutes the Muslim child as being from a 'backward' culture which oppresses women – investments in 'proper' sex-gender subjectivities cross-cut the race and religious identifications of the children in this classroom.

It might be that locating her gender-troubling characters in a mathematics worksheet magnifies the trouble they cause and the children's resistance to it. Perhaps in conversations in the already creative space of story-time on the carpet the children can allow Laura to make incredulous claims about sex-gender. But to do so in the serious and high status terrain of mathematics is to unsettle the disciplinary boundaries of the classroom.

Across her pedagogic practice, Laura persistently intervenes into approved accounts and enactments of sexed-gendered subjects in efforts to trouble these normative subjectivities and their tightly demarcated boundaries. These interventions mark a further step in deconstructive or post-structural pedagogic practice in that they aim to unsettle normative meanings and practices as well as expanding the terms or recognizability. Nevertheless, this does not mean that these interventions have their intended effects. Laura reflects on the impossibility of shifting 'proper' gender, especially its embodiment. This impossibility is evident even as the children simultaneously defend the 'rights' of those outside this sex-gender regime to be 'different', as they do for Elmer of the *Sissy Duckling* (Fierstein 2002) story, in 'Lipstick', and as they do for the alternative fairy tale characters at the centre of the scheme of work that I examined in Chapter 4. In relation to this latter work Laura says:

> I found that across the whole unit of work, a lot of the children were actually very reluctant to explore different identities for fairytale characters . . . Although the children appeared to disapprove of Cinderella's passivity, many found it difficult to be Elizabeth [the Paper Bag Princess] and advise Cinderella on matters of fashion and marriage. They were worried that if they told Cinderella that she does not have to wear ball dresses and glass slippers that may be uncomfortable, and to choose her husband carefully, Prince Charming might reject her.
>
> (Laura, No Outsiders teacher, Explanation of Plan and Unit of Work)

How ever much Laura tries to subtly or not-so-subtly interrupt normative sex-gender-sexuality regimes, the children remain invested in and attached to these gendered bodies, the fixity of the fit between sex, gender and sexuality, and the bodily manifestation of gender. The children learn to cite diversity and equalities and even 'feminist' and 'LGB rights' discourses – Elmer the *Sissy Duckling* has the right to be different, Elizabeth, the *Paper Bag Princess* (Munsch 2003), does not have to wear glass slippers. The children learn that this is the 'correct' discourse in Laura's classroom. But, this is not the same as shifting normative meanings or provoking children to value or believe subjugated or subaltern knowledges and the subjects these constitute. The children are extremely cautious about suggesting to Cinderella that she might be more like Elizabeth, the *Paper Bag Princess*, indeed, they are deeply discomforted by this prospect. Prince Charming might reject Cinderella and it would be their fault. Furthermore, to give such advice would be to identify with Elizabeth, an identification that might risk their own proper place in the sex-gender order and so their own desirability to or recognition as Prince Charming.

Significant here is the everyday-ness of Laura's pedagogic interventions and the everyday-ness of the children's investments and attachments. Laura tries again and again to open up sex-gender and trouble its normative meanings and manifestations. And the children refuse and recuperate this again and again. Just as the pre-school boys in Miss Baxter's nursery deploy normative gender discourse to resist their teacher in Valerie Walkerdine's ground-breaking paper (Walkerdine 1987), so Laura's children deploy normative discourse to resist her gender troubling. The impossibility of the non-normatively sexed-gendered subjects that Laura offers rests, it seems, on the fact that her interventions demand recognition on a discursive terrain where these claims are unintelligible – these are not ways of knowing to which the children have previously been exposed and, it seems, the familiar guides them to refuse the new ways of knowing Laura offers. The sedimentation of enduring discourses, the molar lines of the education and sex-gender-sexuality assemblage are scored deeply in the classroom and the children's lives outside school. These demarcate the limits of recognizability, recuperate subjugated discourses as they are deployed and reterritorialize fine new lines back into the molar lines that they fly from. Furthermore, the liberal rights enshrined and pursued in identity politics are ever present and pervasive in the educational assemblage and are deployed in a moment to shore up 'proper' sex-gender even as these discourses make claims to inclusivity.

Laura's interventions and the children's responses remind me of the traditional English children's game 'Misfits' in which cardboard characters are sliced laterally into hat, head, body, legs and shoes. The purpose of the game is to collect and reassemble the cardboard characters in their proper forms, avoiding them being made 'Misfits' through the improper mixing of body parts and attire. The joy of the game, of course, is the ridiculous impossibility of the lady's hat on the cowboy's head on the nurse's body on the schoolboy's shorts on the clown's shoes. If these 'misfits' could not be rearranged correctly at the end of the game and were instead offered as real subjects then the game's pleasurable absurdity would be replaced by discomforting unintelligibility.

Laura's interventions can be thought of as lines of flight that might scatter the molar lines of the assemblage (Deleuze and Guattari 1983). But the interventions she offers the children are lines of flight that she may take alone. It may well be that she knows as she attempts to take off that she is caught in the binary machine and its molar lines. The force of binary sex-gender, its embodiment and its irrefutability are such that the subject's recognizability as a subject is put at risk by sex-gender trouble (Butler 1999, 2004a). Laura is stuck here with individual sexed and gendered bodies, and with subjects as individuals attached to their subjectivities. Laura's queer pedagogic moves trouble normative subjects and suggest non-normative subjects, but they do not attempt to instate another subject – be it gay, lesbian or queer – in their place. In this sense her practices might be seen as the sort of anti-identity politics that I have discussed in previous chapters. That is, they may be aligned with the anti-subjectivation position suggested by Deleuze and Guattari who, pointing out that subjectivation is one order of those assemblages from which rhizomatic imaginings fly, suggest a politics of affectivity, intensity and becoming-otherwise (Deleuze and Guattari 2008).

With these tools we might ask whether the pedagogic interventions of the teachers in this chapter might be understood as '*assemblage converters*' (Deleuze and Guattari 2008: 358, original emphasis), or even assemblage conversions? Are the assemblages of mainstream education, of 'special' education and its 'difficulties' and 'disorders', of youth culture, of sex-gender converted by these practices? Are these deterritorializations or even just 'en route to deterritorialization'? (ibid.: 358).

The question of the recognizability or impossibility of particular subjects explored in this chapter is bigger than or beyond a teacher's will or desire. Whether we think and act politically in terms of discourses, molar lines, binary machines or assemblages, all exceed the will and the temporality of subjectivated individuals. Furthermore, whether rationality is embraced or rejected, it cannot simply overcome or silence affectivity. Teachers engaging pedagogic politics might want their constitutions to work, their counter-hegemonic claims to take root and run tuber-like through their classrooms and schools, but prevailing meaning may not allow this. These teachers might know conceptually that their constitutive practices and claims are correct, but the affectivities that flow through their classrooms might insist that this is not the case. Foregrounding affectivity and its place in becomings and in the reterritorializations promised by lines of flight has the potential to help us to understand the resistances to and failures of the pedagogic trouble that is evident throughout the scenes of this chapter. The place of feelings and of bodily encounters and their intensities and flows in radical pedagogic politics is the focus of the next chapter.

7 Political feeling in the classroom

There is a strong current of concern in education research over the significance of feelings, or emotions and affectivities, in education. Psychoanalytic theory has offered an important set of conceptual tools for considering the place and significance in education of psychic processes such as recognition, identification, desire and abjection, and for unsettling the usual rational lens through which education is perceived (Benjamin 1998; Britzman 1998; Henriques *et al*. 1998). Alongside and connecting with this, post-structural thinking about discourse, subjectivation and affectivities has offered further tools for moving beyond the usual rational framing of education and engaging with feelings and their political potentials (Braidotti 2005; Butler 1997a, 2004a; Deleuze and Guattari 1983, 2008; Foucault 1990a, 1991a; Laclau and Mouffe 2001). Making use of these conceptual frameworks in various ways, education research concerned with the significance of feelings has foregrounded a subject who is incomplete and who does not and cannot fully 'know' her/himself and emphasized both subjects in relation to each other and the affectivities that flow between them.

The work of Deborah Britzman has made a central contribution to the consideration of the emotional aspects of education. Britzman (1998) argues that in conservative and critical modes alike, education is conceived of as a process of social and personal change and progress, learning is understood as conscious and continuous, and that it is unimaginable that education might be discomforting to learners or educators. In the place of this dominant conception of education, Britzman posits 'the question of education as a psychic event' (ibid.: 3) and argues that conflict between learner and educator as well as within the learner is a central part of education. She suggests we should attend to the difficulties and pleasures of education, considering the significance of the 'inside of actors', their mobile and conflicting wants, their unconscious, their attachments and the wishes and needs of their bodies (ibid.: 6). Yet for Britzman such a psychoanalytic call to the 'inside' of the subject is resisted in education 'because it goes against the wish that consciousness is all, that individuals are masters of their thought, that cognition precedes affect, and that affect should not contradict attitudes' (ibid.: 7). Britzman argues that these psychoanalytic concepts offer education tools for 'turning back on itself' so that it can interrogate the social relations of education, the effects of educational practices on education structures and subjects, and ameliorate the harmfulness of education. She writes:

Psychoanalysis reminds one of the failure of knowledge, the work of forgetting, the elusiveness of significance, the incidental, the coincident, the bungled action, and the psychic creativity of selves: how the self crafts its meanings of the self in the world, what these meanings do to the psyche, and what the psyche does to those meanings. Psychoanalysis interferes with education's dream of mastery, for, through its methods, it catches subjects in the fault lines of inattention: free association, wonderings over the elusive significance of the thing furthest from one's mind, and interpretation of dreams. It risks insights from knowledge devoid of social authority and intelligibity.

(Britzman 1998: 10)

From this she insists that the educator, and education, has an ethical obligation to rethink learning in a way that can apprehend and engage the psychic and affective dimensions of the subject and of learning, including loss, contradiction, resistance and anxiety as well as desire, attachment and love. And she asks whether education can turn from the justification of its institutions and practices to 'take the side of the learner' (Britzman 1998: 47).

The place of psychic processes, feeling and relationality in education has been taken up by a range of education scholars who have demonstrated these at work in a range of institutional and cultural contexts (see Henriques *et al.* 1998; Hey 2005, 2006; Kenway *et al.* 2006; Rasmussen 2006; Ringrose 2007; and Walkerdine 1990). Tamara Bibby, for example, builds on the work of Britzman and makes use of the psychoanalytic work of Bion to think about the emotional dimensions of educative processes. Like Britzman, Bibby is critical of rationalist accounts of education in which relationships, feeling and desires are absent or even disallowed (Bibby 2009). She argues that 'knowing and learning are bound up in the unconscious emotional flows of relationships' (ibid.: 52), drawing on Bion's theorizations of knowledge (K), love (L) and hate (H) to understand the 'blocked pedagogic relationship' (Bibby 2009: 51). Bibby uses these ideas to interrogate empirical data from classrooms and children's accounts of their experiences of schooling, identifying the centrality of relationships with teachers in children's accounts as well as children's feelings of 'anger, hurt and guilt associated with feeling judged, left out and persecuted' when these relationships are absent or 'blocked' (Bibby 2009). She argues for pedagogies in which the relational is foregrounded. Building on the work of Benjamin (1998), Bibby suggests we should look to pedagogies that acknowledge the significance of relationships in the classroom and the emotionality of these (Bibby 2009). In pursuing this she suggests that:

The difficult work of finding ways of thinking and talking non-judgmentally about the unconscious aspects of pedagogic relationships has a long history but does not sit well in the current English policy context. [. . .] What I am suggesting is that there is a need for a language that makes the nature and qualities of relationships visible and enables them to become objects for (non-judgmental) consideration.

(Bibby 2009: 52–3)

Deleuze and Guattari's (1983) critical engagement with psychoanalysis and their insistence on the possibility of desire as productive as well as their thinking about flows of affectivities have also been taken up by education researchers concerned to interrogate feeling in education (Boler 1999; Hickey-Moody 2009; Ringrose in press; Zembylas 2007). In Deleuze and Guattari's (1983, 2008) work, which I explored in detail in Chapters 2 and 3, affectivities are understood as eruptions and flows of bodily sensation and intensities. These affective intensities are posited as exceeding symbolic orders and so being beyond or before subjectivation. As such, Deleuze and Guattari consider affective encounters through these eruptions and flows and between bodies, rather than thinking in terms of affective encounters between individuals. In this sense affectivities are at the centre of their anti-subjectivation thinking. Understood in this way, affectivities are a site and moment of a politics of becoming – lines of flight are pursued through the flows of affectivities, intensities and eruptions of bodies that are anti-subjectivation, flights that have the potential to deterritorialize the assemblage.

Feeling and politics

Just as feeling is located outside the prevailing understanding of education, so it is outside the prevailing account of the Western political tradition. While moral judgements are at the centre of this tradition, these are posited as founded on the development of reason and not reason's opposite – emotion (Butler 2008). This is not to suggest that political discourse does not deploy feeling as it pursues its goals, but this feeling corralled by reason and the moral registers that follows from this. In the liberal-democratic tradition it is this rationality that frees us from the tyranny of sovereign domination or religious dogma. Indeed, Hunter (1994, 1996) suggests that the political state emerged in North Western Europe out of the need to interrupt widespread oppression and bloodshed at the hands of the Church and aristocracies. And this oppositional positioning of reason and feeling can be seen in the contemporary moment in political discourse of the War on Terror. Yet the claim that Western politics, in its radical or liberal forms, is wholly rational and devoid of feeling is problematic. The work of Ernesto Laclau and Chantal Mouffe (2001), which I explored in detail in Chapter 2, makes an important intervention here. They point to the assumption of consensus that underpins prevailing notions of politics and suggest instead that the political should be understood as being shot through with multiple irreconcilable antagonisms. In the light of this they suggest a move away from politics that seeks to build consensus, of whatever sort, and instead suggest a politics of agonistic pluralism. These antagonisms are not reducible to the reasoned good judgements of the liberal tradition – they are fundamentally passionate (Mouffe in Carpentier and Cammaerts 2006).

These lines of educational and political theorizing suggest a wholly feeling educational and political terrain, whether or not this is acknowledged by the discourses, institutions and subjects who constitute and struggle within it, and irrespective of the disqualification of feeling within the discourses that define both education and the political. As I have argued in Chapter 2, teachers engaged in critical pedagogic work do not act against the grain of the education assemblage based just on rational judgement but also because of their passionate commitments.

The elevation of rationality and the separation of feeling from the political and, conversely, the passion of politics is illustrated and brought to life in the 2002 film *Equilibrium* (Wimmer 2002). Written and directed by Kurt Wimmer, the film offers a depiction of Libria, a twenty-first-century post-World War III totalitarian state, where, in order to guard against a further war, all feeling is prohibited. The opening sequence of the film identifies our 'volatile natures' and 'the true source of man's inhumanity to man: his ability to feel'. The prohibition of feeling is achieved through the self-regulation of the population who take a regular dose of the emotion-blocking drug Prosium, alongside the state's repressive deployment of a specialist military force which locates and destroys both 'sense offenders' and outlawed feeling-evoking artefacts.

Equilibrium self-consciously cites anti-authoritarian dystopic science fiction such as Orwell's *1984* (Orwell 2000) and Huxley's *Brave New World* (Huxley 2007) as well as Ray Bradbury's *Farenheit 451* (Bradbury 2008) and its film adaptation (Truffaut 1966) and, of course, the *Matrix* trilogy (Wachowski Brothers 1999, 2003a, 2003b). It has been argued that *Equilibrium* 'outdoes its anti-authoritarian inspirations by proposing not just the *control* of emotions but the *elimination of emotion itself*' (Snider 2003, original emphasis). The film was a success on global release but was not promoted in the USA and had only a very short run in cinemas. And while it has sci-fi cult status, responses from mainstream critics were more mixed (Ebert 2002; Snider 2003).

The restriction of the aesthetic is foregrounded in *Equilibrium*, from poetry and great works of art to patterned fabrics, perfume and sentimental trinkets. These are offered as emblems of the free and feeling life that is denied. Yet the main concern of the film's narrative is the denial of the freedom of *feeling to dissent* intellectually and politically. Indeed, writer and director Wimmer has said that the film was a response to 'the current trend in America to regulate what people can and cannot feel' (Wimmer in Snider 2003: 1). Prosium, the drug self-administered daily by Libria's citizens, prevents the passions, intensities and desires that lead to political commitments, action and conflicts. That Prosium also leads to an absence of relationality and attachment – love, care, joy, pleasure, elation – is a price the state and the citizenry believe to be worth paying.

The film's narrative insists on the centrality of feeling to the political and suggests the dystopian image of absolute political passivity in a world without feeling – the absence of feeling incurs an absence of political will. Counter-positions and politics emerge not from the rational assessments of the disinterested actor exercising (good) judgement, but from the passionate attachments to ideas, modes of life, relations, forms of social arrangement and encounters as well as experiences of the self, of a wholly feeling subject. As such, the film offers a stark counter to a rationalistic conception of knowledge and politics, insisting as it does on the inseparability of feeling from commitment, ethics and politics. The political is fundamentally a matter of feeling.

In the rest of this chapter I make use of the conceptual tools I have outlined above in order to move beyond the rationality that is ordinarily assumed to underpin 'good' politics, education and pedagogy. I explore the affective dimensions of a selection of the scenes from inside schools that have been analysed in terms of their subjectivating effects and resignifying or deterritorializing potentials in the preceding chapters. I engage the intense feelings that educators and students often have in relation to their educational and social locations and their political positions; their feelings of themselves and their lives. In doing this, I explore how feelings shape, influence and make intelligible or unintelligible political pedagogic practices in school.

Approaching the affectivities that circulate in the accounts of pedagogic encounters offered in the previous chapters is not easy. It is difficult to avoid an individuated self-knowing subject ('what did s/he, you, I feel?') as well as the unconscious desires of the split subject of psychoanalysis ('what does s/he, you, I *really* feel?'). Yet engaging feeling as social (Renold and Ringrose 2008; Ringrose in press) and potentially extra-discursive, rather than as the knowable interior experience and property of a singular subject, is what opens up the productivity of affect for pedagogy. Furthermore, it is difficult not to be drawn away from the unruly flows and energies of affectivity and towards the comparatively 'tame' domain of emotion (love, hate, anger, caring) that discourse provides (Zembylas 2007).

Feeling muscles, feeling boobies

In Chapter 6, I engaged with 'Muscles/Boobies', an account of Tomas, aged 7 or 8, announcing to his teacher, Laura, and her teaching assistant, Jenny, that: 'boys have muscles and girls have boobies'. I considered their response – showing female-muscles (Jenny's arm) and asking whether his statement still held true – and its effect – Tomas' hung head, scuffed feet and murmured 'no'. I suggested that this everyday political pedagogic intervention exposes and calls into question normative, but subjugating, masculinity. And that in doing so it (might) unsettle the binary logic of hard male bodies and soft female bodies, but does not unsettle the binary logics of masculinity and femininity. What was left unexplored in Chapter 6 were the affective dimensions of this social and pedagogic scene.

Here I to return to 'Muscles/Boobies' to consider the flows of energy and feeling in this encounter and the relevance these might have for understanding the politics of everyday educational practices. In doing so, I cannot 'know' how the people in 'Muscles/Boobies' feel, Laura did not say anything about how it felt for her in her fieldnotes, and I did not ask her about her feelings later. If these reflections had been present, however, they would have been reflections that corralled the affectivity of the encounter within discourse, within emotion and within the individual. Jenny and Laura might have felt amused, annoyed, attacked, confused, connected, proud. Tomas might have felt pleased, amused, annoyed, attacked, ashamed, confused in any combination in the moment and after it.

Throughout the analysis, I do not want to locate these possible feelings inside these three subjects, either in the rationality of self-reflexive subjects or in the repressed desires of split subjects. And I do not want to attempt (hopelessly) to follow a trail of evidence and analysis to unearth their 'true' feelings. Rather, I want to think about affects that might exceed or precede the symbolic register of 'emotion' and be thought of as productive of and produced by the encounter. And using Ahmed's notion of an emotional economy (Ahmed 2004), I want to think about these affects as circulating in an affective economy in this social and pedagogic encounter. This affective economy impacts the effects of this encounter, which as Chapter 6 shows, are potentially multiple and always provisional. We might imagine that if Tomas felt affects that we might make sense of as 'being pleased' by his statement and 'confused' by his correction, then the affects and effects of the encounter would be different than if Tomas felt 'amused' by his statement and 'pleased' by his correction. And similarly if Jenny felt 'annoyed' by Tomas' statement and 'connected' to Laura by her intervention, or if Laura felt 'amused' by Tomas' statement and 'annoyed' by Jenny's intervention. These potential combinations of affects and interpretive repertoires of emotion circulate in this affective-emotional economy, bringing bodies into relation and/or blocking relationality, and, indeed, bringing bodies into recognizability and/ or blocking recognition. These affective economies and emotional repertoires make and mediate the effects of the encounter.

Borrowing Bibby's (2009) use of Bion's notions of love (L), hate (H) and knowledge (K), and the engagement or blocking of these, might suggest that this pedagogic encounter is one in which relationality is blocked and the recognition sought by the child is foreclosed. Alternatively it might suggest that the intersubjectivity of this encounter is the necessary foundation for the exchange and its apparent affective impact – the intersubjective relationships between the teaching assistant, the teacher and the child allow this encounter, complete with its affectivity to take place. Engaging with Britzman's (1998) argument that education should recognize its interventions into the desires of the child might help us to see the disconnection between the desires of the child for recognition (as potentially masculine-muscular, and so as boy) and the teachers' desire to intervene in and interrupt these normative identifications as part of a critical pedagogy. Engaging this divergence might shed light on the limits of the pedagogic intervention and push for a thinking through of alternative ways of engaging affectivity in this critical work. This might lead to a pedagogy that takes account of the children's desires and acknowledges that learning, or resistance to it, is fundamentally tied up with the psychic and affective life of the child as well as the teacher.

Both Bibby and Britzman locate the affective dimensions of learning that they wish to foreground in the relationality of the educator and the student. Borrowing Deleuze and Guattari's (2008) thinking about affectivity goes further, refusing to take affect as the possession or interior life of individuals, and instead emphasizing the pre-personal flows of energies and intensities that define the boundaries between and mark the contact across bodies. This is not, then, a question of what the affective experiences of the teachers and child might be and how these might impact on the pedagogic encounter. Instead, it is a question of the potentialities opened up by the flows of energies in this encounter.

While these variant accounts of affectivity have different things to say about the scene, all insist that its affective dimension cannot be erased or overlooked. It may be that in 'Muscles/Boobies' we see, ultimately, a pedagogic intervention in which divergent flows of affect come into conflict and in which the teachers' authority closes down certain flows of affect as it closes down a site of identification and subjectivity.

What seems certain is that feelings abound in this scene; that these are important to the learning that may or may not take place here; and that these feelings are, at least in moments, beyond the frameworks of meaning that render these emotions accessible in discourse.

Feeling hungover

'Hungover' – the scene explored in Chapter 5 in which a class of 14-year-old boys in a 'special school' for boys designated as having 'Social, Emotional and Behavioural Difficulties' bounce the idea and the act of being 'drunk' and 'high' around the classroom while their teachers discuss their marked exam papers – offers another useful site for thinking about affectivity in pedagogy. Instead of asking how do the boys and teachers feel, or asking what the boys' and teachers' feelings 'do' here, I want to use Deleuze and Guattari's thinking about affectivity to ask 'what energies are flowing in this space, and what can these bodies do here?' (Deleuze and Guattari 2008; Hickey-Moody 2009; Ringrose in press).

This is a whole classroom scene that gives an account of boys and teachers engaged in a series of collective practice. This perhaps makes it easier to think about the flows of energies here as being social, as circulating amongst bodies, rather than as possessions or interior experiences that belong to each boy and each teacher. It seemed to me at the time, in writing fieldnotes, and in reconstructing the scene that the collectivity and affectivity of the scene was important. And it did feel – I felt the moment bodily, I could civilize it by calling it excitement. But the bodily intensity that I felt was surely an effect of the bodily intensities felt by the boys. The affect created the practices, and the practices created the affect. This is the affectivity of a collectivity – not one boy, two boys, seven boys individuated by their proper given names and their proper distribution at desks around the room. Instead it is a constitutive mass of boy-ness; bodies shaking, shuddering, rolling, calling, connecting, colliding. Perhaps these bodies are taking a line of flight that is precisely the becoming offered by these intensities; becomings that deterritorialize the special school assemblage.

A further affective economy flows between Miss Groves and Miss Appleton and while this might be an exchange between themselves, the meanings and values of that economy are tied up with the affective economy circulating amongst the boys. It feels good to greet each other 'Hi Miss!' because the boys are acting outside their place in school discourse, reveling in the affective intensities of their game, and being allowed to do so by 'Miss' and 'Miss' who joke together. And the intensities of the boys' game are surely intensified by the affectivity of the complicities of the teachers (and researcher) present. It feels good to bounce high-energy prohibited words and practices around the room. Following Deleuze and Guattari, these affects may be seen as life-affirming, and this is a life-affirming moment in this space (Renold and Ringrose 2008).

These bodily intensities are not simply playful and pleasurable – although they surely are those – they are also political. The politics of their affectivity rests in the relationships of power that circulate in and frame this space, constraining what these bodies are able to do and feel here. These bodily intensities refuse the docility and proper comportment of the individualized, hierarchized and normalized schooled body. And they refuse the pathology of the abject, out-of-control emotionally or behaviourally 'difficult' or 'disordered' 'SEBD' body. These bodies are not controlled in the terms of the educational assemblage; they exceed the overcoding of its rigid molar lines. And they fly from the striations of the school space, tracing faint new lines in the smooth surface they evoke. These bodies fly from the subjectivations that limit, constrain and injure them – the 'SEBD' boy – and are instead becoming.

Nevertheless, Mr Newton's intervention exposes the limits of this line of flight, bursting the boys' bubble of becoming and reinstating normative school discourse – affectivity is erased and practice is inscribed not as the affirmation of life, the flow of possibilities, but as the sort of inappropriate behaviour that led the boys to this moment and space in the 'special school'. And the line of flight that is these intensities is tripped back into the deep groove of not just schooled meanings and subjectivities, but 'SEBD' schooled meanings and subjectivities.

Feeling ground-hold

The final scene from the preceding chapters to be revisited is 'Ground-hold', the account from Chapter 6 of the restraint of Matthew by Mr Newton in Assembly at Bay Tree 'SEBD' School which culminated in Matthew being held face-down on the hall floor while the headteacher, Mr Parsons, told the assembled boys that he would pretend that he could not see Matthew. It is a challenge to even approach this account from the vantage point of affectivities and flows of energies. How do we ask 'what intensities are flowing?' and 'what can a body do here?' when confronted by a boy held to the ground by a man? And yet, of course the scene is thick with feeling; intensities are speeding around the room, are inescapable here, are fundamental to what these bodies can do and do.

I created the representation of 'Ground-hold' that appears in Chapter 6 as part of the process of writing this book. That is, it was written with the way it could contribute to responding to the question of politics in education in mind. The content is based on the detailed fieldnotes written sitting in my garden on the afternoon of the encounter. As I wrote them I tried to describe 'what happened', and not what I was thinking or how I was feeling as I watched the events, or how I felt and what I thought as I wrote the notes. As I prepared the account that appears here, I stuck to that approach, trying to represent the events in a way that did not sensationalize, or downplay, or judge, or require a particular mode of engagement from the reader. Of course this is an impossible ambition, but one that felt especially important in relation to this scene given the contentious nature of its material.

As I stood at the front of the assembly hall and watched this scene, I fought back tears that pricked my eyes and accompanied the surging intensity in my body; I fought them back by warning myself that any reaction that could be read as disapproval or failure to behave inside the parameters of the 'professionalism' that frames this place could jeopardize my relationships in the school and perhaps even the research. The flesh on my cheeks crawled, the muscles around my mouth ticked as I demanded of myself the position of the professional educational researcher and battled my body's urge to yell out, to rage, to take flight and instead hold my body in place.

Undoubtedly my entangled experiences, relationships and identifications are projected onto this scene, both in the moment and later (Watkins 2008). Undoubtedly, I identify, or perhaps over-identify with Matthew. I empathize with Matthew. I abhor Mr Newton, who until that moment I liked, and I feel sorry for him because he has to do this to Matthew. I struggle, really struggle, to come to the idea that this is the proper response to Matthew's attempts to flee. As I write about it now my stomach constricts and my chest twists a little, a plum seed sits in my throat; anxiety provoked by revisiting the scene and by the riskiness of stepping outside the boundaries of academic discourse by writing about the scene in this way. Perhaps it is impossible to come to an analysis of the affectivity of the scene through the intensities that erupted on that afternoon, or perhaps it is only possible to come at them in this way. For some readers this account has already undoubtedly called into question my analysis of 'Ground-hold' in Chapter 6, and maybe much of the uncomfortable analysis in this book.

Yet these affects are not 'mine', either right or wrong, balanced or not, exposing professional expertise or failings, personal capacities or shortcomings. Instead, they are a part of this scene, a part of the energies flowing in and between these bodies in this space in these moments. Perhaps the bodies here, children and adults, have seen this collision of bodies before, they have certainly seen bodies collide in 'restraint' many times in the school. Perhaps these bodies have been in such collisions. Perhaps some are excited, amused, angered, defiant. Perhaps some are unmoved by this collision, perhaps some are even tranquil. Were they unmoved the first time they witnessed such collisions or collided in these ways?

What can a body do here? A body can flee, it can rush and struggle, it can lie still and silent; a body can thrust and grasp, twist and hold; a body can sit still, face the front, it can turn and stare and fidget and turn back to the body next to it, also turning, and staring and fidgeting; a body can stand and look, or not look. Is Matthew's attempt to flee, his struggle, his grinning head rising from the floor the life-affirming flow of a body taking flight? Is the capture and ground-hold of Matthew the life-destroying flow of the intensities of authority thwarted, the normative school assemblage refused? Could this bodily collision also be an encounter, a body meeting a body that affirms life despite the meanings that I map onto it here?

Perhaps more radically, could this be a bodily encounter sought by Matthew? Can the pedagogic hopes of this intervention survive these intensities? Is the very humanity of these bodies, children or adults, made vulnerable in this encounter? Can any of these bodies, children or adults, be human in this dehumanizing moment? Can a body learn anything here?

Feelings of a critical educator

In the last section of this chapter I want to turn to the affective and emotional worlds of critical educators, teachers such as Laura and the other teachers who took part in the No Outsiders project. Mainstream approaches to teacher education have little to say about emotions, and when they do approach these it is with a concern for the emotions of learners, not of educators. For instance, in the widely used teacher preparation text *Reflective Teaching* (Pollard *et al.* 2005) beginning teachers are invited to consider the emotions of learners through the notion of 'emotional intelligence', a notion that has already corralled the affective into the rational-scientific discourse of intelligence (Zembylas 2007). Britzman (1998) has critiqued critical pedagogy for being a rationalist project. Yet emotion is an important feature in this – the political commitments to ideas such as justice, equality and democracy that underpin critical pedagogies suggest, if we accept *political feeling*, that educators are emotionally invested in the critical work that they do. Apple and Beane's (2007) collection of the accounts of critical educators is rich with these commitments. Apple and Beane speak only briefly about how it feels to do this sort of work and the professional and personal risks that critical educators take. Yet critical educators' continued struggles and sheer exhaustion in the face of the stresses brought about by marketizing reforms and institutional and administrative systems that both block and discredit critical work, speaks to the depth of feeling that underpins their endeavours. Such feelings have been crucial to feminist pedagogies that have been predicated on the importance of girls' and women's shared experience and the personal. And they have also been developed in Black feminist work, such as that by bell hooks (1984), which emphasizes the feelings of the educator and the learner and their relationship to one another. Freire's later work (Freire 1998, 2001, 2004) foregrounds hopefulness and love, feelings that have been taken up and given centrality by critical scholars drawing on Critical Race Theory and Critical Whiteness studies to envisage race critical pedagogic approaches. For instance, Ricky Lee Allen speaks of the importance of White educators proceeding from a position of love and humility in their pedagogic relations. And love features strongly in both Britzman (1998) and Bibby's (2009) psychoanalytically informed re-thinking of the relationality and affectivity of education. Educators' feelings, then, are a central part of political pedagogic work.

How it *felt* to engage in political pedagogic practices as part of the No Outsiders project was a significant issue for a number of the teachers involved in the project. Laura, whose work has featured already in this book, described how talking about sexualities in the classroom, let alone engaging in the sorts of deconstructive practices that I have described and analysed in previous chapters, left her outside recognizability as a 'good teacher' (or a teacher at all). The impossibility of being recognized as a teacher while engaging in this sort of work was a site of ambivalence for Laura. Laura was committed to her political pedagogies, while also being critical of these interventions through her reading of the limits of their capacity to trouble and reinscribe normative gender-sexuality. She was also critical of the prevailing discourse of teacherly practices and values and experienced its constraints, while also being committed to teaching and to providing her students with the opportunity to succeed in the terms set by the educational system in which they are located.

A useful illustration of this can be found in Laura's account of and reflections on events in Prices Common Primary School after a gay poet, sponsored by the No Outsiders project, led a session in her classroom of 7- to 8-year-old students. Laura's account is thick with a discourse of emotion, with *how it made her feel*. The relationality

of the affectivities and intensities that flow through the bodies of this school community and bring these bodies together in collision and submission can be read within
Laura's accounts. Nevertheless, Laura offers as her own feelings that are framed and
named as recognizable emotional states.

I do not want to suggest that this is a failing or error on Laura's part. Rather,
it underscores the endurance in normative educational and popular discourses of a
conceptualization of feeling as residing in and properly belonging to the interior of
the individual; the responsibilization of the subject who must be self-reflective, self-
knowing and self-correcting in relation to her feelings; and the further individualization of the subject that is effected by this. Laura acts her place in discourse and takes
possession of 'her' feelings as she narrates them.

Poet-gate

Towards the end of the session led by the visiting poet, a child asked the poet if he had
a boyfriend and, subsequently, if he slept with him. The poet answered 'yes' as Laura
stepped in to discuss 'appropriate questions' for students to ask visitors and other
adults in the classroom. The next day, parents began to complain. As Laura begins
to construct a series of accounts of the session and the incidents that followed, she
writes of: 'what I'm sure will become in my school the infamous visit from the poet . . .
I feel a bit like I'm writing a police report' (Laura, web-posting, April 2008). Feeling,
then, is immanent in her experience and reflections, and her feelings are of surveillance and interrogation, of being under suspicion and required to give a satisfactory
account of herself as 'teacher'.

Laura's immediate response to the student's question and the poet's response was
simply that the poet should have fielded the question. She was not overly concerned
by his acknowledgment of his shared bed, however, having already worked with the
storybook *Daddy's Roommate* (Willhaite 1991) which includes an illustration of Daddy
and his 'roommate' in bed together. Laura was more concerned over the fast pacing
and heavy content of the session. Once parents complained, however, Laura was
forced to revise her assessment and act her place in teacher discourse – she took
responsibility and apologized:

> Various parents have come in to complain about yesterday. [One girl's] mum
> asked 'Why was a gay man telling my child he sleeps with men? What on earth hap-
> pened?' So I recounted events and apologized and apologized. [. . .] Apparently
> about 7 parents had been in. Some were upset that their children had been doing
> sex education and others were complaining at the fact that their children had
> been taught about gay people at all.
>
> (Laura, web-postings, April–May 2008)

Parents, acting with feeling, moved from a specific upset over the poet's acknowl-
edgement of his shared bed, to a more general upset that children had been taught sex
education, or even told of the existence of gay men. And in their expression of this
upset, Laura's position as the 'good teacher' is undercut. Laura's ambivalence over the

incident is striking – she is caught between concern, feeling that her lesson had been appropriate, feeling committed to her efforts to do queer work, feeling the weight of others' perspectives press upon her, feeling uncertainty over her queer work: 'I felt really torn between defending what happened or agreeing with [the headteacher]'. She goes on:

> I feel really worried that I've lost the trust of parents AND people in school. [The headteacher] has been supportive of me and when I apologized for rocking the boat, she told me that sometimes boats need rocking. It's tempting to become really defensive, it's tempting to tell myself that I'm doing the right thing . . . but I don't want to do that – become righteous about the rightness of my actions. My perspective is just one perspective and the parents' comebacks reminded me of this very clearly.
>
> (Laura, web-postings, April–May 2008)

The relationality of the feelings circulating here, the centrality of relationships in the pedagogic endeavour, are evident. This relationality is underscored further by Laura's hurt as parents ignore her:

> When I took the kids out at the end of the day, some parents wouldn't make eye contact with me, wouldn't respond to my good wishes for a nice weekend. There were parents whispering in groups. Some parents were the same as always and just as friendly but none of them talked to me about their concerns – friendly ones or hostile seeming ones.
>
> (Laura, web-postings, April–May 2008)

In ignoring and not making eye contact with Laura, the parents do not simply let their feelings be known and so provoke Laura's feelings of hurt and, perhaps, contrition. These not-looking bodies, these flows of affectivities, have the capacity to subjectivate, to put people in their 'proper' place. Indeed, this bodily and affective refusal of acknowledgment has the capacity to refuse subjectivation, to refuse Laura's subjecthood.

As the headteacher shifted from support for 'rocking the boat' to an account that positioned Laura as being in error – a shift that is itself bound up in the affectivity of the events – Laura feels forced to acquiesce to other people's positions, positions that are presented as 'right' professional judgement devoid of feeling:

> Well, [the headteacher] has become less and less supportive. She has basically blamed the poet and has told the parents to be kind to me because 'we all make mistakes'. I don't feel I have any option but to apologize and to tow the line.
>
> (Laura, web-postings, April–May 2008)

Laura's recognizability as a teacher thereby comes to be dependent on her publicly accepting her failings as a teacher – the 'good' (but not-so-good) reflective teacher.

Her feelings of being let-down and unjustly positioned as having made a 'mistake' by her headteacher are also expressed as anger:

> I'm just really cross with [the headteacher]. She likes the project when it is about diversity but runs a mile the moment anything becomes difficult. And it's easy for her to put responsibility back on to me and characterize what happened as my mistake.
>
> (Laura, web-postings, April–May 2008)

Laura offers an account of having felt hurt, let down, regret, anger, defiance, certitude and uncertain over the appropriateness of the session and her management of it. The feelings that she narrates, however, suggest ambivalence; shifting and colliding as the incident, responses to it, and response to those responses unfolded. Ultimately she offers an account to the project team in which her subject-hood as teacher-as-political pedagogue is intact and affirmed, even if this is refused in her school:

> I didn't go to the headteacher to say what had happened because I didn't feel anything awful had happened. Then I really began to doubt myself, my professional judgment, etc., when the parents complained but now I'm back to thinking that what happened was actually ok.
>
> (Laura, web-postings, April–May 2008)

This incident illustrates how political pedagogic work (and all pedagogic work) is not simply a rational act based on 'right' judgement – it is shot through with affectivities. And it is fraught. While such work it is potentially resignifying, it is also subjectivating. Indeed, as the discourses that define what it is to properly be a 'teacher' constrict, work such as this puts subject-hood as 'teacher' at risk. The critical or political pedagogue is not-teacher. And yet the refusal of 'proper' teacher and the practice of the political pedagogue is an enactment of firmly held and *deeply felt* political and ethical positions. These are the life-affirming flows of affects and intensities that far exceed the individual to whom they are attributed and who takes them up as her or his own.

8   Pedagogies of becoming

'Becoming' is an idea that invites us to think about the possibilities for politics in education through the rhizomatics offered by Deleuze and Guattari (1983, 2008). Instead of thinking about the transformation of 'this' school, teacher, pedagogy or student into 'that' school, teacher, pedagogy or student, the rhizomatic move of becoming suggests lines of flight that flee from and potentially scatter the assemblage of meanings, representations, practices and subjectivations that render the 'school', the 'teacher', the 'pedagogic' or the 'student'. These lines of flight suggest a becoming otherwise; a breaking out of or flying from the constraints of the education assemblage and its molar lines, its overcoded meanings and practices, its pervading discourses and its normative and reviled subjects.

Importantly, this is not a becoming otherwise that promises a transformed end point, a new, relatively static state of being. It is a movement from the *middle* and a becoming that is immanent in practice in the present. This is not a revolutionary synthesis or a newly formed abiding subject but a moment or perhaps even an eon in transition, where the desires, energies and affectivities of becoming in the present are the productive possibilities pursued. Coupling the notion of lines of flight with the Foucauldian idea of intervening in the intolerable present to make '*that-which-is*' '*no longer be that-which-is*' invites us to imagine becomings that disrupt the intolerable '*that-which-is*' of the education assemblage and its subjectivations, offering instead the moments of the haecceity of 'this thing' or 'here is' that Deleuze and Guattari (2008) speak of and that were discussed in Chapter 3.

Becomings replace the recognition of the subjugated or disavowed subject with an orientation that is anti-subjectivation. In this sense these are not the becomings of the individual or individual becomings. Rather, this orientation looks for lines of flight from the subjectivities that are part of the constraining assemblage. In this sense, becomings might be seen to move beyond the reinscriptions, the inscribing *again differently*, of the performative politics that we find in the work of Butler (1997a), and which have been pursued as a site of resistance in recent work in education, including in my own (Youdell 2006a, 2006c).

In order to explore the possibilities offered to a radical education politics and pedagogy by becomings, I want to return to Bay Tree 'SEBD' School for boys designated as having 'Social, Emotional and Behavioural Difficulties'. In particular, I want to focus on the headteacher's attempts to remake the abject institution, asking whether his movements in, across and between education, psychiatric and popular assemblages might suggest a becoming-school. I also consider the work of Miss Groves to facilitate the boys' participation in a key national testing programme, asking whether her and the boys' practices might be understood as moments of the 'SEBD' subject becoming-student. And I want to review the practices in Miss Appleton's English classroom to ask whether these are moments in which the abject place, practice and body is becoming-classroom, becoming-pedagogy and becoming-learner.

These sorts of becomings deviate from those explored by Deleuze and Guattari whose anti-subjectivation looks to becoming animal (not human), becoming woman (not man), becoming grass (not tree). The becomings I explore here might suggest simultaneous returns to the binary machines of the education assemblage – school (not psychiatric institution), student (not 'SEBD' or 'disordered' boy), subject (not abject other). These are the risks of rhizomatics that Deleuze and Guattari indicate: collapses into destructiveness, the oblivion of the black hole, reterritorialization. These may well be deterritorializations and reterritorializations that skip from one assemblage to another, that veer from one molar line to another, that call up one regulatory discourse to displace another, and which effect one set of subjectivations to replace another. Here the insistence on the importance of recognizability, of being recognized as human in order to live viable lives, that we find in Butler's (2004b) work perhaps rubs up uncomfortably with a politics that is anti-subjectivation and raises the question of whether anti-subjectivation steps too far beyond a post-identitarian politics (Butler 2007).

If Bay Tree School is understood as a place and a series of people that is constantly threatened with abjection, it seems that the possibility for becomings that may well also be new subjectivations and reterritorializations remains a promise worth pursuing, despite the new constrictions that these bring. It may be that this place is already the black hole; that these people already face the erasure and/or the madness that the black hole threatens. Becoming-school, student, subject on a different line, in a different assemblage, might offer the possibility of livable lives here.

Becoming-school

Bay Tree 'SEBD' School for boys designated as having 'Social, Emotional and Behavioural Difficulties' is set in extensive, but diminishing, grounds with ponds and mature stands of trees. The dense hedgerow perimeter has been thinned out under the current headteacher so that homes and the cricket pitch of the affluent village beyond can be glimpsed from the school, and the school can be glimpsed from the village. Likewise, the high steel fence and gate onto the village side-road that was the main entrance has been removed, offering views into and out of the school through the avenue of trees that flanks the drive. The drive opens onto a large tarmac area bounded on its three sides by a small turn of the century institution; a single-story late 1960s off-the-shelf primary school-style building complete with timber cladding and large square windows; and a row of now well-worn prefab classrooms each with its own access ramp. To the north, waist-high meadow shimmers beyond the timber rail fence that runs behind the prefabs, and beyond the meadow tall natives frame an archetypal English rural scene. Past the old institution and the 1960s school frontage to the south are the dinner hall, gym, and more classrooms, some 1960s and some more recent, as well as a quad, basketball court, 5-a-side pitch, and little-used swimming pool. And beyond these a playing field is being given over to new specialist science and technology buildings, still under construction. These buildings and outdoor spaces are joined together and/or separated by a series of covered walkways, passages, areas of gravel, tarmac, paving and grass, fencing, gates and open and locked doors.

(DY fieldnotes, Bay Tree SEBD School, Summer 2008)

The collection of buildings on this site traces a series of moments in the school's expansion as well as a history of movements and continuities in official conceptions of its population, purposes and pedagogies. This series of moments of expansion give an *ad hoc* feel to the distribution of buildings across the site and to the voids between them: unexpected concreted corners and passages; ways through and dead-ends; inside-outside doors that open freely in one or both directions and others that require a staff-only battery operated fob to unlock. This architectural history and its products make the site challenging to navigate. But it is also constitutive of the multiple and mobile meanings of the place and its people. The institution is school, residential care home, reformatory; it is part of the local community, hidden from it, reviled by it; these are students, patients, inmates; these are teachers, carers, warders. And simultaneously none of these quite 'fit', marking the persistent risk of unintelligibility and continually asking 'what kind of place is this?'

Bay Tree 'SEBD' School can be read as an abject place, a corrupting threat expelled from the education assemblage of proper students and teachers, proper pedagogical practices and relations, proper education endeavours and achievements, proper educational spaces. Located on the fringes of the village and hidden from view, the headteacher's decision to remove fences and thin hedges was reported to have met some local resistance, a resistance that underscores its meaning to the immediate community as a site of containment and concealment for the abject bodies of failed students expelled by mainstream education.

This making visible and new freedom of access and exit, alongside the construction of new specialist facilities for the high-status disciplines of science and technology, might disrupt the assemblages of the psychiatric institution and the 'special' or 'SEBD' school, rejecting their rigid molar lines for more segmented molecular lines – this place is, perhaps, becoming-school. Yet Bay Tree School is a heavily striated space. The dusty grooves of the old institution remain: the Victorian building still stands as home to the boarders and school library; the school retains the series of locked doors that prevent free-movement around the site; and while the high steel perimeter fence has been removed, crossing the now unmarked but still highly visible line of the school's boundary is a heavily disciplined infraction – exit is not 'free' after all.

According to the headteacher, on the removal of the fence a 'deal' was made with the boys that they would not cross the now crossable line, a deal no doubt asserted by the headteacher and promised to the education authority and the local community. The physically constraining and containing fence has been removed, but it continues to do its work in the disciplinary schema of the school – there's running out of lessons, and then there is running *out* – and in the self-disciplining of the boys themselves. Seeing students flee from classrooms to run just inside the line of the unfenced boundary, followed in failing or half-hearted pursuit by teachers, underscores the significance of both the removal of the fence and the reach of the disciplining force of this spatial limit. It also suggests the lure of this line for the body running, fleeing, escaping, in flight.

Taking down the fence, removing the gate, opening up the driveway, building new specialist classrooms might go to remaking or reinscribing this place as school. But it remains on the hinterland of the education assemblage, and within that assemblage it remains inside the 'special' school assemblage: the binary machines, molar lines, striated spaces and subjectivation of these cross-cutting and inter-dependent assemblages are not easy to shake off. Bay Tree might be becoming-school, but this becoming is one that is almost inevitably reterritorialized.

Becoming-student part 1

> We are in the Bay Tree School Music Room where year 9 boys (aged 14) who have chosen to do the National Curriculum test in England for science (SAT) have been brought to complete the test. The details and conditions for the exam are already written on the board: the date, what test it is, the start time, the end time, and the additional time these boys are allocated because of special educational needs. As the boys come into the room and each takes a seat, Lloyd moves behind the seat where Richard has sat down and demands that he moves. 'Hey, that's my chair! Move!' he commands. Richard retorts 'No!' and Lloyd proceeds to grab the chair Richard is sitting in and physically move it, pulling and tipping it to eject Richard from it. Richard squeals and shouts 'Miss!' while holding on to the desk with both hands and wrapping his shins and feet around the chair legs, his face screwed up in determination. Miss Groves intervenes with a firm 'That's enough Lloyd, find somewhere else to sit.' 'It's my seat.' 'No it's not, you don't even come in here, sit somewhere else.' As Lloyd begins to drift away a third boy, Dan, jumps up from his seat and punches Richard hard in the face. Richard screams and begins to cry loudly and the other boys in the room break into energetic laughter. Miss Groves moves quickly, putting herself between the two boys side on and facing Dan she instructs 'No, Dan', holding an arm out towards each boy, her hands flexed, flat palm facing out. As Dan insists he 'hardly hit him', Richard flees the room into the nearby toilet and Miss Groves asks the teaching assistant to follow. Once the class is settled she announces the beginning of the test.
>
> (DY fieldnotes, Bay Tree SEBD School, Summer 2008)

Doing the national science test is not required at Bay Tree School. The then education department, the Department for Children, Schools and Families (DCSF), offers online results tables for this test which include Bay Tree School, but these show that consistently over time the benchmark levels in these tests are attained by zero percent of students here. The table offers the encrypted label 'CYS' to denote that this is a special school, but it does not indicate that the students are not required to take the test. The table simply sucks the data up into the standard form which displays school-by-school results and headlines the absoluteness of the school's and its students' failure in the government department's terms. As standard, the table includes an average point score for the tests and a 'value added' measure. A link to 'value added technical information' allows these results to be decoded and located in the context of other special schools: the low point score is in line with other 'special' schools, the value added is around the national median improvement for 'special' schools. In the constitutive frames of the education assemblage Bay Tree both is and is not recognizable (and recognized) as a school. It is a school – the national indicator is applied and it is included in the tables; but it is not a school – no students ever reach the all-important benchmark; but it is a school – its value added shows its students are learning; but it is not a school – students' improvements are slight, their accomplishments minimal, and would be all but invisible if they were not differentiated out to be measured against other schools of this sort. Bay Tree is not simply one of the education assemblage's abject spaces; its constitutions are inconsistent and mobile, made up of pretences and half-concealed realities.

This is Miss Groves' first year in the school and she has taken on the role of organizing, facilitating and invigilating these tests. In the morning of the test she visits the year 9 tutor rooms inviting and encouraging the boys to take the test, assuring them that it is optional and that they don't have to stay for the whole test, they can just 'give it a try and see how you go'. She manages to collect up about half of the boys in the year group and escorts them to the music room where the test will take place. Across the country all students are required to take the same test on the same day at the same time and Miss Groves' information and instruction on the board indicates that Bay Tree will adhere to this rule. In offering the boys the opportunity to take the national test, at the allotted time and under test conditions Miss Groves opens up a moment for the boys to discard their subjectivation as 'SEBD' boys and 'do normal', in Cath Laws' terms (Laws and Davies 2000). Yet this is not so easily done: the ordinary practices of the 'SEBD' school, teacher and boy designated as having 'Social, Emotional and Behavioural Difficulties' erupt here. Lloyd's demand that Richard give up his seat, and his attempts to physically eject Richard from it are not the practices of the good school student entering an examination room about to embark on a national test. And Dan's punch to Richard's head is far from this. Indeed, even Richard's screaming response to being punched is not that of the 'normal' school boy. Likewise the other boys' laughter at the event exceeds the 'normal' student. Even Miss Groves' rapid move to situate her self physically in the line of Dan's attack is not the practice of the 'teacher'. And for these moments the music room is perhaps no longer even a classroom, let alone an examination room.

This collection of practices, these bodies and their collisions disrupt and fly from their constitution as student and teacher and in doing so they unsettle the fragile constitution of school. These are the practice of the 'SEBD' boy: unruly, violent, threatening; resisting, screaming, fleeing; undisciplined, uncaring, laughing. These are the practices of the warder, police officer, security guard, good Samaritan. This is the street, the park, the unruly space beyond the disciplining reach of authority or social convention. Once the incident has passed, however, Miss Groves resumes the practices of teacher-invigilating-serious-test and the boys, including Richard in a small room across the corridor, take up the practices of student-taking-serious-test with (almost) the still, seated, silent, industrious bodies of the 'good' ('normal') student. As they sit quietly at their desks concentrating on their tests, the boys might be understood as 'doing normal' – Miss Groves has created a smooth space in the striated surface of the 'special' school in which these boys are becoming-student.

Here we see the chaos, failures and aberrant behaviours and corrections of the 'special' school; the madness, diagnoses and therapeutic interventions of the psychiatric institution; the discipline, self-discipline, normalcy and learning of the mainstream school; the hetero-masculine toughness and violence of the places beyond authority's reach. The spaces, systems, practices, subjectivations and affectivities here seem to move across and between assemblages, traversing the education assemblage, and within it the 'special school' assemblage, the psychiatric assemblage, the sex-gender assemblage. This scene is perhaps interassemblage, deterritorializing and reterritorializing these in their movements. Might it be these very movements that open up the possibilities for becomings here?

Becoming-student part 2

As the science test begins I am sitting at the front edge of the classroom observing. A few minutes in, Tom, who is sitting on the front row, makes eye contact with me and puts his hand half up mouthing 'help please miss'. Well-known to the teacher I go over to help him as the exam accommodation allows. Tom waits for me to read the whole text but I suggest that he read the bits he can read and I'll read the bits he can't. I crouch by his desk (later shifting to sit on a chair) and we make our way through the whole text 'whispering aloud' together with Tom tracing the words with his forefinger. As we are doing this a voice calls in the open classroom window 'Tom, you're gay!' and Tom calls back 'So are you . . .' but his retort fades out before he gets to the end of it. [. . .] The teacher has told the boys that they can leave the room and go to another designated classroom as they wish, either when they finish the test or have had enough of doing it. Tom stays for the whole period and by the time he is stopped to go to break he is one of only 2 boys still in the room.

After break time some of the boys come back to take the second part of the test. Tom goes to his previous seat but before he can ask for my help or I can offer it, Martin, the boy sitting at the desk behind him, starts to give him grief saying 'She sat with you all the way through! You had help the whole time!' The teacher interjects saying 'He had a little bit of help' and they repeat the exchange: 'She sat there the whole time!' and 'He had a little bit of help'. Tom shifts around a bit in his chair but doesn't argue it. I wait for him to ask me to help, I look at him, I had anticipated helping him again but now I expect him not to accept my help. He doesn't look at me and turns the test book cover page over to look at the first question. He closes the test book. He opens it again and then closes it, putting his head down on his arm that is lying on the table. I try to offer him eye contact, thinking that maybe I can offer him help once the test has started and the accusations of too much help have passed. But he does not look at me and then says quietly to nobody 'Can't be bothered with this' and leaves. The teacher goes out to him but he doesn't come back in.

(DY fieldnotes, Bay Tree SEBD School, Summer 2008)

The concept of subjectivation invites a reading of the ways in which Tom and the other boys, the teacher and I are made as particular sorts of subjects through these practices. Reading with subjectivation we can see Tom constituted hetero-masculine boy who does not take being cussed, good student who does his test, bad student who calls out in an exam, good-enough student who stops himself calling out, failed learner who cannot read his test book, failed hetero-masculine boy/proto-man who cannot read his test book. The threat of abjection haunts these constitutions: gay bodies have no place in the hetero-masculine assemblage and illiterate bodies or bodies out of control have no place in the education assemblage.

Tom read his exam paper aloud with me inserting assistance as necessary and so acted his place in a discourse of the good (compliant) student, even as his limited reading constituted him a bad (failed) learner. Yet as this failure is pointed out 'he had help' (from a woman) and is defended not by Tom but by the (woman) teacher – his double failure becomes inescapable – he is neither learner nor hetero-masculine boy/man. Yet Tom is not either a good student or a failed learner, he is not either a cool hetero-masculine boy or a good student, he is not either a cool hetero-masculine boy or a recognizable learner. And he is not simply abject. In opting to take his test he, and the others with him, press against the boundary of recognizability, a possibility of identification with and recognition as student-learner that the teacher/school makes possible (perhaps) by offering the test to the boys. And yet in the extra time given, in the help with reading, in working at the boundary of exam conditions the boys' place at the edge of recognizability is reinscribed and the threat of abjection remerges. There is no once and for all resignification or re-subjectivation here, but in this moment and in these practices the boys might be becoming-student, even if this is yet another subjectivating territorialization.

My own place in this scene, my projections and constitutions, are significant. I anticipated assisting Tom during the second test, but as the legitimacy of my help is contested and becomes the site of Tom's subjugation I feel unable to offer it. I see my place in his constitution in this moment as a failed learner-proto-man and I project my own shame and embarrassment at my place in this, and at his failure, and I imagine Tom shamed and embarrassed. In the moment, it does not occur to me that he may well be used to such assistance from teacher figures; used to this assistance being observed by the other boys; and, no doubt, to the teasing from other boys who do not need help. I say in the fieldnotes that I write later the same day that 'I know I'm buying into a masculine-capable construct', but I do it anyway; inscribing the hetero-masculine assemblage, overcoding the moment with its binary machines, imagining that Tom cannot be seen by the other boys to be assisted by me now that the failed hetero-masculine, failed learner has been called up.

I enjoyed helping him during the first test and reflecting on this enjoyment I am reminded of the little teacher that I was as a child when I helped other children to read whenever I visited the primary school classrooms of my mother. I see myself becoming-teacher, complete with normative registers of entangled gender and apti- tude, complete with pity and shame; the well-meaning teacher whose good inten- sions do not compensate for the constraints of her subjectivating practices. Assisting Tom again might have opened another moment for becoming-student, becoming otherwise to the hetero/masculine without need and without need for female assis- tance. Yet I acted my place in hetero-feminine discourse; the woman who acquiesces to the masculine, who does not expose masculinity's limits and shores up its imagined infallibility. And as I act my place I am implicated in constituting these subjects; con- stituting myself and Tom and Miss Groves and the other boys in these terms. These subjectivations bear down on me and I slip into the grooves on the classroom walls and score the room again with the deep striations of sex-gender.

Becoming-otherwise

We are in a year 9 (aged 14) English lesson at Bay Tree School, with two teachers and five boys. Like many of the classrooms of Bay Tree School the tables here are spaced out and lined up one behind the other. Each standard school table is wide enough to accommodate two seats but each has a single chair establishing the convention that the boys sit individually in rows with their backs to each other facing the front. Additional chairs are moved around by the staff who sit neat and contained next to the boys during the lesson. The teachers take turns to read aloud from *Gulf* by Robert Westall (1992), pausing to ask questions and discuss the narrative and literary devices. The boys each have a copy of the book to follow. Ed sits neatly at his desk, square on, feet on the floor, arms on the table-top. As one teacher reads he asks the other if he can draw on the cover of his exercise book. She nods permission and so he asks for coloured pens and gets 'shhh-ed' by the other boys. The teacher gets him coloured pens and sits by him as he draws and colours-in while the other teacher reads. Terry sits leaning his elbows on his table, his face cupped in both hands and his legs outstretched and spread wide but his toes turned in making him knock-kneed under the table. Adam sits relaxed in his chair, legs slightly apart, knees slightly bent, elbows on his table, book open, following as the teacher reads. Anth reclines behind his desk on a soft, low-level comfy chair that he has swopped for his school chair. As the teacher reads he swings round so that he is lying sideways over the chair, his back supported, his head drooping down off one side and his legs off the other. He holds the book in one hand and follows as the teacher reads. Momentarily he puts the book down and reaches his arms back over his head to meet the floor – I recognize his controlled movement as a 'crab' from gymnastics. Richard kneels over his table, with one knee on each of the two chairs behind the desk. He rests on his elbows and leans his body right over the desk and presses the book flat on the table-top with one hand and follows the text with the forefinger of his other hand. He fidgets and shakes his foot rapidly and changes position letting one foot drop down to reach the floor behind him so he is part standing, part leaning, part kneeling. I sit upright and still, following the text, alone at an empty desk.

(DY fieldnotes, Bay Tree SEBD School, Summer 2008)

Thinking about these bodies through the normative discourses of the proper student and her/his proper deportment and practices that frame classrooms, we can see bodies that are intelligible as student, bodies that in some ways approximate student, and bodies that are beyond the bounds of intelligibility in these terms.

Ed's body sits neatly at the desk, the picture of good student deportment. But it also calls out over the top of the teacher reading. Calling out when the teacher is reading, particularly when the call is not related to the set task, is not the proper practice of the 'good' student or learner. Calling out might more often be reserved as response to a teacher's invitation, or perhaps if directly related to the task in hand. This calling out is to request an activity that is on the border of legitimacy; colouring in with felt tip pens is not the proper pursuit of the year 9 English classroom – it is not at the teacher's instruction, and more ordinarily it might be the proper pursuit of a younger child. Furthermore, constituted as a feminine pursuit, this colouring in and its public request might be a feminizing one and so one that puts Ed's hetero-masculinity at risk. Yet while he is 'shhh-ed' by the other boys – who in 'shhh-ing' him constitute their own proper student-hood, or at least their proper place as listeners – Ed is not censured by the teachers. Rather, his request is approved and felt-tip pens provided. While the teacher reads, pausing from time to time to ask questions about the unfolding story and the literary devices that the story-teller makes use of, Ed ignores his copy of *Gulf* and instead listens while he decorates the cover of his English book. That this body is listening, although not reading along, and paying attention to the lesson is evidenced by his participation in the discussions that take place when the teacher pauses. He calls out, does not read, he colours-in, but he remains recognizable as student and as learner in this classroom.

Terry's body might be read as being on the border of the normative student and normative masculinity. The head held in hands might fail to constitute the bright attentiveness of the student body engaged in learning, instead risking the inattentive, post-lunch sleepy just-tolerable student. The turned in toes and knock-knees surely miss the sturdy certainty of hetero-masculinity, instead risking awkward failed masculinity or the failure to manage the body of the subject not-quite in control, or even the pathological. But Terry follows the text and takes part in discussions – he is student and learner.

Adam's body is the archetypal good student-learner body. This body is straight and neat, clear right angles and symmetry. This body follows the text, apparently no forefinger is needed to trace the text and keep the eye in line. Indeed, perhaps this is the body that models the mind's mythical autonomy from and easy control over a subordinate body that sits correctly while the mind learns, as if this body did not learn to do this and will not resist or rebel. Adam is good student and learner.

Anth's body reclines over the low, soft, chair that would ordinarily be reserved for the teacher, or only be accessible at the teacher's invitation. Not only does Anth's body recline, it lies down, it stretches and reaches, it does gymnastic movements in the English classroom. And yet, apart from the few moments when Anth has to set down his book in order to use both hands to support his crab position, this body continues to hold the book, turn the pages, appears to read. This body is undertaking the core task of learning that is asked of students in this classroom. And in so doing, Anth is constituted student and learner.

Richard's body shifts and shakes, it does not sit at the desk, rather it kneels, and mounts, and climbs, bridging the floor, the seat, the desk in an ongoing series of movements. This is not the properly deported, still and docile body of the 'good' student. Indeed, the body that cannot 'simply' sit might not be student at all, but instead in its very movement it might risk being the disturbed body of the pathologi-cal (non-)subject. And yet as this body leans, and climbs, shifts and mounts, it also holds the book and follows the text with a forefinger; Richard is, it appears, reading the text as the teacher reads aloud. Once again, this body is engaged in the core task of learning of this lesson. And so Richard is student and learner.

What can these bodies do here? The normative deportments, movements and practices that these bodies do not enact might, in another space (a mainstream class-room or even another classroom at Bay Tree School), foreclose intelligibility as stu-dent and learner. Indeed, the movements and deportments of these non-normative bodies may well have been taken up as markers of abnormality, cemented in the clas-sificatory systems on which various diagnoses of social, emotional and behavioural difficulties and disorders rest, and deployed as evidence of these boys' proper place in the 'SEBD' school.

In the discourses of mainstream education, as well as in prevailing discourses of 'special educational needs', 'Social, Emotional and Behavioural Difficulties' might be read as the eruption of affectivity – the refusal, failure of, or move beyond the rational self-control of the student-learner. Whether this is through manifestations deemed bad/unacceptable/challenging ('behavioural'?, 'social'?) or deemed aberrant ('social'?, 'emotional'?) it is this excess that renders these subjects unrecognizable as 'student' or 'learner'. Within the constraints of school discourse no such eruptions are acceptable and their recognizability is restricted to/through a constitutive discourse of 'SEBD'.

Yet in this English classroom these bodies can lounge, they can climb, they can shift, they can slump, they can call out, they can be still and straight and crooked. The conventions of the properly deported student body do not delineate who can be stu-dent here. The conventions of the proper student body do circulate in this classroom – variously approximated by the bodies of Ed and Terry and Adam – but the norma-tive body does not constrain recognizability here; this is not all a body can do.

These bodies put me in mind of Paul, a boy at Plains High in Sydney, Australia who was designated as having special educational needs. I wrote in *Impossible Bodies, Impossible Selves* (Youdell 2006a) about how the constant movements of his body – drumming, fidgeting, putting his hands on his head, getting out of his seat, leaning against the wall – were not incorporated into/as the ordinary practices of his English classroom as the variously moving bodies are in the Bay Tree English classroom. Rather his body's movements, his failure to corral his body into the proper stillness of the good student, rendered him an impossible student and led him to being ejected from the classroom.

This English classroom at Bay Tree School, these teachers and their pedagogy are quite different: they allow bodily intensities and affectivities to flow. They do not encourage or entreat these moving, feeling bodies, except perhaps silently through the still, controlled bodies of the teachers, but nor do they censure or constrain them. No attempt to corral bodies into the shape and stillness that would constitute them 'student' in the discourse of mainstream schooling is made here. Instead moving feeling bodies appear to simply be allowed and the lesson takes place. Elsewhere these would be recognized as the unmanageable bodies or bodies beyond management of the 'disordered' or 'SEBD' child, and so would be the objects of correction and discipline. Yet here bodies that are outside meaning, or are only intelligible as abject in the education assemblage, become meaningful. This intelligibility is not just of the subject made meaningful through discourses of 'special educational needs', emotional and behavioural 'disorder' or 'difficulty' and 'SEBD', but also of the subject becoming student and learner. In conducting the lesson while these bodies recline, stretch, reach, climb and shift, as well as remain still, upright and contained, these bodies are avowed and recognized as student and learner. Bodies that elsewhere would be unintelligible as student or learner – the impossible subjects of schooling – are rendered intelligible. These teachers' pedagogy, in this classroom, creates a space for the intelligibility of the non-normative learner.

Key to this pedagogy is the abandonment, on the part of the teachers and students, of a mind/body binary in which the control and constraint of the volatile body is positioned as a prerequisite to recognition as student and to the process of learning. The cognition/body binary machine is overturned, as I sit in this classroom I can almost see it; the faded enamel and bleached timber of a Victorian cast iron and wood machine, its shiny 1960s adaptations dulled, its reels of belched-out neo-liberal paperwork now yellowed, the megaphone that yelled out instruction now silenced, mechanisms jammed, turned over on its side and lying pock-marked and dusty at the edge of the room where the teacher's desk has also been abandoned.

These are not just moving bodies; they are feeling bodies. Affectivities and intensities flow through and between these bodies as they shift and stretch, move and shake. It might be that in its stillness and control, its approximation of the 'good' student body whose constriction allows the mind to learn, Adam's body, for instance, is an implicit bodily censure of the movements of the other bodies here – a bodily equivalent to the 'shhh-ing' of Ed's calling out. But this does not undercut the recognition offered by the teachers' apparently casual, but likely fully intended, continuation with the lesson while these bodies shift and move. In this classroom, then, the flow of affect creates, rather than forecloses, the possibility of learning. Feeling and the bodily motion it precipitates is an integral part of this classroom and of learning inside it.

This pedagogy and this classroom might, then, be understood as one where a line of flight – the gap between cognition and embodiment – is followed into affect; a line of flight that is both a pedagogic becoming and becoming reader, listener, imaginer, student, learner. Smooth surfaces are found within the deep striations of the school space delineated by the education assemblage. Perhaps this might be the pedagogic fold.

The text that the teachers have chosen to read with the boys seems to enhance the possibilities for becoming that this classroom offers. Indeed, as I demonstrate below, the text itself might be understood through the lenses of affectivities, bodily intensities, resignification and anti-subjectivation. Indeed, the text might be read as being a story of becoming.

Gulf, by Robert Westall (1992), is an account of an English boy, Andy, whose connections with others – both human and animal, both present and at a great distance – are so profound that he *becomes* them. The story is told from the perspective of his older brother Tom, who knows him as Figgis – the name of Tom's imaginary friend from before Andy was born. The story takes place during the first Gulf War and its central story is that of Figgis' becoming a boy who is an Iraqi soldier. This becoming consumes Figgis so wholly that for a period he is almost only the Iraqi boy, Latif. This becoming manifests in Figgis speaking Arabic and enacting the behaviours of a young solider in a fox-hole and under attack; in his feelings of anger and disgust at the US/UK military invasion, patriotism towards Iraq, love of the soldiers fighting close by him, discomfort at being infested with lice, and anxiety at the threat of, and terror at the actuality of attack; as well as in physical changes to his body and even face that are so profound that he no longer looks like Figgis.

The manifestation of this becoming are interpreted by the majority of the medical profession, and reluctantly by Figgis' parents, as symptoms of psychiatric illness, and for a time Figgis is committed to a psychiatric hospital. Figgis' brother Tom and his Muslim psychiatrist Dr Rashid, however, refuse this diagnosis – they understand that Figgis is becoming Latif. Rather than resisting this becoming, they accept it and allow it, providing props such as pillows-becoming-sand bags and World War Two rifle-becoming-machine gun to Figgis-becoming-Latif in his psychiatric hospital room. As the becoming intensifies, the narrative does not promise the happy return of Figgis to his 'true' self. Indeed, for a period both brother and doctor entertain as a real possibility the idea that Figgis will die when the soldier Latif is almost inevitably killed by the US/UK air attacks. That Figgis does not die in the moment that Latif is killed is left unexplained but recognition and consolation as Latif, the avowal of this becoming, rather than psychiatric treatment, appears significant. While Figgis survives and is discharged 'healthy' to return home, he is not returned to his former 'self'. The 'self' that survives is Andy; it is Figgis, whose relationality and identification with others is so profound that he becomes them, who is no longer evident, who perhaps did die along with Latif in his fox-hole. In the erasure/death of Figgis-Latif we might read an end to becoming that is some kind of 'cure' – Andy is transformed from a strange and unusual boy into a 'normal' boy. Yet despite the disappearance of Figgis, Andy cannot be 'normal'; and the figure of Figgis continues to offer the possibility of become otherwise to both Andy and to the reader. Andy is *re*-turned, he is, perhaps, continually becoming.

Written in the same moment as Baudrillard's now famous text 'The Gulf War Did Not Take Place' (Baudrillard 1995), a critique of the Western representations of the Gulf War and the easy separation of right and wrong, good and bad, just and unjust, runs through the story. While Figgis' parents have recurrent debates over the properness of the military action, Figgis' becoming demands the recognition of the lived realities of warfare, the humanity of the 'enemy' and the value of lives on both sides that are hidden in mainstream representations. In this sense the story does similar work to Baudrillard's account.

Reviews and synopses of *Gulf* targeted at teachers and resources available on teaching websites often focus on technical aspects of English language learning matched to government-set targets that can be pursued through the book (DCS 2004; HGFL 2008). Less emphasis is placed on the possibilities for social, political, relational or affective explorations and encounters that are opened up by the book, although the conceptual language and media representation of war does feature in these. And in academic engagements with the text, these issues can be found foregrounded (Agnew and Fox 2005; Mallen 2004). In one synopsis (Rosen 2003) the relationship between Figgis and Latif is positioned as one of 'Doppelganger'; a positioning that marks their discreetness and separation through its reduction of their connection to one of likeness. This characterization undercuts the possibility of any more profound connection between the two boys or of them being something other or more than two boys – the certainty and fixity of the unitary subject is assured by this reduction to the 'double'. In another resource (K-State Libraries 2008) the story is offered as part of a collection dealing with 'mental illness'. While this introduces a topic that is not ordinarily the subject matter of the school classroom, it restricts the range of available interpretations of, and encounters with, the text. Understood through a psychiatric discourse the story is reduced to one of descent into and recovery from mental illness, in a developmental discourse it is the proper transition from childhood imagination or fantasy to the rationality and worldliness of the beginnings of adulthood.

In the text itself the relationship between Figgis and Latif and the transformations that Figgis undergoes are left open – Doctor Rashid speculates about 'telepathy' (Westall 1992: 74) and agrees with Tom that it is 'a mystery of nature' (Westall 1992: 81). After Andy's discharge Tom asks Doctor Rashid, 'Do you think he was mad? At all?' and Doctor Rashid replies,

> No, I do not think he was mad at all. I think he was too sane. He felt too much for his fellow men. It is the rest of the world that is mad. But do not dare quote me on that.
>
> (Westall 1992: 91)

The text's openness and its refusal to close down, explain or diagnose offers the possibility to resist reductive interpretations that corral these transformations into normative discourses of psychiatric illness, childish invention, or simply the 'double'. Instead, this openness allows these to be something more productive; to be becomings, even if these becomings are refused by prevailing discourse and open to rapid recuperation and reterritorialization.

A key effect of this openness within the text is that it disrupts the notion of a contained, singular and abiding self. Instead, the self is one of connection and malleability – becoming someone else, someone 'out there' as well as a different self – is possible. The mutability and relationality of the self that the text makes possible means that who/what we have been and who/what we are might not be who/what we will be; we might be something or even someone else. For the boys in this Bay Tree classroom, who have been designated as having 'Social, Emotional and Behavioural Difficulties', the story recognizes the non-normative, aberrant and even 'mad' subject and insists that this subject might not be 'mad' or 'aberrant' after all. And this is a recognition that is similarly offered in this classroom. Furthermore, feeling and its relationality are foregrounded in the story – it is what Figgis-Latif *feels*, not what common sense rationality or psychiatric expertise 'knows' that is central. Feeling and relationality, then, and feeling and relationality that is unrecognizable other than through registers that diagnose, censure or erase, is not only legitimated – it is prioritized over prevailing ways of knowing the subject and knowing itself. And again, feeling, relationality and bodily intensities are legitimated in this classroom.

If we de-pathologize Figgis-Latif and the bodies and boys in this classroom, as their teachers do, and understand movements, affectivities, practices, identifications and subjectivities through affectivities and becomings we might find something of an antidote to the linear, the fixed and rational (or otherwise) subjects of education. This antidote may allow boys such as these to be multiply recognizable and, perhaps, recognizable in new ways. Perhaps here they are becoming-student and learner, a becoming that transforms student, learner and learning itself.

9 Becoming-radical in education

In this book I have considered the shape and nature of education in the contemporary moment and explored a series of analytical tools and forms of politics that might be useful for understanding and intervening in the unjust processes of education. As I have done this I have considered the politics of school knowledge and examined attempts to intervene in and unsettle this. I have examined the ways that students and educators are made inside schools and the implications of these processes. I have explored educators' attempts to deploy political pedagogies on a small scale in the everyday of school and classroom life. I have investigated the place of feelings in schooling and how these are relevant for radical education politics and their enactment. And I have looked for schools, classrooms, teachers and pedagogies that might disrupt the exclusions created by the business as usual of schooling. In this final chapter I draw these threads together in order to begin to map some of the possible terrains that political pedagogies might act on and consider the potential of these tactics to cause school trouble.

So what do the accounts and analyses of the preceding chapters tell us? They tell us that schools are sites of trouble: the trouble that students find themselves in, like the boys whose educational trajectories take them to schools such as Bay Tree School for students identified as having 'Social, Emotional and Behavioural Difficulties' ('SEBD'); the trouble that teachers find themselves in, like Laura who introduced talk of sexualities and implicitly the inference of homosexual sexual desire and practice into her primary school classroom; the trouble that educational institutions and their staff find themselves in as they face the incessant demand for ever-increasing performance in relation to tightly defined and crude measures of achievement; and the trouble that educators might make in and for this education assemblage.

They also tell us that schools are troubling places – they are sites where knowledges, subjectivities and affectivities are produced, regulated and erased and where subjects, both students and educators, are schooled in the acceptable and unacceptable forms that these take. Yet as my analysis has shown, these processes of schooling both students and educators in the normative knowledges, practices, subjectivities and feelings of schools and society can be and are troubled in a range of ways on a daily basis. These practices of troubling schools, however, are no more straightforward or determined than the processes of schooling that they seek to interrupt. They are themselves troubling as they misfire, having unintended or unforeseen effects that reinscribe normative forms or are reterritorialized by the education assemblage. The trouble of troubling schooling then raises further pressing questions of what, precisely, we might seek to trouble, how we might go about this troubling, and how we deal with the consequences, both intended and unintended, of our interruptive practices.

If we accept that the inequalities and exclusions that are faced inside schools are not aberrations but are in fact produced by the very business as usual of education, its taken for granted knowledges and practices, then it is this taken for granted business as usual that we are seeking to interrupt. With this ambition we might look to insert the unknown and the unknowable into the official knowledges of both the curriculum and the institution, recognize as viable learners those students who are designated as beyond the bounds of acceptability, allow disorder to infiltrate the regimen of daily school life and experience and engage affectivities in context framed and contained by rationality.

The question of causing school trouble asks us to consider what forms such a politics might take and what the goals of these politics might be. It also highlights what for me is an as yet unresolved dilemma over the place and significance of intentionality, the individual and collective action. That is, should these politics take as their focus and key concern the micro-level of meaning and practice in everyday life in school or should they be concerned with institutions, systems and structures at the meso- and macro-level? Should these politics be enacted at the level of the concerns, commitments and practices of individuals or should they look to bring people together and mobilize collective actions? And if they remain at the micro-level and/or if they involve only the tactics of an individual, and/or if they flow from tacit understandings or affective desires rather than political analysis and conscious intents, can they be conceived of as politics at all?

Through my engagements with practices in real educational contexts in the preceding chapters I have endeavoured to begin to address these dilemmas. I have done this by drawing on a series of lenses for conceptualizing the political that seem to me to have particular potential to enrich both our thinking and our political practice.

Enacting performative politics

Judith Butler's 'performative politics', which focuses on the potential for meaning to be reinscribed, is one such conceptual tool, as is her work on recognition and the way that a life that is livable means being recognized as human. This way of thinking about political subjects and practices, and the political nature of both subjectivity and practice, invites us to practice in ways that unsettle the normative knowledges, meanings and subjects of school spaces and open-up the possibility for usually disallowed knowledges, meanings, and subjects to become recognizable and legitimate. In the preceding chapters I have shown this unsettling and reinscription in day-to-day school and classroom life. I have shown this effected implicitly through the headteacher's resignification of Bay Tree School. I have shown this effected implicitly through the practices of the students at Bay Tree 'special' School. I have shown this effected through the practices of Miss Groves and Miss Appleton at Bay Tree 'special'

School, not underpinned for them by Butler's framework, but with what seems to be a clear intention to open up the spaces available to the boys to be students and learners. And I have shown this unsettling and reinscription effected through the practices of Laura, the teacher involved in the No Outsiders project, who explicitly sought to take insights from Butler's performative politics and explore and experiment with these in her work with her primary school students.

Three key queries seem to emerge strongly from these instances. One is that the effects of these students' and teachers' practices were not necessarily *only, especially or enduringly reinscriptive*. As Butler has stressed, the effects of the performative are contingent, provisional and subject to misfire *and so are its reinscriptions*. I showed at various points in my analysis the reinscriptive *and* recuperative effects of the practices and discourses that circulate in school spaces.

The second is the apparently *individual* shape of these reinscriptive practices or effects – one headteacher trying to remake the meaning of a school by changing it materially; one small group of students making themselves something in a place that insists they are nothing; one or two teachers setting aside classroom conventions to engage with and include students whose bodies, feelings and practices too often mean they are already beyond schooling; one teacher actively trying to deploy performative politics in her teaching and everyday interactions with students. It is important to recognize that this final teacher, Laura, participated in the No Outsiders research project that involved a team of scholars and teachers in collaborative research into the forms that sexualities equalities work in primary schools might take. In this sense, while Laura was the only teacher in her school involved in the project, her practices were not wholly those of an isolated individual. As my accounts have shown, her pursuit of these politics was in some way understood in her school and received some partial, conditional and at times fragile support there. And she was part of a wider network of educators who in varying ways shared concerns with sexualities equalities. Laura's participation in this project was almost certainly why she engaged these practices in such a sustained way, yet it is possible that with her appreciation of these ideas and her own political commitments she would have engaged in practices of this sort without the project. Furthermore, while the No Outsiders project undoubtedly provided Laura with resources, support and a space for exploring collectively her practices and their effects, participation in the project was not straightforward and was implicated in constituting differently positioned and valued sorts of practices, subjects and politics. In this sense, being part of this network closed down spaces and modes of recognition for Laura as well as opening these up. And ultimately, while the project team did provide extensive support to the participating teachers, when they were practising in their own schools and classrooms the teachers were essentially 'on their own'. The collective political action established and enabled by the project was, then, provisional, contingent and internally contested and it would be difficult to argue that through her involvement in this collective the reinscriptive or other radical political effects of Laura's practices somehow outstripped those of the other teachers I have discussed here.

Following from this, the third query that arises concerns the significance of *conscious intent* in these practices. My research at Bay Tree School for boys designated as having 'Social, Emotional and Behavioural Difficulties' did not include talking in-depth with Miss Groves or Miss Appleton about their own ways of conceptualizing their practices, their motivations for practising in the ways they did, and their hopes for the effects that their ways of working might have. Miss Groves has read and discussed with me my accounts of Bay Tree School and while she found my interpretations provocative and stimulating, she was not working directly with these ideas or seeking primarily or precisely the effects that I suggest the practices I explore might have. The intentions and effects of these teachers' practices, then, are not tied together in a direct or causal way, nor are they are only explicable through a single framework. Nevertheless, exploring motivations, understandings and practices with these teachers could have offered further conceptual frameworks for understanding and interpreting these. Such an exploration might also have offered a further layer of insight into the disconnection between intention, meaning and effect as well as the multiplicity of effects that practices might have, and so *the possibilities for causing school trouble and for developing a politics that is predicated on multiple and even contradictory ambitions, worldviews and politics.* In contrast, Laura explicitly took up performative politics, actively pursued ways of enacting these in her teaching and everyday life in school and was engaged in ongoing and collaborative reflection on this. Yet, as I have shown, the effects of Laura's practices were not guaranteed by her intentions and are open to interpretation not only through the conceptual frame with which she was working.

Enacting a politics of becoming

While performative politics has the capacity to reinscribe meaning and the meanings of subjectivities, the need for recognition and so recognizability remain central. In a move away from a politics of unsettling and shifting subjectivations, Deleuze and Guattari (2008) take up a position that is anti-subjectivation. That is, understanding subjectivation as one of the multiple forces of the assemblage they look for possibilities of moving beyond the constraints of subjectivity and the individual itself. For Deleuze and Guattari, affective intensities, understood as the pre-personal flows of bodily sensations, hold the potential to scatter the subjectivating force of the assemblage and offer a possible way out of the bind of subject positions and identity politics. For them affectivities allow us to escape subjectivities and the limits of working in, with and against them. Affective intensities open up the possibility of becoming-otherwise because they scatter the rigid lines of subjectivations and in so doing promise to deterritorialize the assemblage which subjectivations are a part of. These becomings suggest a change of state, a transition, a passing between. This is not a movement from one thing into another thing, from one state of being into another state of being. Rather, becomings are an invitation to incessant flows and movements.

Studying becomings and their deterritorializations in 'concrete social fields' as Deleuze and Parnet suggest (1983: 90), I have shown how pedagogic encounters are shot through with these affective intensities: the affectivities underpinning and provoked by Laura and her teaching assistant Jenny's contestation of Tomas' assertion about the properly gendered allocation of 'muscles' and 'boobies'; Miss Groves and Miss Appleton's accommodation of the intensities that flow around the classroom as the boys luxuriate in a hangover and Mr Newton's intervention into this; the affective intensities surging around the school hall as Mr Newton grapples Matthew to the ground and Matthew resists this; the force of affectivities as Laura, her students, their parents and the headteacher experience the aftermath of the gay poet's school visit. In all of these instances the significance of affective intensities, their life affirming productivity, their capacity to scatter the education assemblage and deterritorialize it, and the reterritorializing force of the molar lines of this assemblage are evident.

I have also read becomings-otherwise – finding gaps in the molar lines of the assemblage and pursuing lines of flight – in the practices of the headteacher, Miss Groves and Miss Appleton and the boys in Bay Tree 'special' School: I have suggested the abject 'SEBD' institution deterritorialized and becoming-school, the abject 'SEBD' boy deterritorialized and becoming-student and learner and the requirement to contain and correct these abject body deterritorialized and becoming-pedagogy. These becomings are also open to reterritorialization: Bay Tree 'special' School simultaneously remains on the education hinterland, the boys remain schooling's abject and the pedagogies employed in Miss Appleton's English classroom do not undo the prior and future subjectivations of these boys' impossibility as learners.

Just as performative politics raises queries about reinscription and recuperations, so each of these instances suggests both lines of flight and their containment. Each of these becomings is a moment of the deterritorialization of the education assemblage and a moment of reterritorialization. Just as the recuperations of performative politics do not undercut their significance or potential force, so these reterritorializations do not undercut a politics of becoming-otherwise. While these movements do not transform the education assemblage once and for all, attending to them allows us to see the gaps in the molar lines of the assemblage and experience the lines of flight that scatter these. Within my analysis, struggles for recognition, to be recognizable, and the black-hole that is risked when subjectivation is refused, remain evident and suggest an incessant return of the subjectivated subject. Nevertheless, mapping the flows of affective intensities and seeing the moments in which these scatter the subjectivations that are part of the education assemblage offers glimpses of education, its spaces and its subject becoming-otherwise and suggest that the education assemblage might be converted, or even disassembled. While pursuing affective intensities and the becomings that these promise may not act to disassemble the education assemblage on their own, they do offer a further line of flight that we might take. Becomings-otherwise do not posit a transformed future endpoint but are movements from the middle that can be read as deterritorializations and assemblage conversions that are immanent in the present. Nevertheless, becomings-otherwise do offer a way of understanding and engaging with these practices and demonstrate the possibilities for lines of flight to deterritorialize the education assemblage in this moment.

These analyses also raise again the pressing question of the place of the individual and intentionality in enacting these becomings as a politics. That is, what is the place of the individual, the subjectivated subject, and its intentions in a politics that is anti-subjectivation. Can politics *be* anti-subjectivation, and if it can, 'who' practises these politics when it is the very subjectivation of and as an individual, and the will and rationality mapped onto them, that lines of flight flee from? This is more than a post-identitarian politics that refuses to move from or place at the centre a call to an abiding subject; it is a politics that refuses to move from even a subjectivated subject, it refuses to move from a subject at all. Despite this, Deleuze's politics are populated. Deleuze's work with Parnet posits the possibility that lines of flight might equate to a becoming-revolutionary. Rather than thinking about individuals organized into groups to pursue political action or looking to a future moment of revolutionary endeavour, they posit those engaged in these becomings as a 'mutant machine' that is 'becoming-revolutionary' (Deleuze and Parnet 1983: 113–14). The figure of the mutant suggests not a group of allied individuals, but a multiplicity that follows lines of flight. Nevertheless, the people of this machine are evident. Deleuze and Parnet discuss these 'men of the line' (ibid.: 98) – or better people of the line – moving with prudence, curiosity and as experimenters, and deterritorializing the assemblage again and again and at myriad points and in myriad ways. Are these teachers and students becoming-revolutionary? Is the practice of writing and reading this book the act of becoming-revolutionary? Are we, as educators, education researchers and activists, already becoming-revolutionary? And might we understand further contemporary resistant practices in this way? For instance, when teachers collectively critique high-stakes standardized tests and their impacts or when teachers like Miss Groves insist on offering these tests to their students, are they becoming-revolutionary?

The question of collective action: mutant machines, new collectivities and agonistic pluralism

Returning to Butler's suggestions that 'radical acts of public misappropriation' (Butler 1997a: 100) have the potential to shift meaning over time and that a shift from a focus on personal freedom to a focus on the operations of the state (Butler 2007, 2008) might bring together multiple interest groups in new alliances or collectivities in response to pressing contemporary public concerns is helpful for thinking through matters of misfire and recuperation or reterritorialization, intentionality and collective action. In a performative politics misfire and potential recuperation are both an opportunity and a cost, just as reterritorialization and descent into the black hole of meaninglessness are risks intrinsic to a politics of becoming-otherwise. These are the condition of possibility for both performative politics and becomings, the limits that mean the effects of these politics are provisional and uncertain. Nevertheless, the idea that alternative, currently disavowed meanings might and do become recognizable, subjugated meanings might and do become legitimate, and that these might and do congeal to become a new normativity, demonstrates the contingent certainties that the *public repetition* of performative politics offers. Likewise, that becomings-otherwise can and do deterritorialize the assemblage suggests that a myriad of such becomings might scatter the lines of the assemblage in ways from which it cannot recover and, therefore, convert it.

This suggests that the public repetition of performative politics or a politics of becoming-otherwise, and their *repetition in public spaces*, cannot be conceived of as taking a singular form. Rather, these politics might be achieved through the practices of groups coming together in collectivities; they might be achieved through the practices of individuals, like Laura, Miss Groves and Miss Appleton; they might be achieved through the practices of subjects following lines of flight that are anti-subjectivation; or they might be achieved through flows of affective intensities that cannot be said to belong to individual subjects at all.

Political tactics such as these underscore how knotty the question of collective action remains. Building on Butler's (2007) call to new collectivities, collectivities and collective action might be consciously organized – as in the case of the No Outsiders project – or these might emerge out of otherwise disconnected individuals engaging simultaneously with particular ideas and practices. Such collectivities might be as much, or more, about *thinking* collectively as they are about organizing and practising collectively. Formally organized collectivities might offer opportunities to think tactically together and be sustaining for those involved, or they might reign-in thinking and subjectivate their members in ways that restrict recognizability. This conception of political practice, then, is not necessarily a call to forming, belonging to, and taking action as a group – although this may well be one tactical move. Indeed, Butler states that she is 'not at all sure we need to gather . . . struggles within a unified framework' (Butler 2008: 20). Such a politics is about the proliferation and dispersal of ideas and practices, a proliferation and dispersal that is itself the making of a new collectivity even though the constituents of this collectivity may well be temporally and geographically remote and remain wholly unknown to each other. Thinking about collectivities in this way, then, is neither a return to formalized counter-political organizations nor to identity politics. Instead, it is a call to collectivities that cross-cut single issue politics and include but stretch beyond the confines of organized collective action. Also useful here is Laclau and Mouffe's (2001) proposition of collective radical politics built on agonistic pluralism in which the particular concerns of individuals and groups are tethered together in chains of equivalence which do not pit concerns against each other in a struggle for primacy or seek to identify a singular, homogenizing primary concern.

The notion of new collectivities and alliances built on an agonistic pluralism demands a consideration of how the individuals who engage in this are conceived of; the place of both rationality, intentionality and affectivities in these politics; how the contradictions and incommensurabilities inherent in these collectivities are expressed and worked with; and the *what this might look like in practice*.

For instance, how might any claims made in relation to boys designated as having 'Social, Emotional and Behavioural Difficulties' in an English rural 'special' school be connected to any claims made in relation to gender and sexuality in multi-ethnic primary schools in London? And how do we respond when confronted with further and contradictory claims, based on alternative or conflicting identifications of class, gender, sexuality, race, ethnicity and religion that are intrinsically bound to these claims and counter-claims? For instance, some resistances to the sexualities equalities work of the No Outsiders project were grounded in the religious and ethnic affiliations and identifications of some members of school communities, and some of the Bay Tree School boys' resistances to 'SEBD' subjectivations were grounded in their classed, sexualized and gendered identifications. Do we need to try to find ways to bring the boys in Bay Tree School into alliances with minoritized race and religious communities when the negation of these communities is the very ground on which these boys resist their own abjection? Conversely, do we need to try to find ways to bring the minoritized race and religious communities into alliances with minoritized sex-gender communities when the disavowal of these communities is intrinsic to some race and religious identifications? And if we do think this is a necessary political endeavour, is it possible? For instance, can boys whose identifications are deeply invested in hyper-heterosexualized and classed forms of Whiteness that are intrinsic to their very recognition of themselves and each other be brought into alliance with queer teachers or minoritized race and religious communities? And vice versa. Might these constituencies be brought together in new collectivities predicated on chains of equivalence within an antagonistic pluralism? Considering the possibility of alliances between sexual and religious minorities Butler writes: 'certainly, I want to be able to kiss in public – don't get me wrong. But do I want to require that everyone watch and approve before they acquire rights of citizenship? I think not' (Butler 2008: 5).

In the current moment new collectivities seem necessary, but they also seem deeply unlikely unless we shift what we mean when we think about collectivities. Rather than envisaging all of these groups sitting together in a community centre or, given their geographical dispersal, in an on-line group organizing collective political action, we might envisage each of these constituencies engaging in a range of political practices with a range of political hopes, but all orientated towards deterritorializing dominant assemblages.

On the basis of the analysis that I have pursued in this book there is some evidence of *tacit* alliances already being enacted at the micro-level and in particular spaces. For instance, we might read tacit alliances, albeit provisional and fleeting, in the collective practices of the boys at Bay Tree 'special' School, Miss Groves and Miss Appleton, as well as Miss Groves, Miss Appleton and the boys together. If these are tacit alliances, they seem fragile and to have inherently contradictory effects. That is, the teachers' complicity with the boys' practices acts to constitute the boys 'student' and draw them into recognition as 'learner' at the same time as it undergirds the boys' claims to hyper-heterosexual, White, working class masculinity. Yet by simultaneously allowing recognition of the boys' sexed, gendered and raced subjectivities the teachers risk once again the boys' recognizability as student and learner. While this might seem to undercut the possibility of understanding these practices as either a politics or a tacit alliance, this might be the inevitable terrain of an agonistic pluralism that engages cross-cutting modalities of life.

How might we respond to the apparent inevitability of one set of practices undercutting the effects of another set of practices? I made this argument in relation to the incompatibility of identity politics and performative politics in the No Outsiders project where political practices concerned with ostensibly the same set of interests were shown to undercut each other. How then might counter-political practices that have clearly contradictory interests not be expected to do this? How can these contradictory counter-concerns be brought together in a new collectivity? How can agonistic pluralism be made to work? And how can new collectivities and even tacit alliances be made to work when these are shot through with feeling?

Enacting a politics of feeling

These concerns raise as a key question the place of affectivities in politics. That is, does a turn to affectivities represent a new political opportunity or a slippage into the interiority of fragmented subjects? It seems to me that in the work of Laclau and Mouffe, Foucault, Butler and Deleuze and Guattari we can find resources that enable us to recognize the politics of affectivities in different ways. Laclau and Mouffe's work enables us to move beyond a politics rooted in rationalism and science, and embrace the passion of the political commitment that underpins political practices. Foucault's consideration of resistance implies the passionate politics of the subjectivated subject who engages in resistant practice; likewise Butler's work on performative politics. Foucault's later work on an ethics and practice of self, grounded not in a moral position already steeped in particular prevailing knowledges but in our responses to the 'intolerable' nature of aspects of the present, also suggests a subject who, while constrained by their subjectivation, is deeply moved and holds a deep commitment to the ethics of resistance that underpin their practices. The passion that this rests upon is particularly evident in Foucault's discussion of *parrhesia*, or fearless speech. Butler's recent work on the recognition of the Other and our fundamental dependence on the Other for our own recognition also suggests passionate attachments and their place in politics. And Deleuze and Guattari's conceptualization of affectivities does not see these passionate commitments as simply belonging to individuals, but flowing as intensities that are politically productive in their flights from the molar lines of the assemblage.

All of these lines of thinking help us to recognize the affective as a fundamental dimension of the political, whether in the form of the prepersonal intensities of the body or the discourse of emotion that code these as outrage, concern, disgust and so on. They assert a passionate politics that takes account of the place of affectivities in our own political investment; the passionate attachments of others to their political investments; and the political potentialities of affectivities themselves. This series of recognitions suggests agonistic pluralism or new collectivities that cross-cut various modalities as fundamental to any sort of organized politics. This underscores the deep problems within any political thinking or practice that is based on a politics of rescue, exposing the colonizing and normalizing moves implicit in such politics and, therefore, the way that these operate as a further moment of abjection. Diane Reay's work (2004), along with her work with Helen Lucey (2000) that contests the constitution of working class positions and spaces as abject and Silvia Grinberg's reading (Grinberg in press) of a Buenos Aires shanty town not as an abject space, as dominant readings would have it, but as a space of desire and life demonstrate these conceptual moves put to work in relation to real, situated lives and politics. These conceptual and analytic moves all suggest strongly that we engage, are already engaged in, *passionate politics*.

Converting the education assemblage: a social movement of becoming

The effects of the assemblage and of counter-politics are contingent, but we do have a degree of certainty about many of these. Particular social structures, systems, institutions, discourses, meanings, practices and subjectivities are enduring and entrenched. Likewise, we understand that the sorts of counter-politics I have been discussing here have real affective, symbolic and material effects, even though these are constrained and open to recuperation. How might we build on these contingent certainties to develop a politics that is fit for assemblage conversion and that might even dismantle the education assemblage?

Essential here is an understanding of power and its operations – we need to know as clearly as possible what it is that we are up against. Social and political theory has posited a range of conceptualizations of power and the way that power works. These include zero-sum conceptions of power that see uneven power shares as the source of dominance and subordination. Flowing from this, power is conceived of as repressive, coercive; a power wielded that bears down on those subjected to it by the sovereign, state or judicial system through which it is legitimated and enacted. Power has also been conceived of as a product of economic or social status, of particular forms of social, cultural and symbolic capitals, and as a function of ideology or hegemonic forms. Inserted into this thinking that, even when contextually located, posits power as something that one either does or does not have, have been ideas about power as contingent, circulatory, produced and productive, and distinctions have been drawn between sovereign power that is seen as repressive and disciplinary power that is seen as productive. There has been significant debate over the relative analytical force of these conceptualizations, which have often been taken up as alternatives or pitted against one another. For instance, rejections of Foucault's reading of disciplinary power have generally been based in an assumption that it replaces a concern with or appreciation of sovereign power. These contestations appear to misunderstand Foucault's move, which was to augment an understanding of the repressive power of the sovereign or state with an understanding of how this was elaborated, and potentially undercut, by the disciplinary technologies that act to govern populations at the level of everyday life and provoke their self-management. The multiplicity of forms of power and their operations is simply but effectively expressed by Deleuze and Guattari's reference to power set ups. They suggest of power and the assemblage:

> Very specific assemblages of power impose significance and subjectification as their determinate forms of expression . . . there is no significance without a despotic assemblage, no subjectification without an authoritarian assemblage, and no mixture between the two without assemblages of power that act through signifiers and act upon souls and subjects.
>
> (Deleuze and Guattari 1987: 180 cited in Hickey-Moody 2009: 13)

The readings of power offered by Foucault and by Deleuze and Guattari invite us to engage the multiple manifestations and effects of power and insist on politics across all orders of the assemblage from systems, policies, institutions, institutionalized knowledge and processes to everyday practice, subjectivities and identifications and feelings. In this sense, Foucault's power/knowledges can be understood as an order of the assemblage, circulating, forming molar lines through their regimes of truth and striating education spaces. As such, while analyses of the everyday and a concern with performative politics or a politics of becoming may appear in tension with larger-scale politics focused on the state, policy and social movements, politics at all of these levels are called up by this work. As Blaise (2009) usefully highlights, micro- and macro-politics are seen not simply as complementary but as simultaneous in Deleuze and Guattari's thinking.

My analysis suggests that at the level of micro-politics, individuals' enactments of performative politics and their lines of flight into becoming-revolutionary can work. But do these also offer the potential to shift the apparatuses of the state and its over-coding machine? Thinking in terms of the assemblage helps us to move past debates over whether notions of disciplinary power and discourse have any explanatory force in relation to material conditions or inequality. Hierarchy and subjugation are embedded in the material *and* the symbolic, in the structures of the state *and* in the practice of everyday life. The persistence of hierarchy, subjugation and inequality means enduring material circumstances of want, insecurity, pain and disenfranchisement, on the one hand, and enduring material circumstances of plenty, security, comfort and enfranchisement on the other. This persistence suggests not only supporting structures and overcoding machines, but also fields of meaning and conscious or intentional and unconscious or unrecognized investments and affectivities that are *mutually* justifying, normalizing and sustaining. People, groups and institutions are invested in particular ways of being, status positions, privileges and even marginalizations, and are implicated in the ongoing production and remaking of these. Thinking with the assemblage reminds us again that we should not approach meaning and materiality as if they were distinct orders and invites us to imagine that as we find gaps between and scatter the molar lines of the assemblage we also deterritorialize, even if only momentarily, the assemblage itself (DeLanda 2006).

But have we any hope of disassembling education, of converting the education assemblage, and can the tools I have been exploring here achieve this? Putting becoming-otherwise and a performative politics together alongside a move to new collectivities based in agonistic pluralism flags a bigger political project for educators that looks to a politics of meaning as well as a structural politics that is concerned with interrupting material and lived inequalities and converting, or even disassembling, the education assemblage.

Individual educators might deploy performative politics and becomings in isolation; knowingly or not, they might be doing this simultaneously; and they might come together in new collectivities to do this in synchronized ways. Taking up an approach of agonistic pluralism and accepting and forming chains of equivalence, these new collectivities might organize more formal coalitions. Blaise (2009) draws attention to the notion of 'major' and 'minor' politics (Dahlburg and Moss 2005 cited in Blaise 2009), that is, politics at the levels of government and local context and, importantly, how these are connected to each other through political practice. The political practices that I have suggested might have in their sights the transformation of social structures, formal political institutions and processes, public institutions such as schools, as well as the meanings and practices of everyday life – and all of these will have the potential to deterritorialize the assemblage.

As my analysis has shown, as the mind/body distinction, rationality and individualization are refused and the flow of affective intensities is allowed, the potential for becoming-otherwise comes into view. And while reterritorializations remain evident, assemblage conversions, however transitory, are also possible. The deterritorializations that I suggest through my reading of practices in schools take place at the micro-level and are temporally and spatially constrained. Yet the molar lines that these practices unsettle and scatter are intrinsic to the education assemblage as it works at the level of the state and its apparatuses, its systems and structures, its discourses and representations, as well as its subjectivations. How then might we think about deterritorializing the state and its apparatuses that Deleuze and Guattari see as the overcoding machines of the assemblage? Perhaps these passing conversions, that are temporally and locally situated, might congeal over time, just as perfomative resignifications might, to effect a fundamental conversion of the education assemblage. Are these micro-level becomings simultaneously scattering the overcoding machine? Can the assemblage continually and consistently draw its scattered components back together seamlessly without evidence of its fractures and fault-lines? If the micro-instances of becoming-revolutionary that I have mapped are to impact on knowledges, subjects and affects outside the immediate field and moment of practice, and if we are to proliferate these, if we are to convert the education assemblage, then new collectivities, perhaps informed by agonistic pluralism will be important.

One such collectivity might be found in the *Revolutionary Planning Group*, or RPG, a collective of early years educators in Australia whose collaborative thinking about political tools and their deployment in everyday professional practice looks to shift early years education at the micro- and macro-levels (Blaise 2009). The No Outsiders project might also be understood as such a collectivity. Both of these collectives have a common issue as their overarching concern and in this sense might not immediately appear to be the sort of new collectivity that Butler speaks of or based in the sort of agonistic pluralism that Laclau and Mouffe posit. Yet in the case of both collectives, a multiplicity of ways of conceptualizing the issues at stake are evident, multiple and sometimes conceptual and political framings are drawn on, multiple and potentially incommensurate tactics flow from them, and competing goals are prioritized. In this sense, in both cases dissensus is at the core of these collectivities that we might ambitiously want to think about as mutant machines in the making.

In Laclau and Mouffe's terms (2001) a politics grounded in agonistic pluralism requires an overarching strategy realized through its dialogic spaces and practices. In turn, this may demand that political practice in the form of the tactics of everyday life be augmented by more structure-focused and coordinated effort for change. The need for those with divergent and potentially agonistic concerns to ultimately identify the state as their shared concern, even if they do not all have to accept class-based subjugation as the key axis of their oppression, seems to remain central for Laclau and Mouffe. This might seem incompatible with both performative politics and new collectivities whose political practices may well be localized and whose concerns may well be more particularistic. Similarly, it may place intentionality of the subjectivated subject too firmly in the centre of politics to be thought alongside the mutant machine of the people of the line. Yet it may be possible to place Butler's renewed focus on the contemporary interplay of disciplinary and sovereign power, and Deleuze and Guattari's positing of the apparatus of the state and its overcoding machine as an intrinsic part of the assemblage, alongside Laclau and Mouffe's ambition for an agonistic and heterogeneous collective movement. Bringing these together has the potential to assist us in thinking about a range of political practices that are concerned with structures and material concerns as well as the discursive, symbolic and affective.

While the call to deterritorialize, convert and even disassemble the education assemblage invokes the need for political practices that can reach all of the orders of the assemblage, it does seem to me that these may need to take particular forms. For instance, liberal politics based on reform and identity politics seeking an incorporating form of recognition seem to both be a *part* of the assemblage and its molar lines, concerned as they are with adapting the overcoding machine and putting subjects in their (new) places. In contrast, performative politics might be conceived of as the 'explosion' of a molecular line 'dragging along segments like no longer recognizable blocks that have been torn away' (Deleuze and Parnet 1983: 84). And becomings-otherwise suggest 'a third type of line, even stranger still, as if something were carrying us away, through our segments but also across our thresholds, toward an unknown destination, neither foreseeable nor pre-existent' (ibid.: 70–1). What *sort* of political tactics we deploy in our work as people of the line, then, seems crucial.

I remain convinced by Foucault's accounts of productive power, the inseparability of power/knowledge, the subjectivation of the subject, and the multiplicity of resistances. I am also convinced by Butler's account of the way that the subject is constituted again and again by performative practices, its need for recognition and its capacity to enact a performative politics. And I remain deeply aware of the very real and material ways that inequalities play out, making some lives livable, or in Judith Butler's words viable, and some intolerable. I want to take up a commitment to fearless speech, after Foucault's account of those who speak unpalatable and uncomfortable truths in the face of power set ups that can disavow and even destroy them. And I want to look for and engage, in contexts of deep division and even annihilation, practices that, in Butler's terms, let the other live (Butler 2005). Putting these ideas together with Deleuze's work with Guattari and Parnet on lines of flight and becomings that have the potential to deterritorialize the assemblage seems to me to bring together a collection of generative tools for thinking about and enacting political practices. Furthermore, conceptualizing Laclau and Mouffe's agonistic pluralism as potentially representing a new collectivity that might underpin the pursuit of public acts of misappropriation or lines of flight that may, in turn, unsettle the existing hegemony and convert the assemblage in ways that make possible a new hegemony of contingent certainties, seems to offer a model for collective action that holds real promise.

In all of this the struggle over meaning that has been at the centre of radical and post-structural politics remains key, meaning which informs and bounds all of these orders of the assemblage, from the structural to the symbolic and affective and to subjectivity and recognizability. Fundamental to these processes is the matter of how we live and practise in the everyday; the practices of self of Foucault's work.

This suggests the need for us to endeavour to continually practise in ways that open up spaces for recognition. It is also a matter of the contexts in which we live, from meanings and practices in our personal lives, our engagements with others and in communities, to the institutions, systems and structures in which we are situated and which frame and constrain the possibilities for recognition.

This may seem an unlikely, incoherent and unwieldy set of starting points and guides to political tactics. But it is important to remember that many of these thinkers were one another's contemporaries whose work was and continues to be in dialogue. The points where these ways of thinking about the political rub-up uncomfortably with each other are surely points of possibility, not closure. In all this I want to hold onto the idea of radicalism and the revolutionary. Taking inspiration from Deleuze and Parnet's notion of becoming-revolutionary in their thinking about the politics intrinsic to becomings and the RPG's take up of the revolutionary and its manifesto, and in the face of the appropriation of radicalism within deeply imperialistic and Islamaphobic discourse of radicalization and violent extremism, I want to hold onto the notion of the radical and radicalism for a heterogeneous counter-politics and I want to join in the contemporary *re*citation of the revolutionary.

Re-imagining education

The idea of converting the education assemblage, or even disassembling education, invites us to re-imagine education. This re-imagining has been a central concern of progressive education, critical pedagogy, feminist pedagogy, critical race pedagogy and queer pedagogy, each identifying ways ahead and mapping spaces where a re-imagined education is already being practised. This thinking, and the practices that it maps, provokes and calls for, looks to teachers to work as organic intellectuals (Apple and Beane 2007); explores the possibilities of education being a space of desires and pleasures (Talburt 2009); foregrounds the place of feeling in the education (Britzman 1998; Bibby 2009); builds pedagogies grounded in affectivities (Zembylas 2007); places recognition of the global workings and impacts of Whiteness at the centre of education (Leonardo 2009); foregrounds the position of the Other as a 'genuine inter-locutor' and insists on the centrality of recognition of the suffering of Others and our implicatedness in this (Smith 2006); and calls for a focus on 'critical knowing' (Blaise 2009) or on 'educated hope' (Giroux 2006: 50). This sort of thinking and practice in education invokes Foucault's 'heterotopias' – not just a multiplicity of utopian spaces in the future, but a multiplicity of real counter-spaces in the present (Foucault 1967; Peters and Freeman-Moir 2006; Soja 2000). This thinking also underscores the mul-tiple and potentially deeply incommensurable conceptual framings for and concerns of such pedagogies. In so doing, it highlights again that if we want to move our prac-tices beyond our own classrooms and proliferate, develop and extend these, we may well need to build new collectivities that proceed from an agonistic pluralism. For instance, it is difficult to re-imagine schools as spaces where a predominantly White and middle class teaching workforce takes up *en masse* the role of the organic intel-lectual to practice as race-traitors as they explore with their students the operations of Whiteness at the same time as they promote the recognizability and legitimacy of queer pleasures and desires. But it is not impossible. Some of the education spaces that I have described and interrogated in this book and some of the education spaces that others have identified might suggest that such heterotopias can and do exist in the present.

One area of education scholarship that is focusing on the practice of re-imagining education is 'education futures', where utopianism is being reengaged in order to imagine 'edutopias' (Peters and Freeman-Moir 2006). This approach to utopianism foregrounds openness and provisionality, avoiding blueprints of a brave new educational world. Instead, it uses utopianism as an invitation, where we are, to imagination about educational possibilities 'free from the constraints imposed by the now' (ibid.: 4). Taking our thought out of the 'now' and finding spaces for thinking that are not constrained by the sedimented forms and ways of knowing that situate and constitute us is clearly difficult. But while current forms and knowledges are no doubt potentially limiting they are not determining – we are not simply the dupes of history, contemporary social forms, or normative meanings – the spaces and tools for re-imagining education do exist.

I opened this book with a story I called 'Falling'; a composite account that depicts the multiple and nuanced ways in which education as it is currently configured and enacted closes down not just opportunities for certain sorts of students, but also 'who' these students can be. I close the book with the hope of re-imagining education as a space of open-endedness, dialogue and possibility; as a space of becoming. This is no easy task. Constrained as we are by the limits of our own experience of normative meanings and sedimented practices, the sort of education that we might hope for can easily remain spectral; a glimmer that remains just out of sight and cannot be drawn into focus. Or the imaginings that come into view feel hollow, naive and flawed. And avoiding tightly defined prescriptions for an 'edutopia' that can never prove to be that for all people in all settings renders naming the component parts of such an 'edutopia' problematic (Peters and Freeman-Moir 2006). While I want to avoid a blueprint or check-list of 'must-have' elements of an 'edutopia', I do want to suggest some of the practices, forms, subjects and feelings that might help to create education spaces of possibility. Based on what we know about schools and schooling as it stands, building on the heterotopias that can already be glimpsed in contemporary education spaces and pursuing the promises of the radical politics that I have been exploring, the education space that I imagine does seem to be underpinned by some contingent certainties. It is a semi-formal space that is physically accessible, welcoming and comfortable; it is a space of listening, exploration and openness; it is a space of dialogue where consensus and disagreement are both important, where uncomfortable truths are spoken and where the intolerable is named and responded to; it is a space where there is time for and interest in children and young people's lives, ideas, experiences, feelings, imaginings and hopes; it is a space where trust circulates; it is a space where feelings of all sorts, whether thought through and translated into the language of emotions or in the form of flowing affective intensities, are not simply allowed but are acknowledged as a vital part of living and learning; it is a space where both engagement and disconnection are valid and where participation is elective; it is a space that is interdisciplinary, where learning moves from children and young people's pressing concerns, where teachers map connections to existing knowledges as well as the gaps in this, and where the possibility of new ways of knowing and new knowledges is real; it is a space where identifications and subjectivities are heard, explored and offered recognition, even as this recognition includes critical interrogation and problematization; it is a space where tests, performance indicators, league tables and the terrors these bring with them are insignificant; it is a space that is recognized as being deeply political and deeply significant. It is a classroom that I have seen glimpses of in my own research and that has been documented elsewhere. In this sense it is a heterotopia. It is a classroom that I would like to teach and learn in.

References

Abel, J. (2008). *The Thought Crime Law*. Retrieved 20/01/09, from http://www.hartfordadvo-cate.com/article.cfm?aid = 5068

Agnew, K., and Fox, G. (2005). *Children at War*. London: Continuum.

Ahmed, S. (2004). *The Cultural Politics of Emotion*. Edinburgh: Edinburgh University Press.

Ahmed, S., Castaneda, C., Fortier, A., and Sheller, M. (Eds). (2003). *Uprootings/Regroundings: questions of home and migration*. Oxford: Berg.

Ali, M. (2004). *Brick Lane*. London: Black Swan.

Ali, S. (2003). *Mixed-Race, Post-Race: gender, new ethnicities and cultural practices*. Oxford: Berg.

Allen, B. (2003). *Changing Minds: the psychology of managing challenging behaviour within an ethical and legal framework*. St Leonards: Steaming/Team-Teach.

Allen, H. E. (1931). The Fire of Love. In H. E. Allen (Ed.), *English Writings of Richard Rolle, Hermit of Hampole*. Oxford: Oxford University Press.

Allen, J. (1999). *Actively Seeking Inclusion: pupils with special needs in mainstream schools*. London: Falmer Press.

Allen, R. L. (2004). Whiteness and Critical Pedagogy. *Educational Philosophy and Theory*, 36(2), pp. 121–36.

—— (2005). Whiteness and Critical Pedagogy. In L. Leonardo (Ed.), *Critical Pedagogy and Race* (pp. 53–68). Oxford: Blackwell.

Althusser, L. (1971). Ideology and Ideological State Apparatuses (B. Brewster, Trans.). In *Lenin and Philosophy* (pp. 170–86). London: Monthly Review Press.

Anyon, J. (2005). *Radical Possibilities: public policy, urban education and a new social movement*. London: Routledge.

Apple, M.W. (1990). *Ideology and Curriculum*. London: Routledge.

—— (1996). *Cultural Politics and Education*. Buckingham: Open University Press.

—— (2000). *Official Knowledge: democratic education in a conservative age*. London: Routledge.

—— (Ed.). (2003). *The State and the Politics of Knowledge*. London: RoutledgeFalmer.

—— (2006). *Educating the 'Right' Way: markets, standards, God, and inequality*. Second Edition. London: RoutledgeFalmer.

Apple, M. W., and Beane, J. A. (2007). *Democratic Schools: lessons in powerful education*. Second Edition. Portsmouth, NH: Heinemann.

Atkinson, E., and DePalma, R. (Eds). (2009). *Interrogating Heteronormativity in Primary Schools*. London: Trentham.

Atkinson, P. (1990). *The Ethnographic Imagination: textual constructions of reality*. London: Routledge.

Atwood, M. (1990). *The Handmaid's Tale*. London: Virago.

AVID. (2004). *From Dawa to Jihad: the various threats from radical Islam to the democratic legal order.* The Hague: General Intelligence and Security Service.

Awanuiārangi. (n.d.) *Te Whare Wānanga o Awanuiārangi.* Retrieved 20/01/09, from http://www.wananga.ac.nz/

Bakunin, M. (1990). *Statism and Anarchy.* Cambridge: Cambridge University Press.

Ball, S. J. (1990). *Politics and Policy Making in Education: explorations in policy sociology.* London: Routledge.

—— (1994). *Education Reform : a critical and post-structural approach.* Philadelphia: Open University Press.

—— (2003a). *Class Strategies and the Education Market: the middle classes and social advantage.* London: RoutledgeFalmer.

—— (2003b). The Teacher's Soul and the Terrors of Performativity. *Journal of Education Policy,* 18(2), pp. 215–28.

—— (2005). *Education Policy and Social Class: the selected works of Stephen J. Ball.* London: Routledge.

—— (2006). The Necessity and Violence of Theory. *Discourse,* 27(1), pp. 3–11.

—— (2007). *Education Plc: understanding private sector participation in public sector education.* London: Routledge.

Ball, S. J., and Youdell, D. (2008). *Hidden Privatisation in Public Education.* Brussels: Education International.

Barton, L. (Ed.). (2001). *Disability, Politics and the Struggle for Change.* London: David Fulton.

Baudrillard, J. (1995). *The Gulf War Did Not Take Place.* Bloomington, IN: Indiana University Press.

BBC1 (2009). *Inside Out,* 25/02/09.

Benjamin, J. (1998). *Shadow of the Other: intersubjectivity and gender in psychoanalysis.* London: Routledge.

Bibby, T. (2009). How Do Children Understand Themselves as Learners? Towards a learner-centred understanding of pedagogy. *Pedagogy, Culture and Society,* 17(1), pp. 41–55.

Blaise, M. (2005). *Playing it Straight: changing images of early childhood.* London: Routledge.

—— (2009). Revolutionizing Practice by Doing Early Childhood Politically. In *Professional Learning in Early Childhood Settings* (pp. 27–47). Rotterdam: Sense.

Boggs, C. (1976). *Gramsci's Marxism.* London: Pluto Press.

Boler, M. (1999). *Feeling Power: emotion and education.* London: Routledge.

Bosche, S. (1983). *Jenny Lives with Eric and Martin.* Gay Men's Press.

Bradbury, R. (2008). *Fahrenheit 451.* London: Harper Voyager.

Brah, A., and Phoenix, A. (2004). Ain't I a Woman: revisiting intersectionality. *Journal of International Women's Studies,* 5(3), pp. 75–86.

Braidotti, R. (2005). A Critical Cartography of Feminist Post-postmodernism. *Australian Feminist Studies,* 20(47), pp. 169–80.

Brand, R., Fregonese, S., and Coaffee, J. (2008). *The Urban Environment – Mirror or Mediator of Radicalisation?* Retrieved 01/03/09, from http://www.sed.manchester.ac.uk/architecture/research/radicalisation/resources/information/documents/FCO-report-18092008_Brand-Coaffee-Fregonese_for-website.pdf

Brittain, V., Christian, C., and Crow, B. (2009, 11/03/2009). A New Agenda for Political Change. *The Guardian.*

Britzman, D. (1998). *Lost Subjects, Contested Objects: towards a psychoanalytic inquiry of learning.* Albany: State University of New York Press.

Britzman, D. P. (1995). Is There a Queer Pedagogy? Or, Stop Reading Straight. *Educational Theory,* 45(2), pp. 151–65.

Brown, P., and Lauder, H. (2006). Globalisation, Knowledge and the Myth of the Magnet Economy. In H. Lauder, P. Brown, J. Dillabough and A.H. Halsey (Eds), *Education, Globalization and Social Change* (pp. 317–40). Oxford: Oxford University Press.

Bulbeck, C. (1998). *Reorientating Western Feminisms: women's diversity in a postcolonial world.* Cambridge: Cambridge University Press.

Burgess, J. P. (2008). Radicalization and the Critique of Liberal Tolerance. *6th CHALLENGE Training School.* Paris.

Burns, K. (2005). Practicing Queer Theories: queer image-based texts in the tertiary classroom. *Curriculum Perspectives,* 25(3), pp. 65–8.

Butler, J. (1990). *Gender Trouble: feminism and the subversion of identity.* London: Routledge.

—— (1991). Imitation and Gender Insubordination. In D. Fuss (Ed.), *Inside/Out: lesbian theories, gay theories.* London: Routledge.

—— (1992). Contingent Foundations: feminism and the question of 'postmodernism'. In J. Butler and J. W. Scott (Eds), *Feminists Theorize the Political* (pp. 3–21). London: Routledge.

—— (1993). *Bodies That Matter: on the discursive limits of 'sex'.* New York: Routledge.

—— (1997a). *Excitable Speech: a politics of the performative.* London: Routledge.

—— (1997b). *The Psychic Life of Power: theories in subjection.* Stanford: Stanford University Press.

—— (1997c). The Uses of Equality. *Diacritics,* 27(1), pp. 3–12.

—— (1999). Revisiting Bodies and Pleasures. *Theory, Culture and Society,* 16(2), pp. 11–20.

—— (2004a). *Undoing Gender.* London: Routledge.

—— (2004b). *Precarious Life: the powers of mourning and violence.* London: Verso.

—— (2005). *Giving an Account of Oneself.* New York: Fordham University Press.

—— (2007). Sexual Politics: the limits of secularism, the time of coalition. *British Journal of Sociology,* Public Lecture. LSE, London.

—— (2008). Sexual Politics, Torture and Secular Time. *Sociology,* 59(1), pp. 1–23.

Califia, P. (1996). *Doc and Fluff: the dystopian tale of a girl and her biker.* Los Angeles: Alyson.

Callinicos, A. (1976). *Althusser's Marxism.* London: Pluto Press.

Carpentier, N., and Cammaerts, B. (2006). Hegemony, Democracy, Agonism and Journalism: an interview with Chantal Mouffe. *Journalism Studies,* 7(6), pp. 964–75.

Carter, A. (1992). *The Virago Book of Fairy Tales.* London: Virago.

Castle, D. (n.d.). Hearts, Minds and Radical Democracy (Interview with Ernesto Laclau and Chantal Mouffe), *Red Pepper: spicing up politics.*

Chandler Harris, J. (2002). *Uncle Remus: his songs and his sayings.*

Choudhury, T. (2007). *The Role of Muslim Identity Politics in Radicalisation (a study in progress).* London: Department for Communities and Local Government.

Christensen, C., and Rizvi, F. (Eds). (1996). *Disability and the Dilemmas of Education and Justice.* Buckingham: Open University Press.

Cixous, H., and Clement, C. (1986a). Sorties: Out and Out: Attacks/Ways Out/Forays. In H. Cixous and C. Clement (Eds), *The Newly Born Woman* (pp. 63–134). Minneapolis: University of Minnesota Press.

Cixous, H., and Clement, C. (1986b). *The Newly Born Woman.* Minneapolis: University of Minnesota Press.

Collins, C., Kenway, J., and McLeod, J. (2000). *Factors Influencing the Educational Performace of Males and Females in School and Their Initial Destinations after Leaving School.* South Australia: Deakin University.

Collins, P. H. (2000). *Black Feminist Thought: knowledge, consciousness and the politics of empowerment,* (Tenth Anniversary Edition). London: Routledge.

Communities and Local Government (n.d.) Prevent. Retrieved 01/02/10, from http://www.communities.gov.uk/communities/prevent

Compass. (2007). Compass Constitution. Compass: Direction for the Democratic Left.

Connell, R. W. (n.d.) *Identity*. Unpublished paper.

Connolly, P. (2006). Summary Statistics, Educational Achievement Gaps and the Ecological Fallacy. *Oxford Review of Education*, 32(2), pp. 235–52.

—— (2008). A Critical Review of Some Recent Developments in Quantitative Research on Gender and Achievement in the United Kingdom. *British Journal of Sociology of Education*, 29(3), pp. 249–60.

Corbett, J. (1996). *Bad Mouthing: the language of special needs*. London: Falmer.

—— (2001). *Supporting Inclusive Education: a connective pedagogy*. London: RoutledgeFalmer.

Cornell, D. (2000). *Just Cause: freedom, identity and rights*. Lanham, MD: Rowman & Littlefield.

Crenshaw, K. (1991). Mapping the Margins: intersectionality, identity politics and violence against women of color. *Stanford Law Review*, 43(6), pp. 1241–99.

Davies, B. (2003). *Shards of Glass: children reading and writing beyond gender identities*. Hampton.

DCS (2004). *Key Stage 3: English – improving writing 2003–2004 follow up materials*. Retrieved 01/04/09, from www.devon.gov.uk/dcs/literacy/ks3/improve/improving%20writing%202003–4%20Follow%20Up%20Materials.do

DCSF (n.d.) *The Gender Agenda*. Retrieved 10/02/09, from http://www.teachernet.gov.uk/wholeschool/equality/genderequalityduty/thegenderagenda/

—— (2007). The Use of Force to Control or Restrain Pupils: non-statutory guidance for schools in England. London: DCSF.

—— (2008). *Statistical First Release: special educational needs in England January 2008*. London: DCSF.

—— (2009a). *Statistical First Release: GCSE and equivalent examination results in England 2007/8 (revised)*. London: DCSF.

—— (2009b). *Deprivation and Education: the evidence on pupils in England Foundation Stage to Key Stage 4*. London: DCSF

—— (2009c). *Gender and Education Myth Busters: addressing gender and achievement myths and realities*. Nottingham: DCSF.

—— (2009d). *Statistical First Release: GCSE and equivalent examination results in England 2007/8 (revised)*. London: DCSF.

de Certeau, M. (1988). *The Practice of Everyday Life*. Berkeley: University of California Press.

De Haan, L., and Nijland, S. (2002). *King and King*. Berkeley, CA: Tricycle Press.

—— (2004). *King and King and Family*. Berkeley, CA: Tricycle Press.

Delamont, S., and Atkinson, P. (1995). *Fighting Familiarity: essays on education and ethnography*. New Jersey: Hampton Press.

DeLanda. (2006). *A New Philosophy of Society: assemblage theory and social complexity*. London: Continuum.

Deleuze, G., and Guattari, F. (1983). Rhizome. In G. Deleuze and F. Guattari (Eds), *On The Line*. New York: Semiotext(e).

—— (2008). *A Thousand Plateaus*. London: Continuum.

Deleuze, G., and Parnet, C. (1983). Politics. In G. Deleuze and F. Guattari (Eds), *On The Line*. New York: Semiotext(e).

Delgado, R. (1989). Storytelling for Oppositionists and Others: a plea for narrative. *Harvard Law Review*, 87(2), pp. 411–41.

—— (1995). *The Rodrigo Chronicles: conversations about race and class*. New York: New York University Press.

Delgado, R., and Stefancic, J. (2000). Introduction. In R. Delgado and J. Stefancic (Eds), *Critical Race Theory: the cutting edge*. Second Edition. Philadelphia: Temple University Press.

—— (2001). *Critical Race Theory: an introduction*. New York University Press.

DePalma, R., and Atkinson, E. (2009). 'No Outsiders': moving beyond a discourse of tolerance to challenge heteronormativity in primary schools. *British Educational Research Journal*, 35(6), pp. 837–55.

Derrida, J. (1978). *On Writing and Difference*. London: Routledge.

—— (1988). Signature Event Context. In J. Derrida (Ed.), *Limited Inc* (pp. 1–23). Elvanston: Northwestern University Press.

—— (1997). *Of Grammatology*. Baltimore: Johns Hopkins University Press.

Desai, S. R., and Marsh, T. (2005). Weaving Multiple Dialects in the Classroom Discourse: poetry and spoken word as a critical teaching tool. *Taboo: The Journal of Culture and Education*, 9(2), pp. 20–90.

Devine, D. (1996). *Maximum Security: the culture of violence in inner city schools*. Chicago, IL: University of Chicago Press.

Dick, P. K. (1991). *Ubik*. New York: Vintage.

Dollimore, J., and Sinfield, A. (1985). *Political Shakespeare: new essays in cultural materialism*. Manchester: Manchester University Press.

Dworkin, A. (1988). *Letters from a War Zone: writings 1976–1987*. London: Secker & Warburg.

Eagleton, T. (1983). *Literary Theory: an introduction*. Oxford: Blackwell.

Ebert, R. (2002). *Equilibrium*. Retrieved 10/02/09, from http://rogerebert.suntimes.com/apps/pbcs.dll/article?AID=/20021206/REVIEWS/212060303/1023

Eliasoph, N. (1998). *Avoiding Politics: how Americans produce apathy in everyday life*. Cambridge: Cambridge University Press.

Epstein, D., Elwood, J., Hey, V., and Maw, J. (Eds). (1998). *Failing Boys? Issues in gender and achievement*. Philadelphia: Open University Press.

Fielding, M. (2005). Alex Bloom, Pioneer of Radical State Education. *FORUM for promoting 3–19 comprehensive education*, 47(2), pp. 16–134.

—— (2007). On the Necessity of Radical State Education: democracy and the common school. *Journal of Philosophy of Education*, 41(4), pp. 539–57.

Fierstein, H. (2002). *Sissy Duckling*. New York: Simon & Schuster Children's Publishing.

Foucault, M. (1967). *Of Other Spaces, Heterotopias*. Retrieved 20/02/09, from http://foucault.info/documents/heteroTopia/foucault.heteroTopia.en.html

—— (1988a). Critical Theory/Intellectual History. In L. Kritzman (Ed.), *Michel Foucault – Politics, Philosophy, Culture: interviews and other writings 1977–1984* (pp. 17–46). London: Routledge.

—— (1988b). An Aesthetics of Existence. In L. Kritzman (Ed.), *Michel Foucault – Politics, Philosophy, Culture: interviews and other writings 1977–1984* (pp. 47–56). London: Routledge.

—— (1990a). *The History of Sexuality: an introduction* (Vol. 1). London: Penguin.

—— (1990b). *The Care of the Self: the history of sexuality* (Vol. 3). London: Penguin.

—— (1991a). *Discipline and Punish: the birth of the prison*. London: Penguin.

—— (1991b). Governmentality. In C. Gordon, G. Burchell and P. Miller (Eds), *The Foucault Effect: studies in governmentality* (pp. 87–104). Chicago: University of Chicago Press.

—— (1992). *The Uses of Pleasure: the history of sexuality* (Vol. 2). London: Penguin.

—— (2001). *Fearless Speech*. Los Angeles: Semiotext(e).

—— (2002). *The Order of Things*. London: Routledge.

—— (2007). *The Politics of Truth*. Los Angeles: Semiotext(e).

Francis, B., and Hey, V. (2009). Talking Back to Power: snowballs in hell and the imperative of structural explanations. *Gender and Education*, 21(2), pp. 225–32.

Freedom-Writers-Foundation. *The Freedom Writers Foundation*. Retrieved 01/04/09, from

http://www.freedomwritersfoundation.org/site/c.kqIXL2PFJtH/b.2259975/k.BF19/
Home.htm

Freesmith, D. (2006). The Politics of the English Curriculum: ideology in the campaign against critical literacy in The Australian. *English in Australia*, 41(1), pp. 25–30.

Freire, P. (1970). *Pedagogy of the Oppressed*. New York: Herder & Herder.

—— (1998). *Pedagogy of the Heart*. London: Continuum.

—— (2001). *Pedagogy of Freedom: ethics, democracy and civic courage*. Oxford: Rowman & Littlefield.

—— (2004). *Pedagogy of Hope*. London: Continuum.

Freud, S. (1990). The Uncanny, in *Art and Literature*. London: Penguin.

Fuss, D. (1990). *Essentially Speaking: feminism, nature and difference*. London: Routledge.

Gadher, D. (2007). *The Battle For Hearts and Minds*. Retrieved 20/01/09, from http://www.timesonline.co.uk/tol/news/uk/crime/article2042548.ece

Gandin, L. A. (2003). Educating the State, Democratizing Knowledge: The Citizens School Project in Porto Alegre, Brazil. In M. W. Apple (Ed.), *The State and the Politics of Knowledge* (pp. 193–220). London: RoutledgeFalmer.

Gewirtz, S., Ball, S. J., and Bowe, R. (1995). *Markets, Choice and Equity in Education*. Buckingham: Open University Press.

Gillborn, D. (2008). *Racism and Education: coincidence or conspiracy?* London: Routledge.

Gillborn, D., and Youdell, D. (2000). *Rationing Education: policy, practice, reform and equity*. Buckingham: Open University Press.

Ginsborg, P. (2005). *The Politics of Everyday Life: making choices, changing lives*. Bury St Edmunds: Bury St Edmundsbury Press.

Giroux, H. (1981). *Ideology, Culture and the Process of Schooling*. London: Falmer.

—— (2006). Dystopian Nightmares and Educated Hopes: the return of the pedagogical and the promise of democracy. In M. A. Peters and D. J. Freeman-Moir (Eds), *Edutopias* (pp. 45–64). Rotterdam: Sense.

Giroux, H., and McLaren, P. (Eds). (1994). *Between Borders: pedagogy and the politics of cultural studies*. New York: Routledge.

Glasscoe, M. (1976). *Julian of Norwich, A Revelation of Divine Love*. Exeter: Exeter University Press.

Gorard, S. (2000). One of Us Cannot Be Wrong: the paradox of achievement gaps. *British Journal of Sociology of Education*, 21(3), pp. 391–400.

Gorard, S., and Smith, E. (2008). (Mis)Understanding Underachievement: a response to Connolly. *British Journal of Sociology of Education*, 29(6), pp. 705–14.

Graham, L. (2007). Out of Sight, Out of Mind/Out of Mind, Out of Sight: schooling and attention deficit hyperactivity disorder. *International Journal of Qualitative Studies in Education*, 20(5), pp. 585–602.

Gramsci, A. (2003). *Selections from the Prison Notebooks*. London: Lawrence & Wishart.

Grande, S. (2004). *Red Pedagogy: native American social and political thought*. Lanham, MD: Rowman & Littlefield.

Grinberg, S. (in press). Schooling and Desiring Production in Contexts of Extreme Urban Poverty: everyday banality in a documentary by teenage women. *Gender and Education: Resistance and Regulation*, Special Issue. 22(6).

Grosz, E. (1995). *Space, Time, and Perversion*. London: Routledge.

Guardian Editorial. (2009, 27/05/2009). A New Politics: an optimist's charter. *Guardian*.

Guile, D. (2006). What is Distinctive about the Knowledge Economy? Implications for education. In H. Lauder, P. Brown, J. Dillabough and A. H. Halsey (Eds), *Education, Globalization and Social Change* (pp. 355–66). Oxford: Oxford University Press.

Harwood, V. (2006). *Diagnosing 'Disorderly' Children: a critique of behaviour disorder discourses.* London: Routledge.

Hayden, C., and Pike, S. (2005). Including Positive Handling Strategies Within Training in Behaviour Management. *Emotional and Behavioural Difficulties*, 10(3), pp. 173–87.

Henriques, J., Holloway, W., Urwin, C., Venn, C., and Walkerdine, V. (1998). *Changing the Subject: psychology, social regulation and subjectivity.* London: Routledge.

Hey, V. (2005). The Contrasting Social Logics of Sociality and Survival: cultures of classed be/longing in late modernity. *Sociology*, 39(5), pp. 855–72.

—— (2006). Getting Over It: reflections on the melancholia of reclassified identities. *Gender and Education*, 18(3), pp. 295–308.

HGFL. (2008). *Hertfordshire Grid for Learning: Teaching and Learning – English and Literacy – KS3 – Schemes of work year 9.* Retrieved 01/04/09, from http://www.thegrid.org.uk/learning/english/ks3/sow/year9.shtml

Hickey-Moody, A. (2009). *Unimaginable Bodies: intellectual disability, performance and becomings.* Rotterdam: Sense.

Hickey-Moody, A., and Malins, P. (2007). *Deleuzian Encounters: studies in contemporary social issues.* Basingstoke: Palgrave.

Hoffmann, E. T. A. (1992). The Sandman. In E. T. A. Hoffmann (Ed.), *The Golden Pot and Other Tales* (pp. 85–118). Oxford: Oxford University Press.

Home Office. *Prevent*. Retrieved 01/01/10, from http://www.homeoffice.gov.uk/counter-terrorism/what-we-are-doing/prevent/

hooks, b. (1994). *Teaching to Transgress: education as the practice of freedom.* London: Routledge.

Hunter, I. (1994). *Rethinking the School: subjectivity, bureaucracy, criticism.* St Leonards NSW: Allen and Unwin.

—— (1996). Assembling the School. In A. Barry, T. Osborne and N. Rose (Eds), *Foucault and Political Reason: liberalism, neo-liberalism and rationalities of government* (pp. 143–66). London: UCL Press.

Huxley, A. (2007). *Brave New World.* London: Vintage.

ICSR. (n.d.) *The International Centre for the Study of Radicalisation and Political Violence.* Retrieved 20/01/09, from http://www.icsr.info/

Illich, I. (2000). *Deschooling Society.* London: Marion Boyars.

Jacobs, H. (1987). *Incidents in the Life of a Slave Girl: written by herself.* Cambridge, MA: Harvard University Press.

Joseph, P. E. (Ed.). (2006). *The Black Power Movement: rethinking the civil rights-black power era.* London: Routledge.

K-State Libraries. (2008). *Subject Guides: special education – children's and young adults' books about disabilities.* Retrieved 01/04/09, from http://www.lib.k-state.edu/subguides/specialed/disability.html

Kahn, R., and Kellner, D. (2007). Paulo Freire and Ivan Illich: technology, politics and the reconstruction of education. *Policy Futures in Education*, 5(4), pp. 431–48.

Keddie, A. (2008). Playing the Game: critical literacy, gender justice and issues of masculinity. *Gender and Education*, 20(6), pp. 571–83.

Kehily, M. J. (1995). Self-Narration, Autobiography and Identity Construction. *Gender and Education*, 7(1), pp. 23–31.

Kelly, C. (2009). *MPs' Expenses and Allowances: supporting Parliament, safeguarding the taxpayer Cm 7724.* London: HMSO.

Kennedy, D. (2001). The International Human Rights Movement: part of the problem? *European Human Rights Law Review*, 3, pp. 245–67.

Kenway, J. (1987). Left Right Out: Australian education and the politics of signification. *Journal of Education Policy*, 2(3), pp. 189–203.

Kenway, J., Kraack, A., and Hicky-Moody, A. (2006). *Masculinity Beyond the Metropolis*. Ashgate.

Kitching, K. (2009). *Justifying School and Self: an ethnography on race, recognition and viability in education in Ireland*. Institute of Education, London.

Laclau, E., and Mouffe, C. (2001). *Hegemony and Socialist Struggle: towards a radical democratic politics*. Second Edition. London: Verso.

LaGravenese, R. (Writer) (2007). *Freedom Writers*. Paramount.

Lather, P. (1991). *Getting Smart: feminist research and pedagogy with/in the postmodern*. New York: Routledge.

Laws, C., and Davies, B. (2000). Poststructural Theory in Practice: working with 'behaviourally disturbed' children. *Qualitative Studies in Education*, 13(3), pp. 205–21.

Leahy, D. (2009). Disgusting Pedagogies. In V. Wright and V. Harwood (Eds), *Biopolitics and the 'Obesity Epidemic': governing bodies* (pp. 172–82). London: Routledge.

Lee, J. (2007). *Kicinich on HR 1955*. Retrieved 20/01/09, from http://www.indypendent.org/2007/12/02/kucinich-on-hr-1955/

Leonardo, Z. (2004a). The Souls of White Folk: critical pedagogy, whiteness studies and globalisation discourse. In G. Ladsen-Billing and D. Gillborn (Eds), *The RoutledgeFalmer Reader in Multicultural Education*. London: RoutledgeFalmer.

—— (2004b). The Color of Supremacy: beyond the discourse of white privilege. *Educational Philosophy and Theory*, 36(2), pp. 137–52.

—— (2005). *Critical Race Pedagogy*. Oxford: Blackwell.

—— (2009). *Race, Whiteness and Education*. London: Routledge.

Levitas, R. (1998). *The Inclusive Society? Social Exclusion and New Labour*. Basingstoke: Palgrave Macmillan.

Levy, A. (2004). *Small Island*. London: Review.

Lewis, R., and Mills, S. (Eds). (2003). *Feminist Postcolonial Theory: a reader*. London: Routledge.

Lingard, B. (Ed.). (2007). *The RoutledgeFalmer Reader in Education Policy and Politics*. London: Routledge.

Lucey, H., and Reay, D. (2002). A Market in Waste: psychic dimensions of school choice policy in the UK and children's narritives on 'demonized' schools. *Discourse*, 23(3), pp. 253–66.

Luke, A. (1997). Critical Approaches to Literacy. In V. Edwards and D. Corson (Eds), *Literacy* (pp. 143–51). Dordrecht: Kluwer.

Luke, C., and Gore, J. (1992). *Feminism and Critical Pedagogy*. London: Routledge.

Lund, P. (1977). Forgotten Messiah? On the influence of the ideas of Ivan Illich on the English school system. *Times Educational Supplement* (3216), 24–5.

Lyotard, J. (1984). *The Postmodern Condition: a report in knowledge*. Minnesota: University of Minnesota Press.

Maclure, M. (2004). *Discourse in Educational and Social Research*. Buckingham: Open University Press.

Maiden, S. (2007). *National Curriculum Would Drive Out Sludge: Howard*. Retrieved 01/04/09, from http://www.theaustralian.news.com.au/story/0,20867,21195773–2702,00.html

Malcolm X. (1968). *The Autobiography of Malcolm X*. London: Penguin.

Mallen, K. M. (2004). *Changing World Orders and Children's Fiction: constructing communities of critical or compliant readers*. Paper presented at the Constructing Communities of Learning and Literacy, Zillmere.

Mann, M. (Writer) (2001). *Ali*. Columbia Pictures Corporation.

Martin, J. (2004). Contested Knowledge: Mary Bridges Adams and the workers' education movement. In J. Goodnam and J. Martin (Eds), *Gender, Colonialism and Education* (pp. 124–47). London: Woburn Press.

Martin, P., and Phelan, S. (2002). Representing Islam in the Wake of September 11: a comparison of US television and CNN Online messageboard discussions. *Prometheus*, 20(3), pp. 263–9.

Massumi, B. (2008). Translators' Foreword: pleasures of philosophy. In G. Deleuze and F. Guattari (Eds), *A Thousand Plateaus* (pp. ix–xvi). London: Continuum.

Maupin, A. (1993). *Tales of the City*. London: Black Swan.

McDowell, L. (2009). Old and New European Economic Migrants: Whiteness and managed migration policies. *Journal of Ethnic and Migration Studies*, 35(1), pp. 19–36.

McLaren, P. (1994). *Life in Schools: an introduction to critical pedagogy in the foundations of education*. Second Edition. London: Longman.

—— (1995). *Critical Pedagogy and Predatory Culture: oppositional politics in a postmodern era*. London: Routledge.

McSmith, A., and Savage, M. (2009, 21/05/2009). Political change we can believe in. *The Independent*.

Mirza, H. S. (Ed.). (1997). *Black British Feminism: a reader*. London: Routledge.

Moore, A. (2004). *The Good Teacher: dominant discourses in teaching and teacher education*. London: Routledge.

Morrison, T. (1999). *The Bluest Eye*. London: Vintage.

Morrow, R. A., and Torres, C. A. (1990). The De-Schooling Thesis: a reassessment of Illich's proposals two decades after. *New Education*, 12(1) pp. 3–17.

Moss, G. (1999). Texts in Context: mapping out the gender differentiation of the reading curriculum. *Pedagogy*, 7(3), pp. 507–22.

—— (2007). *Literacy and Gender: researching texts, contexts and readers*. London: Routledge.

—— (2009). The Politics of Literacy in the Context of Large-Scale Education Reform. *Research Papers in Education*, 24(2), pp. 155–74.

Mughal, M. (2008, 20/01/09). *Opinion: the Horn of Africa and radicalisation*, from http://www.libdemvoice.org/opinion-the-horn-of-africa-and-radicalisation-5912.html

Munro, P. (1999). Political Activism as Teaching: Jane Adams and Ida B. Wells. In M. S. Crocco (Ed.), *Pedagogies of Resistance* (pp. 19–45). New York: Teachers College Press.

Munsch, R. (2003). *The Paper Bag Princess*. New York: Scholastic.

NCTB. (n.d.) *National Coordinator for Counterterrorism: radicalisation and recruitment*. Retrieved 20/01/09, from http://english.nctb.nl/what_is_terrorism/introduction/Radicalisation/

Nelson, A. R. (2001). *Education and Democracy: the meaning of Alexander Meiklejohn, 1872–1964*. Madison: University of Wisconsin Press.

Neumann, P. R. (2008). Introduction. In *Perspectives on Radicalism and Political Violence: papers from the first international conference on radicalism and political violence*. London: International Centre for the Study of Radicalisation and Political Violence.

Nieto, S. (2004). Critical Multicultural Education and Students' Perspectives. In G. Ladsen-Billing and D. Gillborn (Eds), *RoutledgeFalmer Reader in Multicultural Education*. London: RoutledgeFalmer.

Nieto, S., and Bode, P. (2008). *Affirming Diversity: the sociopolitical context of multicultural education*. Fifth Edition. Pearson/Allyn and Bacon.

Nind, M. (Ed.). (2005). *Curriculum and Pedagogy in Inclusive Education*. London: RoutledgeFalmer.

No Outsiders. (2009). *No Outsiders: researching approaches to sexualities equalities in primary schools*. Retrieved 02/02/09, from http://www.nooutsiders.sunderland.ac.uk/

Ofsted. (2007). *Summerhill School, Independent School Inspection report*.

Ollman, B. (2003). *Dance of the Dialectic: steps in Marx's method.* Chicago: University of Illinois.

Orwell, G. (2000). *Nineteen Eighty-Four.* London: Penguin.

Oshinsky, D. (2005). *A Conspiracy So Immense: the world of Joe McCarthy.* Oxford: Oxford University Press.

Owens, L. (2006). *The Complete Brother Grimm Fairy Tales.* Robert Beard Books.

Paechter, C. (2001). *Knowledge, Power and Learning.* Paul Chapman.

Perkins-Gilman, C. (1992). *The Yellow Wallpaper.* London: Virago.

Peters, M. A., and Freeman-Moir, D. J. (Eds). (2006). *Edutopias: new utopian thinking in education.* Rotterdam: Sense.

Piercy, M. (1991). *Woman on the Edge of Time.* London: The Women's Press.

Pillow, W. S. (2003). Confession, Catharsis or Cure? Rethinking the uses of reflexivity as methodological power in qualitative research. *International Journal of Qualitative Studies in Education,* 16(2), pp. 175–96.

Pollard, A., Collins, C., Maddock, M., Simco, N., Swaffield, S., Warin, J. (2005). *Reflective Teaching.* Second Edition. London: Continnum.

Purkiss, D. (Ed.). (1994). *Renaissance Women: the plays of Elizabeth Cary, the poems of Aemilia Lanyer.* London: Pickering and Chatto.

Rasmussen, M. L. (2001). Queering Schools and Dangerous Knowledge: some new directions in sexualities, pedagogies and schooling. *Discourse: Studies in the Cultural Politics of Education,* 22(2), pp. 263–72.

—— (2006). *Becoming Subjects.* London: Routledge.

—— (2009). Beyond Gender Identity. *Gender and Education,* 21(4), pp. 431–77.

Rasmussen, M. L., and Crowley, V. (Eds). (2004). *Discourse: Sexualities Special Issue.* 25(4).

Reay, D. (2004). 'Mostly Roughs and Toughs': social class, race and representation in inner city schooling. *Sociology,* 35(4), pp. 1000–23.

Reay, D., and Lucey, H. (2000). 'I Don't Like it Here but I Don't Want To Be Anywhere Else': children living on inner London council estates. *Antipode,* 32(4), pp. 410–28.

Rees, J. (1998). *The Algebra of Revolution: dialectic and the classical Marxist tradition.* London: Routldge.

Reeves, T. (1983). *The Life and Times of Joe McCarthy.* Henry Holt and Co.

Reiss, M. J. (2009). Imagining the World: the significance of religious worldviews for science education. *Science and Education,* 18(6/7), pp. 783–91.

Renold, E. (2005). *Girls, Boys and Junior Sexualities: exploring children's gender and sexual relations in the primary school.* London: RoutledgeFalmer.

Renold, E., and Ringrose, J. (2008). Regulation and Rupture: mapping tween and teenage girls' resistance to the heterosexual matrix. *Feminist Theory,* 9(3), pp. 335–60.

Rich, A. (1980). Compulsory Heterosexuality and Lesbian Existence. *Signs,* 5(4), pp. 631–60.

Richardson, J., Parnell, P., and Cole, H. (2005). *And Tango Makes Three.* London: Simon & Schuster.

Richardson, J. E. (2004). *(Mis)representing Islam: the racism and rhetoric of British broadsheet newspapers.* Amsterdam: John Benjamins.

Riddell, S. (1992). *Gender and the politics of curriculum.* London: Routledge.

Ringrose, J. (2007). Rethinking White Resistance: exploring the discursive practices and psychical negotiations of whiteness in feminist, anti-racist education. *Race,* 10(3), pp. 323–44.

Ringrose, J. (in press). Beyond Discourse? Using Deleuze and Guattari's schizoanalysis to explore affective assemblages, heterosexually striated space, and lines of flight online and at school. *Educational Philosophy and Theory.*

Rose, N. (1998). *Inventing Our Selves: psychology, power and personhood.* Cambridge: Cambridge University Press.

—— (2000). Government and Control. *British Journal of Criminology*, 40, pp. 321–39.

Rosen, M. (2003). *Micheal Rosen's Top Ten Books*. Retrieved 01/04/09, from http://www. guardian.co.uk/culture/2003/mar/03/bestbooks.booksforchildrenandteenagers

Rowse, A. L. (1976). *The Poems of Shakespeare's Dark Lady: Salve Deus, Rex Judeorum by Emilia Lanyer*. London: Cape.

Roy, A. (1998). *The God of Small Things*. London: Flamingo.

Said, E. (1997). *Covering Islam: how the media and the experts determine how we see the rest of the world*. New York: Vintage.

—— (2003). *Orientalism*. London: Penguin.

Scott, J. W. (1992). Experience. In J. Butler and J. W. Scott (Eds), *Feminists Theorize the Political* (pp. 22–40). London: Routledge.

Seel, P. (1995). *I, Pierre Seel, Deported Homosexual*. New York: BasicBooks.

Shepherd, J. (2007). *So, Kids, Anyone for Double Physics? (But no worries if you don't fancy it): official approval at last for the school where almost anything goes*. Retrieved 20/01/09, from http://www. guardian.co.uk/uk/2007/dec/01/ofsted.schools

Silverman, D. (1997). Towards an Aesthetics of Research. In D. Silverman (Ed.), *Qualitative Research: theory, method and practice* (pp. 239–53). London: Sage.

Sinfield, A. (2005). *Cultural Politics/Queer Reading*. Abingdon: Routledge.

Smith, D. G. (2006). On Enfrauding the Public Space: the futility of Empire and the future of knowledge after 'America'. In M. A. Peters and D. J. Freeman-Moir (Eds), *Edutopias* (pp. 65–78). Rotterdam: Sense.

Smith, J. (2008). *Home Secretary's speech on the threat of international terrorism*. Retrieved 20/01/09, from http://security.homeoffice.gov.uk/news-publications/news-speeches/speech-to-ippr

Snider, J. (2003). *Sci-fi Dimensions: Equilibrium – interview with Kurt Wimmer*. Retrieved 01/03/09, from http://www.scifidimensions.com/May03/kurtwimmer.htm

Soja, E. (2000). *Thirdspace: journeys to Los Angeles and other real-and-imagined spaces*. Oxford: Blackwell.

St. Pierre, E. A., and Pillow, W. S. (Eds). (2000). *Working the Ruins: feminist poststructural theory and methods in education*. London: Routledge.

Stanley, J. (1989). *Marks on the Memory: experiencing school*. Milton Keynes: Open University Press.

Stanley, J., and Wise, S. (1993). *Breaking Out Again: feminist ontology and epistemology*. London: Routledge.

Sullivan, N. (2006). *A Critical Introduction to Queer Theory*. Edinburgh: Edinburgh University Press.

Summerhill. (2004). *A.S. Neill's Summerhill*. Retrieved 20/01/09, from http://www.summer-hillschool.co.uk/

Talburt, S. (2000). Identity Politics, Institutional Response, and Cultural Negotiation: meanings of a gay and lesbian office on campus. In S. Talburt and S. Steinberg (Eds.), *Thinking Queer: sexuality, culture, and education* (pp. 61–81). New York: Peter Lang.

—— (2009). Toys, Pleasures, and the Future. In R. DePalma and E. Atkinson (Eds), *Interrogating Heteronormativity in Primary Schools*. Stoke on Trent: Trentham.

Talburt, S., and Steinberg, S. (Eds). (2000). *Thinking Queer: sexuality, culture, and education*. New York: Peter Lang.

Tamboukou, M. (2008). Machinic Assemblages: women, art education and space. *Discourse*, 29(3), pp. 359–75.

Team-Teach. (2003). *Team-Teach Workbook*. St Leonards: Steaming.

Telegraph. (2009). *MPs' Expenses*. Retrieved 30/04/09, from http://www.telegraph.co.uk/news/newstopics/mps-expenses/

Thompson, E. P. (1980). *The Making of the English Working Class*. London: Penguin.

Truffaut, F. (1966). *Fahrenheit 451*. US: Universal.

UKREN. *Anti-Terrorism and Racism: the impact of EU and UK policy on black and minority ethnic communities*. Retrieved 01/01/10, from http://www.runnymedetrust.org/uploads/projects/europe/UKREN%20counter%20terrorism.pdf

Unlock Democracy. (2009). *Unlock Democracy incorporating Charter 88*. Retrieved 15/04/09, from http://www.charter88.org.uk/

Wachowski Brothers (1999). *The Matrix*. US: Warner.

—— (2003a). *The Matrix Reloaded*. US: Warner.

—— (2003b). *The Matrix Revolutions*. US: Warner.

Walby, S. (1986). *Patriarchy at Work: patriarchal and capitalist relations in employment*. Cambridge: Polity.

Walker, A. (1982). *Meridian*. London: The Women's Press.

Walkerdine, V. (1987). Sex, Power and Pedagogy. In M. Arnot and G. Weiner (Eds), *Gender and the Politics of Schooling* (pp. 166–74). Hutchinson: Open University Press.

—— (1989). *Counting Girls Out*. London: Virago.

—— (1990). *Schoolgirl Fictions*. London: Verso.

Waters, S. (1998). *Tipping the Velvet*. London: Virago.

Watkins, M. (2008). Teachers' Tears: affect and the emotional geography of the classroom. *The Emotional Geographies of Education Conference*. London, November 2008.

Weis, L. (2007). *The Way Class Works: readings on school, family and the economy*. London: Taylor & Francis.

Westall, R. (1992). *Gulf*. London: Mammoth.

Whitty, G. (1985). *Sociology and School Knowledge: curriculum theory, research and politics*. London: Methuen.

Whitty, G., Power, S., and Halpin, D. (1998). *Devolution and Choice in Education: the school, state, and the market*. Buckingham: Open University Press.

Willhaite, M. (1991). *Daddy's Roommate*. Los Angeles: Alyson.

Wimmer, K. (Writer) (2002). *Equilibrium*. Dimensions.

Winterson, J. (1991). *Oranges Are Not the Only Fruit*. London: Vintage.

Woolf, V. (2005). *A Room of One's Own*. Harcourt.

Wray, R. (1997). *Shakespeare and Ireland: history, politics, culture*. Basingstoke: Macmillan.

Yates, L. (1990). *Theory Practice Dilemmas: gender, knowledge and education*. Waurn Ponds Vic: Deakin University.

Youdell, D. (2003). Identity Traps or How Black Students Fail: the interactions between biographical, sub-cultural, and learner identities. *British Journal of Sociology of Education*, 24(1), pp. 3–20.

—— (2004a). Engineering School Markets, Constituting Schools and Subjectivating Students: the bureaucratic, institutional and classroom dimensions of educational triage. *Journal of Education Policy*, 19(4), pp. 408–31.

—— (2004b). Wounds and Reinscriptions: schools, sexualities and performative subjects. *Discourse*, 25(4), pp. 477–94.

—— (2006a). *Impossible Bodies, Impossible Selves: exclusions and student subjectivities*. Dordrecht: Springer.

—— (2006b). Diversity, Inequality and Post-Structural Politics for Education. *Discourse*, 27(1), pp. 33–42.

—— (2006c). Subjectivation and Performative Politics – Butler Thinking Althusser and Foucault: intelligibility, agency and the raced-nationed-religioned subjects of education. *British Journal of Sociology of Education*, 27(4), pp. 511–28.

—— (2009). Lessons in Praxis: thinking about knowledge, subjectivity and politics in education. In R. DePalma and E. Atkinson (Eds), *Interrogating Heteronormativity in Primary Schools*. Stoke on Trent: Trentham.

Young, M. F. D. (1971). *Knowledge and Control: new directions for the sociology of education*. Collier-Macmillan.

—— (1977). *Society, State and Schooling: readings on the possibilities for radical education*. Brighton: Falmer Press.

Younger, M., and Warrington, M. (2007). Closing the Gender Gap? Issues of gender equity in English secondary schools. *Discourse*, 28(2), pp. 219–42.

Yuval-Davis, N. (2007). Intersectionality, Citizenship and Contemporary Politics of Belonging. *Critical Review of International Social and Political Philosophy*, 10(4), pp. 561–74.

Zembylas, M. (2007). *Five Pedagogies, A Thousand Possibilities: struggles for hope and transformation in education*. Rotterdam: Sense.

Zizek, S. (2008). *Violence*. London: Profile.

Author index

Subject index